GASTON BACHELARD

GASTON BACHELARD

AN INTELLECTUAL BIOGRAPHY

STEVEN CONNOR

REAKTION BOOKS

Published by
Reaktion Books Ltd
2–4 Sebastian Street
London EC1V 0HE, UK
www.reaktionbooks.co.uk

First published 2025

EU GPSR Authorised Representative
Logos Europe, 9 rue Nicolas Poussin, 17000, La Rochelle, France
email: contact@logoseurope.eu

Printed and bound in Great Britain by Bell & Bain, Glasgow

A catalogue record for this book is available from the British Library

ISBN 978 1 83639 087 9

CONTENTS

Note on translations

Except where otherwise indicated, all translations of texts not originally in English are my own.

Introduction: A Writing Life

The book has just spoken to us of ourselves.[1]

This book inhabits and is energized by a paradox. Although biographies have been written about Bachelard (though none up to this point in English), the biographer quickly comes up against a strange and frustrating blank when it comes to the evidence of that life. Bachelard's life was far from uneventful, but those events seem not to have left the kind of traces that one would expect, and that would allow the biographer to weigh the life against the work, or set the work in the context of the life from which it emerged. It is not that Bachelard lived a markedly withdrawn or reclusive life, for he was active as a post-office worker, First World War combatant, student, teacher and writer. What is more, he had by the end of his life achieved considerable celebrity as a writer and public figure.

And yet, to set about writing the life of one who, like Gaston Bachelard, spent most of their life writing and, once embarked on that work of writing, seems to have made time for little else, is also to risk a tautology. For it may appear that the one who has spent their life writing has already turned their life into their *Life*, ghost-writing in advance any attempt by another coming after to write it. But if writing a life that has itself been taken up in writing is a tautology, it also comes close to perpetuating a perjury: the perjury of the belief that every life has some act of writing as its destiny, since a life is a story that we are enjoined to tell or have told by others. We write, and read, the lives of writers, in part to make doubly sure the assurance of this doubling of life by writing. According to this view, to devote your life to writing is to transform the mere expenditure of time into the patient splendour of an accrual, as the mere sequence of days lived from day to day is curved into the shape of 'a life', intently and intricately meant. This myth of the writing life is that, no matter what the alleged subject of one's writing may be, it must always in the end amount to an autobiography, a work of double-entry book-keeping that will fold work and life together without arrear or residue. As his biographers, who have been very few, have tended to note, in Bachelard's case one will search the life in vain for the external source or truth of the work, since Bachelard's seems to have been a life lived wholly in the service of its work of writing. François Dagognet wrote that, in the case of Bachelard, 'thought energized his life, rather than the other way round.'[2] Jean-Michel Wavelet has put it somewhat more expansively:

> With Bachelard, it is not in the life that one should seek the truth of a work, since the life does not reflect it, it is the work which produces the life . . . More than a life's work, it is the life of the work, the life made into a work which takes its place, to the point sometimes of making it almost unlivable.[3]

In fact the paradox is even tauter and more toothed than this. Bachelard, we might say, perfected, or, to use the word to which he reverted throughout his life, *rectified* himself by a work that could not but be at odds with that life. Far from rounding out his life into completeness, the act of writing is the enemy of full and satisfactory living. As Bachelard wrote in his final months: 'To live life well is to express life poorly; if one expresses life too well, one is living it no longer.'[4] 'Bachelard could very well not have been Bachelard,' notes Jean-Michel Wavelet.[5] Astute observation though this is, it is in fact also a banal and almost universal verity, the opposite of that announced in the response to Shane MacGowan's vainglorious line in the Pogues song 'The Fairytale of New York', 'I could have *been* someone,' traditionally echoed back in sardonic jubilation by his audiences: 'Well, so could *any*one.' In Bachelard's case, however, the one subject to contingency makes himself the subject of it, making of his life an indirect meditation on the non-necessity that it should have been this particular life.

At the same time, and perhaps even for the same reason, to write is to confirm the necessity of the unnecessary. To write seems like a doubling of whatever must have been the first real thought that any human being can have had, and must have made themselves human by having: the stirring of demur in the feeling that things do not necessarily have to be like this. If to write, whether or not one writes of one's own life, is thought of as rounding out one's life, giving it its defining silhouette, to write is also to break into the unconscious continuity of mere unfolding. It is to make one's mark, and by making a mark, to mark a parting of the ways, in a life come about in coming apart from itself. If writing fulfils a life, it does so by fracturing it. In his *The Dialectic of Duration*, Bachelard writes, 'thought is always in some respects a trying-out of or a first move towards a new life, an attempt to live differently, to live more or even . . . a will to go beyond life.'[6] Such a viewpoint can be regarded as the evidence of a will, flexed against habit, duty or destiny. But it can also be the product of a life that has been repeatedly derailed, nudged or shouldered, by opportunity or its lack, into 'what something hidden from us chose'.[7]

It is easier to see this partition when writing begins late in life, as it did with Bachelard, whose first publication appeared in 1928, when he was 44 years old. Bachelard's life of writing is a life paradoxically looped together from ruptures, refusals, suspensions and dissentings. Indeed, he would make of this kind of rupture simultaneously a method and a recurring subject, to which one of his books would give the name 'the philosophy of no' – though it might also be called the philosophy of *yes, but*. If in one sense this makes for a drastic division between the actions and events of Bachelard's life and the act of writing that occupied so much of it, it will be the work of this book to suggest that, in a more profound sense than usual, Bachelard's abiding subject in his work was always, implicitly or subliminally, this very relation between living, thinking and writing, in its moral, psychological and philosophical dimensions.

Though himself taken up in a life of writing, Bachelard was profoundly unimpressed by the writing of lives, and seems as he grew older to have become increasingly hostile to the idea of biography. Though there are autobiographical glimpses and interludes throughout his writings on poetry and the imagination, they form, as it were, an anonymous autobiography, shorn of names, dates and places. *Lautréamont*, the only book he wrote devoted to an individual writer, seems to be given impetus, and was perhaps even made possible for him, by the fact that so few biographical facts seem to be available about the life of his subject, Isidore Ducasse, who might therefore be thought to have given rise to his own life in his writing. Bachelard seems never to have succumbed to the temptation to write any more connected kind of autobiography, not even of an intellectual kind, though the opening chapter of the book published after his death as *Fragments of a Poetics of Fire*, 'Retrospective Glance at the Life Work of a Maker of Books', indicates the faint stirring of this kind of ambition. Even here, though, the opening sentence resists the idea of a life reducible to an orderly almanac of events:

> When some twenty years ago (or is it twenty-five – where the life of the mind is concerned, who can say just when a lasting change occurs?) I first became interested in the problem of literary imagery, quite in the margins of my regular work as a science teacher, I believed so narrowly defined a concern might be simply treated and did not require the tools of philosophy.[8]

One must be wary of the temptation to which all those undertaking to write the life of a writer must be subject, to construe that writer's life-work as necessarily a form of life-writing. And yet the temptation is particularly strong in the case of Bachelard to see his whole output as a disguised or displaced effort of autobiography, never carried through to completion, but never completely abandoned either. One of the very earliest witnesses to Bachelard's personal investment in the abstract work of epistemology was Léon Brunschvicg, Bachelard's doctoral dissertation adviser, who wrote in his review of Bachelard's *Essai sur la connaissance approchée*:

> Mr. Bachelard, for his part, was admirably prepared for the task he set himself, both by a scientific culture of the highest quality and by a rare integrity of mind, which restrained him from presumptuous generalities and school-level prejudices and led him back constantly not only to minutely question the facts, but also to question himself, in a direct and scrupulous way, on the exact limits of his interpretations. Like any disinterested and profound work, the *Essay on Approximate Knowledge* is a kind of autobiography through which an evolution is taking shape.[9]

Bachelard's life as a thinker and writer is devoted to the work of understanding what it means to devote (unless it is to delegate) one's life to thinking and writing. One might find an image of this enterprise in what he would later write about Henri Bergson's theory of the progress of evolution in his *Creative Evolution* (1907), that it is 'a vast intuition that is more the image of a soul than it is a portrait of things'.[10] This is not a subject that Bachelard very often addressed directly, but I will try to show that the more manifest objects of his writing, in the history of science, the philosophy of scientific knowledge, the role of education and the nature of the poetic imagination, were in fact driven by this central concern with the nature of the life of thought. In his *Lautréamont*, Bachelard abruptly poses the question that he spent much of his life haggling over: 'why did God make life when he could have made thought directly?'[11]

I

Hostile Novelty, 1884–1919

Gaston Bachelard was born and brought up in the small rural town of Bar-sur-Aube. The town itself has scarcely changed its population since the late eighteenth century, and that population still hovers between 4,000 and 5,000 inhabitants. It is situated to the southwest of the region in the east of France in which champagne is produced, and indeed the region known as the Aube, from the river that traverses it, produces around a quarter of all champagne. Though winemaking had been a continuous tradition for centuries when Bachelard was young, the Aube region was not given approval to use the champagne name until after the First World War. Hardship caused by bad harvests and the incursions of the phylloxera louse led to conflict and unrest that erupted in widespread rioting in 1910 and 1911.

Although Bachelard himself never wrote directly about his rural upbringing, its significance has repeatedly been emphasized in those who have written about his life. At the beginning of the twentieth century, the division between the country and the city in France was much more marked than it was in Britain, in which industrialization and urbanization were much more developed. It was therefore even more unusual for a person with a rural upbringing to achieve eminence in the prestigious institutions of the capital.

Although Bachelard's family had small vineyards, they were not agricultural workers. His grandfather had been a shoemaker, and his parents ran a small newsagent-tobacconist on the rue Nationale, the main street of the town. Bachelard studied at primary school and then, from 1895 to 1902, pursued secondary education at the Collège de Bar-sur-Aube. Born in 1884, Bachelard was an early beneficiary of the educational reforms introduced by French prime minister Jules Ferry in laws enacted in 1881 and 1882, which aimed to reduce the influence of the Catholic Church and made primary education mandatory, free and secular. Boys and girls were both required to attend primary school between the ages of six and thirteen, where they were taught reading and writing, civics, French literature, geography, history, basic law and politics, and elementary natural science and mathematics. Though there is no evidence as to how able or assiduous Bachelard was as a student, or where his principal areas of interest or aptitude lay, he did remain in school until the age of eighteen and completed what was known as the 'modern' baccalaureate. This had been instituted in 1882, and had evolved from a programme of secondary education instituted by Victor Duruy in 1865 that was intended to provide more practically focused instruction for members of the middle class and lower middle class who were likely to proceed into industrial, commercial and agricultural occupations. The modern baccalaureate was distinguished from the 'classical' baccalaureate, which tended to be taken by students from wealthier backgrounds who were expecting to progress into elite professions, and was centred on the study of ancient languages and classical antiquity. The modern baccalaureate was regarded as distinctly second-best, even by the prestigious Ecole polytechnique, set up following the Revolution in 1794 to provide technical training for various occupations.[1] The distinction between the two baccalaureate streams

59 rue nationale, Bar-sur-Aube, where Bachelard was born and grew up.

approximates to the distinction that existed in Britain from 1945 to 1965 between grammar schools and 'secondary modern' schools, though the French system did not divide students into these two academic and 'vocational' streams as early as in Britain, where the separation took place at the age of eleven.

Bachelard's studies did not include any Latin, which he therefore had to learn on his own in order to pass an examination in it for his *agrégation* in philosophy in 1921. Bachelard would presumably have benefited from the provision, from 1911, that allowed candidates for the *agrégation* who had advanced scientific qualifications to substitute linguistic competence in English or German for Greek, but competence in Latin remained a requirement until 1968.[2] Bachelard's schoolfriend Daniel Giroux reproduced his description of how he went about it:

> His method? Very simple: 'You buy a *De Bello Gallico*: you read the first page of the Latin text, with the translation in good French, and opposite, you read it word-for-word. The next day you reread the first page and move on to the next.' Sceptically, I ventured: 'And the grammar?' The reply came straight away: 'The grammar? You deduce it!'[3]

The story lends authority to the reputation that Bachelard gained for fearless and indefatigable autodidacticism. The method described, however, could be relied upon only as long as one had a translation to hand to verify one's deductions, a provision that would therefore make the actual learning of the structure and conventions of use in Latin superfluous. The story may not have much to tell us about the best way to learn Latin, or even the way in which Bachelard may have gone about it, successfully or not. But, even assuming as one probably should that the story was in fact a gentle tease, it does seem to dramatize a striking faith in the powers of rational deduction, operating in an abstract and *a priori* fashion. Throughout his life, Bachelard would maintain his high estimation of these powers. No matter how complex and contextually dependent the processes of human reasoning and deduction might seem to be, Bachelard retains a kind of magical confidence in the power of moving from observation through analysis and deduction to understanding. Like René Descartes, who similarly invested hugely in a philosophical programme of reform of rationality from the bottom up and from the inside out, unaccommodated by anything but his reason, the idea that reason can form and reform itself independently of its circumstances is never relinquished by Bachelard.

Though Bachelard was no Jude the Obscure, locked away inescapably from any hope of acceding to the powers and privileges of education, it is instructive to put this account alongside the episode in Thomas Hardy's novel in which the young Jude receives the first great blow to his intellectual ambition, when he discovers that the second-hand Latin grammar he has ordered does not simply provide a magical formula for understanding the language. Opening the book, he

> learnt for the first time that there was no law of transmutation, as in his innocence he had supposed (there was, in some degree, but the grammarian did not recognize it), but that every word in both Latin and Greek was to be individually committed to memory at the cost of years of plodding . . . What brains they must have in Christminster and the great schools, he presently thought, to learn words one by one up to tens of thousands! There were no brains in his head equal to this business; and as the little sun-rays continued to stream in through his hat at him, he wished he had never seen a book, that he might never see another, that he had never been born.[4]

Jude's despair here is that of the uninstructed child who expects there to be an easy abracadabra that would turn incomprehension into understanding. The apparently more mature form of intellectual confidence claimed (or mischievously dissimulated) by Bachelard lies in a method that itself seems to operate as a magical 'law of transmutation', capable of turning glamour back into grammar. The power of deduction as assumed by Bachelard is as magical a key as that longed for by the young Jude.

Though he would retain a sense of the contingency of all thought, the ways in which the act of thought was conditioned, inflected and instrumentalized through material conditions, Bachelard's tendency was always to be aware of the power to abstract away from appearances and assumptions, and indeed to identify rationality with abstraction itself. To think was always to break with what was given or immediate in experience. Thinking was what freed you from a life lived unreflectively from day to day, and so in a sense was a refusal of mere life. The drama of thought asserting itself against all the obstacles and possibilities of life would provide the tone and texture of Bachelard's whole life.

The Collège de Bar-sur-Aube, where Bachelard was a student from 1897 to 1902 and a teacher from 1919 to 1930.

Bachelard's education at the Collège de Bar-sur-Aube from thirteen to eighteen would have had to be paid for somehow by his family, but their resources were not sufficient for him to proceed to higher education, so it was necessary for him to support himself from the age of eighteen. Bachelard's first employment was as a 'répétiteur', or classroom assistant, at a college in Sézanne, 100 kilometres off. Bachelard never recorded anything about this experience, and no other traces of it survive. If, however, it was intended as the first step towards a career as a schoolteacher, we may surmise that the experience was not positive enough to encourage the young Bachelard in this direction, at least not until his return to teaching seventeen years later.

The function known as *repetitio* was traditional in European universities. In the University of Bologna, it referred to the practice in which an assistant would attend a lecture given by a master and then repeat it to students and examine them upon it.[5] It was common for senior students to be given this role in European schools and universities. In Germany, the term *Repetitor* was used to refer to a private tutor in law or medicine, who would set up in university towns to provide accessory instruction.

Something similar happened in Oxford, Cambridge and London in Britain, where coaches or 'grinders' assisted in the preparation of students for examinations. The term survives largely in opera and ballet schools, where *répétiteurs* usually provide instrumental accompaniment during rehearsals (*répétition* can be used to mean rehearsal in French), and continue to have an important function in coaching and mentoring.

Although the intention in French schools, admirable in principle, was to provide a kind of mediation of abstract or advanced material to schoolchildren by somebody closer to them in age and experience, the docile function embodied in the name *répétiteur* would in fact epitomize everything that the later Bachelard would recoil against in education, at all levels – the uncritical transmission of settled knowledge to passive learners. He would later scornfully distinguish what is known and understood in science from what is taught, the latter meaning what is blindly and incuriously repeated. In *The Formation of the Scientific Mind*, he complained about 'the teaching of a physics where there are no problems but just oral questions: such reforms misunderstand the real meaning of the scientific mind'.[6] He persisted in his critical view of teaching where it is founded on error or imprecision, writing in 1953 that a mistaken theory, 'if it is taught, if it is given the dignity of a doctrine – if it is really teachable – retards culture'.[7]

Following his experience in Sézanne, Bachelard decided not to persist in school teaching, which would have required attendance at one of the *écoles normales* for the training of teachers set up by the Ferry reforms in education. It seems likely that financial constraints prevented this in any case, meaning that Bachelard would need to find a more practical and sustained way to earn his living. Even today, with greatly increased education and career opportunities, most people still do not choose the way in which they end up making their living as a conscious and once-and-for-all lifetime decision, and we can assume that this would have been even more true for the young Bachelard, for whom the options were not limitless. In 1903 he decided instead to enrol as supernumerary worker for the Postes et Télégraphes and was assigned to the office in Remiremont, 200 kilometres to the east.

Bachelard's experience as a postman-turned-philosopher has sometimes been taken as an index of his dramatic rise from provincial obscurity to metropolitan eminence, though this may be to scorn unreasonably the nature of the job and the prospects that it seemed to offer. Though there is a certain poetic satisfaction in the idea that one might proceed from the condition of being a mere carrier of others' letters to being oneself an exponent of 'belles lettres', Bachelard seems not to have been a postman for very long, if at all. It seems likely that one of the attractions of working for the French Post Office was that it offered the possibility of further education and training, even if this possibility was not immediately apparent to the young Bachelard. The growth in communications in industrialized nations like Britain, France and the USA was accompanied by, and itself produced the need for, new kinds of technical and educational understanding and training, in areas such as electrical engineering that were much better represented in the fields of industry than in universities. The equivalent today to the opportunity offered by joining the Postes et Télégraphes might be the case of a young person ambitious to learn about computation or genetics who must judge between the rival attractions of a long and expensive university training and a better-paid job in a software or biotech company working at the forefront of technical developments.

Certainly, the young Bachelard seems to have responded promptly to the educational and training opportunities of his new occupation. From 1903 to 1906, he began to study for the specialized baccalaureate in mathematics, arranging his life in order to compress two days into every one, as described by his friend and long-term correspondent Daniel Giroux: he would go to bed at 9.30 p.m. and wake at midnight, in order to study until 4 a.m., before going back to sleep until 7.30 a.m, when he would rise and go to work at the post office in Remiremont.[8]

Bachelard maintained his commitment to communications by serving as a telegraphic rider in the 12th Dragoons regiment stationed at Pont-à-Mousson for the period of his national service, which lasted from 1906 to 1907. Following this, aged 23, he returned to the Postes et Télégraphes, and was assigned to the office of the Gare de L'Est in Paris. Here, he became a senior executive in the telephonic exchange. He worked a night shift, which enabled him to study during the day, supported by bursaries that he won for the Ecole Polytechnique Saint-Louis and the Faculté des sciences of the University of Paris. In 1909 he began studying for the Engineers' Competition, but narrowly missed gaining a bursary, being placed third when there were only two scholarships available. Despite this disappointment, he had accumulated by 1914 a number of diplomas and certificates in mathematics, general calculus and physics. The most important of these was his *licence* in mathematics and in physics, which he completed in 1912. This is equivalent to an undergraduate degree, the standard qualification in France for teaching in a college (students aged eleven to fifteen) or lycée (students aged fifteen to eighteen).

There are striking parallels between the young man working in a provincial post office and another young man who had commenced work around the same time, in June 1902, as an Expert III class in the Swiss Patent Office in Zurich: Albert Einstein. Einstein was somewhat further on his academic career, having graduated from the University of Zürich, completed a doctoral thesis and even published a couple of scientific articles, even though his academic prospects could not be said to be very strong. But Einstein nevertheless sustained himself in this occupation for seven years, working six eight-hour days a week in the Patent Office while pursuing his scientific research.[9]

Bachelard alluded several times later in his life to his ambitions of becoming an engineer, though he never achieved this aim. In many ways, however, he retained his orientation towards engineering. Although he would develop a specialism in the history and philosophy of science, never having the opportunity to be an experimental scientist, Bachelard's scientific interests never became wholly theoretical. His writing is strongly attuned to the fact that the pursuit of scientific knowledge always takes the form of a struggle between pure rationality and the impediments represented by the real, which casts doubt on the idea of purity, either in nature or in the work of understanding it. This may explain why Bachelard should have been drawn not just to the philosophy of physics, which, until the beginning of the upsurge in the reputation of biosciences with the discovery of DNA in the 1950s, had the reputation of being the ultimate or foundational science, but to the philosophy of chemistry, a science that, largely because of the enormous success and impact of industrial chemistry from the nineteenth century onwards, has often been thought of, and indeed looked down on, as more instrumental and so 'impure' than other sciences. Bachelard's optimistic interest in the synthesis of new chemical compounds took him towards the field of chemical engineering, a scientific specialism that became established over the course of his life. His theories of scientific knowledge depended upon application and invention as much as upon abstract knowledge. The emphasis on active scientific doing is what might be expected from somebody who had retained an engineer's interest in making things happen. From his first book onwards, Bachelard insisted that knowledge must depend on instruments, which both open possibilities of knowing, and yet also limit the form of that knowledge. This emphasis comes to the fore in a remarkable chapter of his doctoral thesis on approximate knowledge, which is devoted to the work of modern industry, which, he writes, 'does not individualize the object it creates: strange creation, in which the general surpasses the particular . . . The archive of moulds in a foundry or glassworks is a veritable collection of platonic ideas.'[10] For Bachelard, 'The engineer is not an artist who chooses and signs a work which is full of personality, he is a geometrician, a guardian of rational methods and a veritable representative of the *technical society* of his epoch.'[11]

Jean-Michel Wavelet sees a distinct turning away in Bachelard's work from the late 1930s onwards, after which time 'His references to industrial history become ever rarer, while his references to the physical sciences and mathematics increased. From now on, Bachelard is more scientist than engineer, more epistemologist than technologist.'[12] While this is true in a superficial sense, what Wavelet calls the 'progressive disincarnation' of Bachelard's philosophy of science is never continuous or complete.[13]

Bachelard remained committed to the idea that scientific discovery was bound up with the work of invention and synthesis rather than instruction and analysis. In an essay of 1932, Bachelard introduced the concept of 'phenomenotechnics', as a name for the process in which 'new phenomena are not only merely discovered, but also made up, and not merely discovered but made up from scratch'.[14] He would return to this idea repeatedly over the next three decades, most emphatically in the arguments in favour of what, in the title of a book he published in 1949, he called 'applied rationality'.[15] Bachelard's unfailing emphasis on the work of science might also have been driven by the engineer's sense that what is important is how things work rather than what things exist. 'The lever is a theorem,' he affirmed, implying that the inverse may also hold.[16] This prejudice may also lie behind his preference for the open and evolving practice of 'mechanics' over the closed and abstract formality of 'mechanism'.[17] In the final books on scientific epistemology that he published, he emphasized ever more strongly the importance of applied rationality, and maintained the need for philosophy to be led by science rather than the inverse, since 'science in effect creates philosophy'.[18]

In the years before the First World War, Bachelard had met up again with a childhood friend named Jeanne Rossi, who was a schoolteacher in the little village of Maisons-lès-Soulaines, 10 kilometres from his birthplace in Bar-sur-Aube. Like many others on the eve of war, they decided to marry, the wedding being on 8 July 1914, just weeks before Bachelard was called up into a combat unit as a Dragoon Brigadier on 2 August, in anticipation of Germany's declaration of war against France. Bachelard was unable to obtain leave to rejoin his new wife for sixteen months, for Christmas 1915. Jeanne seems to have had recurrent ill health, for there is a record that, returning home during the war for another period, Bachelard took over some of her duties as a temporary teacher in 1916 and 1917. During the course of the war, she moved to another school, in Voigny, a little closer to Bar-sur-Aube.

Bachelard was a combatant in the trenches for four-and-a-half years. He applied for officer training in 1917, as he was entitled to by his licenciate, and performed with sufficient distinction to be awarded a Croix de Guerre. Although there were more than 2 million citations for it, the Croix de Guerre was not a merely commemorative medal, for it was instituted for acts of conspicuous bravery, and so corresponds to being 'mentioned in despatches'. Bachelard's own citation, of 19 May 1918, records that 'for some days at the end of March 1918, actuated by a sense of duty, and ignoring the noise of battle, he established and repeatedly reestablished telephone lines that were constantly being broken by enemy fire, providing for his engineers a fine example of calm, determination and energy.'[19]

The combined town hall and primary school in Maisons-lès-Soulaines where Bachelard and Jeanne Rossi were married on 8 July 1914, and where she was a schoolteacher.

Bachelard's war years are perhaps the most singular and intriguing area of reticence in his later life. He does not seem ever to have referred to this episode or his wartime experiences more generally in writing or conversation of which there is a record. Jean-Michel Wavelet judges that Bachelard's silence regarding his experiences in the First World War, 'overturning the course of his existence, and exposing him daily to the tragedy of death', must be 'without doubt the unspoken of collective trauma. It is the silence that translates the unspeakable.'[20] The further in time we get from the mass civilian mobilizations of the two world wars in the twentieth century, the more extraordinary this kind of silence comes to seem, even as the symptomatology of unspeakable trauma comes to seem so familiar as almost to be expected. However, though we are now more strongly aware of the traumatic effects of war experience – though perhaps mostly from the contemporary extension of the idea of post-traumatic stress disorder to experiences other than those in armed conflict or combat – many of those who returned from extended military service overseas in the two world wars similarly did not speak or write about it at length, and it is probably sentimental to assume that such silence must always be the sign of repressed trauma. There are many more kinds of unspeakability, or ways of leaving nothing to be said, than the conventional deployment of the word *unspeakable*, as an ornament or apotheosis of an act of speech, seems to imply.

In Bachelard's case, as in that of many others, this may have to do with the fact of the responsibilities that he found himself having to undertake very soon after his return from military service. He was not demobilized until 16 March 1919, when he was able to rejoin his wife in Voigny. Bachelard's degree helped him to obtain a position as a lecturer in physics and chemistry in the Bar-sur-Aube College, completing every day on foot the 12-kilometre round trip from Voigny. Jeanne was pregnant with their first child shortly after Bachelard's demobilization, which must already have focused his mind on the question of his future employment. He might possibly have been considering a return to the Postes et Télégraphes (P&T), shortly to be renamed the Postes, Télégraphes et Téléphones (PTT), but the question of his future employment became pressing following the birth of a daughter, Suzanne, on 18 October 1919, and the sudden death of his young wife only a few months later. There is some uncertainty as to the cause of Jeanne's death. She had been unwell for some time, and was possibly suffering from tuberculosis, though she may also have been a victim of the influenza epidemic that ravaged Europe after the First World War, to which young people proved to be extremely susceptible.

As with Bachelard's war experience, there is little evidence of how the savage shock of the death of his wife affected him. The most direct reference may occur in the course of his *Intuition of the Instant*, the first book on philosophical themes he published in 1932, after a sequence of four books on the history of science. The book centres on the experience of sudden discontinuity and at one point abruptly asserts that

> the cruelest mourning is the awareness of a future betrayed. When that shattering instant arrives as the eyes of a cherished being close forever, we immediately feel the hostile novelty of the next instant that comes to pierce the heart.[21]

Following Jeanne's death, Bachelard left the schoolhouse in Voigny and took his daughter back to live with his parents in Bar-sur-Aube. Those whose lives have been subject to interruption and deformation can find considerable solace and satisfaction in ensuring that others are shielded from such experiences. Certainly Bachelard undertook his parental task with an undemonstrative but unabating devotion that lasted for the rest of his life. Teaching in the college from which he had himself graduated seventeen years before enabled Bachelard to be close to his young daughter. That this was in practical terms a necessity for the young man who was required suddenly to be both paternal provider and maternal carer may have given impetus to the psychological motivation to take over the life of a wife whose daughter's immediate needs gave him little time to mourn. Just as Bachelard had stood in as a schoolteacher during his wife's illness in 1916, so now, having to fulfil her parental place permanently, it may have seemed natural for him also to take over her occupation. If so, he would not be the first who has dealt with a loss by mimetic incorporation of the one who has been lost, attempting thereby to live for two. Certainly, Bachelard never remarried, and gave no evidence of any inclination to settle with another partner who would help him raise his daughter, though if he had done so it would not, at this period or any other, have been cause for surprise. Late in his life, Bachelard wrote to the poet Louis Guillaume, himself a schoolteacher, thanking him for recommending a book of his:

> It is very kind of you to recommend my book to an educational public. I have lived my whole life as close to those who teach as to

> those who are taught. My wife was a village schoolteacher and my daughter was born in a school house.[22]

Repeating his thanks in another letter a couple of years later, he adds a comment that makes the identification with his wife even more apparent: 'I would have wished to have passed my whole life in a village school.'[23]

For the next ten years, Bachelard would be a teacher in the Bar-sur-Aube College, teaching at first physics and chemistry and then philosophy. To begin with, he was able to rely on the help of his parents, but the loss of his wife was followed by the death of his father in 1923 following an abscess of the neck, and then of his mother in 1925, leaving his five-year-old daughter exclusively in his care. The daughter whom he had brought up on his own continued to share his life, living with him as a companion, and not only following him into a career as a philosopher of science but succeeding him as a professor of philosophy at the Sorbonne and director of the Institute for History of Science and Technology.

Bachelard wrote in a letter to the poet Pierre Jean Jouve, 'all my life has been under the sign of the latecomer' – 'Toute ma vie est sous le signe du tardif.'[24] No doubt Bachelard means by this that he came later than would be expected to the most important experiences and achievements of his life: he did not attain his licence, equivalent to a bachelors degree, until the age of 28, or his doctorate until the age of 43. His first university appointment was at the age of 46, and he took up his chair at the Sorbonne at the age of 56, at an age when established academics might have begun to look forward to shaking cares and business from their age in retirement. And then, having established himself in the field of history and philosophy of science, it was only in the last twenty years of his life that Bachelard turned to the writing on art, dream and imagination for which he is most well known, especially outside France.

But there is another way of understanding this latecoming. For Bachelard, what came early in his life seems to have lain latent, to be acknowledged and absorbed much later, at a point at which the experiences had been concentrated, as early memories tend to be, into images rather than coherent sequences. Just as Bachelard's early life was subject to involuntary interruption, by financial necessity, by military service and by the responsibilities of parenthood, so his later life, during what might be expected to be the more settled course of his academic career, was subject to interruption from the past rather than from the future, in the form of intense but by this time necessarily fragmented memories, in a benign kind of trauma that allowed him to experience a sort of deferred revenge of joy. So Bachelard not only came late to what he might have wanted to have come earlier, but the significance of what had come earlier also had to wait until later to be revealed.

Bachelard promotes this kind of belatedness to an epistemological principle in his first book, in which he writes that '*the given is from our point of view essentially retarded* [*tardif*]', since what may appear to be given in nature must always wait on its explication to be understood, and so can never be wholly given, absolutely and all at once.[25] If Bachelard encountered Freud's idea of *Nachträglichkeit*, 'deferred action' or 'afterwardness', he never made reference to it in writing, but the necessary looping together of the early and late, as evoked by Andrew Barnaby's explication of lateness in psychoanalysis, both provides the dynamism of scientific rationality and seems to describe the complex syncopation of living and writing in Bachelard's own life: 'the later event of retrospective meaning-making produces what is "primal" in the primal scene even as its own conceptual priority or precedence is thereby converted into a lateness, a lateness then (re)enacted in various substitutions.'[26]

It is as though Bachelard's life had been subject to some catastrophe, a sort of slow, gentle tornado that blew apart the natural connections between his life and his experience of that life. So Bachelard's is a life that was never fully contemporary with itself. Late in his life, in a letter of 1957 to the poet Louis Guillaume, Bachelard evoked the disorder of his cluttered shelves in his Paris apartments, a disorder confirmed in many photographs:

> I live amid a great chaos of books and notes. It has become a problem to relocate a book on my shelves. I have a large library in Dijon. But here I live in a single room 4 metres by 4 metres. My memory fades, my projects intertwine and time is often short. How many poems I would wish to reread. It is with great melancholy that I find unused notes, notes which might have supported the arguments of my book.[27]

2

Realizations, 1919–32

The habits of self-application that Bachelard had learned in Paris as he studied alongside his work for the P&T were now drawn on to continue his academic development. Even before his elevation to his magisterial position in the Sorbonne for the last twenty years of his life, Bachelard was living intellectually in two worlds at once. On the one hand, he was teaching students at the beginning of their understanding of the principles of science, and on the other, he was reflecting on the convulsive intellectual changes that had come about in the world of science through relativity and quantum physics. Bachelard seems in a sense always to have remained on this threshold, convinced that a thinker can never entirely leave school behind, precisely because the experience of school is, or should be, one of such profound intellectual convulsion. His dissertation supervisor, Léon Brunschvicg, asked him, when he had just completed his doctorate in 1927, 'How is it that someone of your accomplishment can be content with teaching physics and chemistry to children?' Bachelard replied, 'I am a teacher taught.'[1] Late in his life, he would repeat the formula in describing himself as no more than 'the subject of the verb "to study"'.[2]

In a notable change of focus, Bachelard began studying philosophy, taking on the challenge of an *agrégation* in philosophy. The *agrégation* has no obvious equivalent in English academic training, or indeed elsewhere in Europe. Equivalent in some ways to a master's degree, in that it lies between the licence and the doctorate, it is designed to provide a thorough grounding in the history of philosophy for teachers in colleges and lycées. The examination called for intensive study of a number of named philosophers, with a very strong emphasis on Plato, Aristotle, Descartes and Kant. In 1921, when Bachelard may have begun his systematic philosophical studies, Leibniz was the most modern philosopher named, though in subsequent years Locke, Schopenhauer, Hobbes, Berkeley and Fichte also featured. The examinations for the *agrégation* were both exacting and conservative, with little credit given for original or creative argument. Henri Bergson, to whose work Bachelard would allude critically throughout his career, was one of the only twentieth-century philosophers to be specified for close study. Bachelard would demonstrate thereafter a strong grasp of the history of philosophy, which never hardened into slavish devotion to philosophical tradition.

Bachelard's success in the *agrégation* meant that he was able to add the teaching of philosophy to senior students in the college in Bar-sur-Aube. In 1924 he began work for a doctorate, which would be awarded for the two dissertations he submitted to the Sorbonne in 1927, which would constitute his first two academic publications. The principal dissertation was a study in the epistemology of scientific knowledge, *Essai sur la connaissance approchée*, and was supervised by Abel Rey, who held the chair of history and philosophy of sciences at the Sorbonne, the chair to which Bachelard would succeed on Rey's death thirteen years later in 1940. The second, or minor, dissertation, *Étude sur l'évolution d'un problème de physique: la propagation thermique dans les solides*, supervised by Léon Brunschvicg, a study of the development of ideas about the propagation of heat, was a more conventional exercise in the history of science.

The first of these is a work of remarkable range and authority for a scholar who, in academic terms at least, was at the beginning of his career. Its most striking feature is how very unlike an apprentice work it seems. In its range of reference, its theoretical expansiveness and the mature confidence of its writing, assured enough to be able to range across detailed and situated arguments but also to cinch them together in sudden, arresting claims, it reads like the work of a scholar drawing on a great range of experience and mature reflection. Perhaps its scope and powers of philosophical decision are partly a reflection of the fact that Bachelard was already 43 when it appeared. Bachelard would later describe philosophy as 'royalty without a kingdom', but the sovereignty a schoolteacher becomes accustomed to exercise in the limited realm of his or her classroom might be described as the reverse.[3] Perhaps most striking is the cool audacity of his judgements, often rendered in concentrated aphorisms. Writing, for example, of 'le donné', or what might seem to be 'given' in experience, whether in what Bergson had influentially called the 'données immédiates' of consciousness, or what nowadays is hazily and incuriously called 'data', Bachelard insists that by the given, one can only understand what is *taken* to be given, in different ways and in different circumstances. So the giving depends upon the taking, rather than vice versa. Bachelard's crisp ruling that 'A given must be received [Il faut qu'un donné soit reçu]' enunciates in six words a principle that will guide much of his writing about science.[4]

The *Essai sur la connaissance approchée* opens by setting out the problem that will preoccupy Bachelard for much of his writing life, of how the real and the rational are to be aligned. The challenge is that knowledge of the real must be both complete and clear. Either completeness or clarity on their own are much easier to conceive, and achieve, than their combination. Every clear statement, that might appear to give integration to a body of phenomena, risks omitting or glossing over things that do not completely fit the model. A mere aggregation of contingent phenomena, on the other hand, approaches the condition of unintelligibility. The 'philosophy of the inexact' that Bachelard projects in the book aims to place knowledge 'in its oscillation, at the point where the spirit of finesse converges with the geometric spirit' (*Connaissance*, 8, 10). Bachelard alludes here to the contrast drawn by Blaise Pascal between the 'spirit of geometry' and the 'spirit of finesse'. By the 'spirit of geometry', Pascal means the tendency to combine particulars by rigorous analysis and logical synthesis into general principles of universal validity. Pascal's contrasting 'spirit of finesse', which is sometimes understood as 'intuition' in English explications, refers to the capacity to see things synoptically and at a glance.[5] The distinction between geometry and finesse will be returned to across Bachelard's work, though here it seems to mean something more particular, and even idiosyncratic than in Pascal's usage. Bachelard seems to imply that finesse involves fidelity to precise particulars, even to the point of a kind of fascination with them, where geometry involves the search for the abstract laws and principles that govern those particular processes and phenomena. The English use of the word *finesse* flickers between the idea of fineness, as in the making of delicate or nuanced distinctions, and the display of a somewhat flashy or exhibitionist sophistication. Bachelard's concern is not so much with the contrast of calculation and proof on the one hand and immediate intuitions on the other, but with the contrast between the absoluteness of general laws and the contingency of appearances and experimental results. In saying that knowledge is to be understood as 'oscillation, at the point' of the convergence of geometry and finesse, Bachelard is engineering a teasing paradox of geometry. How, after all, can an oscillation be a point?

Bachelard proposes that 'the whole being [of reality] resides in its resistance to knowledge', meaning that 'we therefore take as an epistemological postulate the fundamental incompleteness of knowledge' (*Connaissance*, 13). One of the problems that Bachelard considers is that of whether, under such conditions, one may only speak of knowledge in approximate terms, or whether exact knowledge of one's approximation might be possible:

> If the place of the pole is in fact fixed, one would be able to measure the degree of the approximation, but in that case one would have no need of approximation because the value sought would in fact be known. One must not lose sight of the fact that the approximation is itself only knowable by approximation. (*Connaissance*, 233)

Bachelard makes it clear that the very notion of exactness is itself variable, depending on the particular conditions under which it is understood:

> Exact knowledge in one domain becomes inexact in relation to other analytic procedures. So the number π is defined very exactly by the relation of the circumference to its diameter as long as one takes geometrical intuition as a given. It is in its evaluation by arithmetical means that this notion is assailed by inexactitude, making approximation necessary. It is not a matter of an unknown in itself, but an unknown in relation to a specific mode of knowledge. One might say, for example, that the diagonal of a square is a geometrical known but an arithmetical unknown. (*Connaissance*, 188)

Such a view seems to anticipate what has come to be called 'constructionism', the view that phenomena do not exist in themselves, but are only intelligible within, and perhaps also the productions of, socially constructed frames of understanding. Constructionism can easily lead to scepticism regarding the limits and possibilities of scientific rationality. In fact, however, Bachelard sees approximation, and the possibility of an ever closer approach to objectivity that it seems to allow, as the dynamic principle that validates scientific enquiry. He quotes from his supervisor, Abel Rey, the view that 'the fact that there are errors, and consequently necessary rectifications, seems rather to be the proof that there is an object. The existence of subjective error proves the existence of objective truth.'[6] Bachelard goes further:

> Moreover, an *a priori* and so to speak massive objectivity is only conceivable as a dialectical value. It amounts to opposing an object to the subject as a necessary condition for the exercise of thought. The self necessarily arises as determined by a non-self, before attempting the assimilation of this non-self. (*Connaissance*, 248)

So, for Bachelard, there is only scientific progress insofar as there is also oscillation between error and truth, a concept that will recur through Bachelard's writing about scientific epistemology.

The second dissertation Bachelard wrote for the award of his doctorate was an historical study of the idea of thermal propagation in physics. Just as he concluded in his study of approximation that 'Reality and knowledge are joined in their very oscillation and dynamic reciprocity' (*Connaissance*, 250), so, rather than simply complementing it, this second dissertation enters into dynamic reciprocity with the first. The study of approximation arrives at what might be thought of as asymptotic realism, in which, even as a complete and final understanding of reality remains inaccessible, there is nevertheless always the possibility of further 'rectification', a word that recurs throughout Bachelard's writing. In this sense, the real is what pulls rationality into being, just as the resistance of objects is necessary for the formation of subjectivity. But the study of the understanding of thermal relations in Bachelard's companion dissertation can be seen as being pulled in the other direction, towards the pole of thought rather than that of reality. It describes the process whereby a vague understanding of heat, which, well into the nineteenth century, was routinely conceived of as the mysterious kind of stuff or substance known as 'caloric', gives way to an understanding based on mathematical relations rather than an idea of physical substance. Traditionally, mathematics has been taken to be an economical and inclusive way of generalizing the relations and processes to be found in reality. Bachelard argues that mathematics adds something to the reality that it formalizes:

> The prediction which rests on a theory rather than on facts could be accused of temerity. But one is forced to admit that the prediction which derives from mathematics succeeds physically and enters intimately into phenomena. It is not a matter of generalization, but rather of an idea that, by anticipation of the fact, discloses detail and brings out specificities. *It is the idea that sees the particular in all its richness, going beyond sensation which grasps only generality.*[7]

Such relations do not merely lie latent in reality, since they cannot really be said to exist as any kind of given before their formalization. Rather than existing in a simple past tense, they are a kind of future perfect that, once articulated, will be what will have intelligibly emerged from the past. The real and the rational are therefore linked by the kind of temporal looping that Bachelard referred to as the 'signe du tardif'.

The possession of the *agrégation* conventionally qualifies its holder to teach in a lycée rather than a college, and it appears that Bachelard turned down an offer of such an advancement, replying, 'No, no, I am doing fine in Bar-sur-Aube, I am doing fine.'[8] That Bachelard continued to teach in the college in his home town for as long as he did may have been in part to avoid uprooting his young daughter. Accounts of Bachelard's time as a teacher in Bar-sur-Aube mention his devoted, and sometimes anxious, attentiveness to Suzanne, even to the point of having her accompany him into the classroom. A remarkable photograph from some time in the 1920s gives evidence of this. In it the forty-year-old Bachelard, his hair and beard already luxurious, stands in a classroom in front of a backboard and behind a desk strewn with books and papers. He has three white-coated colleagues, or possibly senior students, around him, and, standing on a chair, to lift her up to the level of the group, and gently supported at her elbows by her father, the young Suzanne directs a level, candid look straight back into the camera. Almost all of the photographs of Suzanne as a girl show her in company with her father, with whom she would continue to share her life and her accommodation all the way through to Bachelard's death in 1962. Jean-Claude Margolin, who reproduces this photograph, dates it to 1924, which would make Suzanne only four years old, though in it she seems two or three years older.[9]

Though he taught continuously in Bar-sur-Aube for almost ten years, Bachelard's independent studies meant that he was also a fortnightly visitor to the library of the University of Burgundy in Dijon – still today a complete day's round trip by public transport – from which he would bring back a suitcase full of books to support his studies for the philosophy *agrégation*.[10] One of the most extraordinary stories of Bachelard's self-education is that he copied out in longhand the whole of an otherwise unobtainable scientific book in German that he had been given special permission to borrow for a fortnight.[11] Copying out, a practice that has been familiar among literate humans for centuries and even millennia, but began quickly to disappear during the second half of the twentieth century, is a magical as well as practical procedure. It condenses a whole world of labour, servility, rapture and sublimated dissidence. It is at once a stupefying slavery of the hand and a phantasmal exaltation, in which the sorcerer's apprentice can take the place of his imaginary master.

The close relationship between school and university teaching in France means that it would not have been at all unusual for Bachelard to have proceeded to a university position from a lycée on attainment of his doctorate in 1927: Henri Bergson published his first works as a lycée teacher, before his appointment at the Collège de France.[12] It was rather more remarkable for a teacher of younger students in a college, of lower prestige than a lycée, to be invited, as Bachelard was in 1928, to teach courses in the University of Burgundy, and subsequently to be offered a professorship, which he accepted in 1930.

Once embarked on sustained writing of his own for publication, Bachelard found that he had a rich seam to work. Having been for so long the patiently accumulative 'subject of the verb "to study"', Bachelard was eager to reverse the direction of flow, interrupting the simple decantation of knowledge from its container into its studious containing vessel.[13] In the process, Bachelard would find in the principle of interruption, to which he had himself for much of his life been frustratingly subject, his great animating preoccupation, and the source of his most distinctive contribution to the history and philosophy of science.

By the time he and Suzanne had made the move to the University of Burgundy in Dijon, Bachelard had already published a third book, *La valeur inductive de la relativité*, in which he moved from the history of science to an appraisal of the effect of the revolution in scientific thought initiated by Einstein's theory of relativity. By 1929, when Bachelard's book appeared, there was no shortage of explications of the theories of relativity, encouraged by the debate on the topic that had taken place in Paris between Einstein and Bergson, and by popular works published in English by Bertrand Russell and Arthur Eddington. Nevertheless, relativity remained, as it still is today, a kind of standing affront to common sense and experience, even given the many practical and experimental confirmations of the theory, and perhaps because of them. If Bachelard's first book had emphasized the continuing need for 'rectification' of theories in the light of experimental results, this book articulates a more fundamental sense of discontinuity in the development of science. In the opening words of his book, Bachelard made it clear that the break made by the theory of relativity was only the inauguration of a continuing effort of rethinking:

> the newness of relativity is not static in nature. It is not things which surprise us, but the mind which constructs its own surprise and submits itself to the play of questions. Relativity is more than a definitive renewal in the way in which the physical phenomenon is thought, it is a method of progressive discovery.[14]

Bachelard's next book, *Le pluralisme cohérent de la chimie moderne*, his first to be written from the security of an academic position in a university, turned from contemporary physics back to chemistry – back, in the sense that his aim is to show how chemistry became a modern science during the late nineteenth century. It is a transition that Bachelard would recapitulate repeatedly in his writing during the 1930s. As in his first book on approximation, Bachelard characterized chemistry in terms of an oscillation, homologous with his earlier oscillation between 'finesse' and 'geometry', between detail and system, or 'plurality on the one hand and the reduction of plurality on the other'.[15] This will require Bachelard to explain how a science focused on the idea of substances, or of independent, unrelated and self-sufficient entities, moves towards a coordinated 'geometry of substance' or 'harmony of substances' (*Pluralisme*, 8). Contemporary chemistry, Bachelard advises, has discovered 'the general plan of elementary substances' (*Pluralisme*, 9), founded essentially on mathematical relations, rather than essential forms of matter. For modern chemistry, 'chemical substances appear as examples of laws rather than examples of things' (*Pluralisme*, 23). This licenses and mandates a move from realism to rationalism, Bachelard's aim being to show how 'the primitive realism of experimental chemistry has finally opened up the routes to the rationalism of mathematical chemistry' (*Pluralisme*, 27).

Such a history, in which the conception of a plurality of distinct, heterogeneous substances yields to an understanding of general orders of material relations, gives every appearance of a reduction or simplification. But Bachelard's point, as in the conclusion to his doctoral dissertation on the mathematics of heat propagation, is that this methodological reduction actually multiplies chemical possibilities:

> One demands of a general perspective not just that it be extensive, but also that it be extensible. Diversity springs up anew, with a revived power and prodigality, from the very thought which had drawn an antecedent diversity into unity. (*Pluralisme*, 12)

The governing example here is the discovery by Dmitri Mendeleev of the principles of the periodic table of elements, announced in 1869, which showed that elements followed recurring cycles of properties corresponding to their atomic weights when ranged in order. Mendeleev not only provided a periodic grouping of the properties of existing elements but predicted the existence, in vacant positions in the table, of other, hitherto unknown elements, which were duly discovered between 1875 and 1886, being given the names scandium, gallium and germanium. This seemed for the first time to give chemistry the same predictive powers as astronomy and physics, allowing for the movement 'from an idle pluralism, which accepted all the elements isolated in the laboratory as unrelated individualities, to a coordinated pluralism' (*Pluralisme*, 120).[16] The essential principle of regular recurrence allows for the coordination of differentiation and similarity according to the principle that will come to seem ever more prominent in Bachelard's writing, of rhythm. Although the word 'rhythm' does not appear in *Le pluralisme cohérent de la chimie moderne*, it would be a governing preoccupation of the book *Intuition of the Instant*, which Bachelard published in the same year. The adaptation by William Crookes in 1887 of Mendeleev's two-dimensional table into a spiral model, which took account of the historical evolution of elements from the primal matter of stars, made for an open rather than closed rhythm, suggesting that 'chemistry had found its Darwin' (*Pluralisme*, 125).

Bachelard traces in his book an evolution from the ancient Pythagorean idea of the harmony of the elements, in a direct relation with the divine plans of the Creator, towards a harmony of reasoning (*Pluralisme*, 226). The capacity to make possible a renewed diversification is what constitutes the active nature of chemistry. It provides a framework, not of unalterable laws, but of possibility, allowing for the synthesis of new elements and compounds: 'In the world of the chemist, one may certainly not say that everything that is possible exists naturally, but one can affirm that everything that is possible can be made' (*Pluralisme*, 228). Bachelard's view, which may seem more unsettling now, is that 'In chemistry, whatever may be coherently thought, whatever is systematically possible, can be *realized*, in the full sense of the term' (*Pluralisme*, 228). Bachelard is less concerned with the burden of scientific responsibility that this opening of possibility brings than more recent writers have been, in the light of the developments in nuclear physics, genetic engineering and automated computation.

The principle of the realizability of scientific theory is introduced in 'Noumenon and Microphysics', an essay that Bachelard published in 1931, in which he characteristically bends the usual meaning of the word 'noumenon' to his purposes. A noumenon is usually distinguished as something that exists fully in itself and independently of human perception, as opposed to a phenomenon, which is something that appears or is shown through the senses. In Platonic and neo-Platonic usage, the idea of the noumenon often has a mystical shimmer, as reflected in the ways in which the word 'numinous' is employed to convey the sense of the sublime or divine. Bachelard's usage draws attention to the fact that *noumenon*, from νοῦς, *nous*, mind, understanding, literally means that which is known rather than that which merely appears, *phenomenon* being formed by contrast from φαίνεσθαι, *phainesthai*, to appear or be shown. Where, for the Platonic tradition, the realm of the numinous is eternal and immutable, such that for Immanuel Kant it was not at all clear that human beings could ever be equipped with the special kind of intuition required to apprehend noumena, for Bachelard noumena are actively formed through the work of mathematical reasoning, and thereby denuded of their spiritual aura. The reasoning required may not be easy, and its outcomes may often, especially in atomic or subatomic physics, be counterintuitive, but there is nothing unworldly or otherworldly about its practice or outcomes. It is for this reason that noumena, though not apprehensible as real by the senses, can nevertheless be subject to *realization* – and, indeed, for Bachelard, must be. This is the central principle of what he called *phenomenotechnique*, 'by means of which, new phenomena are not only merely discovered, but also invented [inventés] and made up from scratch'.[17] The idea that physics is involved in the production of the kind of second nature constituted by Boyle's vacuum – which is both unnatural, in that it does not seem to occur naturally, and yet also arises from and is obedient to natural laws – produces one of the temporal inversions that are characteristic of Bachelard's thought:

> newly discovered theorems must always end up being realized. In order to do so, it is no longer a question, as our predecessors of the 19th century incessantly repeated, of translating the facts obtained from experience into the language of mathematics. It is rather a question of doing the opposite. We need to express in the common language of experience a deep reality, which is mathematically meaningful before it is phenomenally significant.[18]

In the final words of 'Noumenon and Microphysics', Bachelard proclaims the productive powers of mathematical rationality, governed by the modified Cartesian motto '*cogitatur, ergo est*', it is (can be) thought, therefore it exists (can be).[19] This seems just a twitch away from the 'omnipotence of thought' defined by Freud:

> we find ourselves, for the first time, in the presence of a metaphysics that is positive because it can be experimented with. It is the metatechnique of an artificial nature. Present day atomic science is more than a description of phenomena, it is a production of phenomena. Mathematical physics is more than an abstract thought, it is a naturalized thought (*pensée naturée*).[20]

As intimated earlier, this orientation to the realizing function of mathematical rationality may be seen as a sign of the lingering force of the idea of engineering for Bachelard. The apparent abandonment of the ambition to become an engineer in favour of the abstract work of philosophy of science in fact leads Bachelard's philosophy to curve round into the kind of higher engineering, the 'description' that is also a 'production', that is proposed in the idea of *phenomenotechnique*. It is another of those strange loops of thought and life, in which early and late criss-cross over each other, of which Bachelard's life was so full.

Five years out from his doctorate, Bachelard already had four books to his name, which substantially solidified his reputation as a historical philosopher of science. The books would continue to come, at a rate of almost one a year. Although Bachelard continued to address particular problems in the history of science – atomism, space, electricity – his work in epistemology from 1930 onwards became steadily more ambitious and encompassing.

3

Cadence of Instants, 1932–6

Given how long a road it had been, and how strewn with obstacles, and bearing in mind that he was already 44 when he took up his post in the University of Burgundy, Bachelard might have been forgiven for taking a few years to settle in to his newly acquired security and authority, cementing his reputation with a few more works of historical overview and synthesis. Bachelard was not at this point an intellectual trailblazer, for the history and philosophy of science had already become established as what Gary Gutting has described as 'a nearly autonomous domain' in the French university.[1] The early twentieth-century work of Henri Poincaré, Pierre Duhem and Emile Meyerson, all of them, like Bachelard, relative outsiders to the world of mainstream French philosophy, anticipated by some decades the interest in the history of science in the Anglophone world from the 1970s onwards.[1] One of its leading representatives, Léon Brunschvicg, had been the supervisor for one of Bachelard's two doctoral dissertations, and Bachelard's work has seemed to many to exhibit strong continuities with Brunschvicg's views of the historical importance of the challenge posed by scientific discoveries to philosophy.[2]

Even though he would take his place in a lineage that seemed to run through him to his successor Georges Canguilhem and then, through the work of Michel Foucault, outside France, Bachelard was never entirely comfortable with this position as representative of French history and philosophy of science. Indeed, his achievement of professional status seemed to stimulate in him a kind of intellectual intemperance that propelled him into new areas of thought and styles of writing. This pattern of intemperate recoil from security would be repeated a decade later, when he moved on from Dijon to a position of even higher distinction in the Sorbonne.

This is not to say that, having spent so long in the solitary position of the autodidact, Bachelard did not relish the new intellectual sociability that working in a university offered him. Bachelard's encounter with the work of his colleague Gaston Roupnel, the professor of Burgundian history, provided particular stimulation. Roupnel's books on the history of Burgundy have been described as promoting 'an essentialized, rustic, and traditional cultural identity that could provide an alternative to generic models of "modern," anonymous, urban, and bureaucratic national French identity'.[3] Coming in the train of two popular novels of Burgundian life, *Nono* and *Le Vieux Garain*, Roupnel's *Histoire de la campagne française* (1932) was part of a strong tradition of French rural social history that emphasized locality and long durée, and was most influentially embodied in the work of historians associated with the journal *Annales d'histoire économique et sociale*, founded in 1929 by Lucien Febvre and Marc Bloch. Roupnel's book shares the emphasis of these historians on collective mentality, ending with an evocation of the stoic endurance of the peasant, locked into the movement of the seasons, as epitomized in the patience required to cultivate the vine, keeping intact an ancient way of being and relation to the natural world: 'Here', wrote Roupnel, 'the soul is more ancient than the oldest of fields.'[4] Although Gaston Bachelard's own life was proof that rural life was anything but timeless and unchangeably enduring, least of all in the France of the first half of the twentieth century, Roupnel's work may have articulated an idealized vision of a past enduring into the present that would be a powerful influence on his later thinking.

Although twenty years later, in *The Poetics of Space*, Bachelard would recall 'having learned the dialectic of fields and woods from my unforgettable friend Gaston Roupnel', it was, however, neither as an historian nor as a novelist of peasant life that Bachelard drew most from the work of his colleague.[5] Instead, Bachelard found his provocation in Roupnel's *Siloë*, a book of metaphysical speculations published in 1927, which drew eclectically on contemporary physics and evolutionary biology to formulate a pantheistic doctrine of Universal Spirit, everywhere immanent, yet appearing suddenly in instants of intense vision. Both in its evocations of immutability and in its emphasis on the time-out-of-time of revelatory moments, *Siloë* seems like an unpredictable production from a professor of history, even one also known for two successful novels of rural life, and Philip Whalen's judgement that it is 'quite forgotten nowadays and little read in its day' does not seem unduly severe.[6] But it provided Bachelard with a new perspective on the psychology of time, which he would retain and develop for the remainder of his writing life.

Although Bachelard's *L'intuition de l'instant*, his strange and intense meditation on *Siloë*, appeared in the same year as his book on the evolution of modern chemistry, in 1932, it looks forward to the books on the imagination that Bachelard would write during and after the Second World War, while not stylistically resembling them at all. The aim and method of the book is anticipated in an odd passage from Bachelard's 1928 dissertation in which he compares the 'rapid unity' that might often seem to be provided by a scientific description of disparate phenomena to 'the intuition which integrates poetic diversity in the sentiment of a single subject' characteristic of religious or artistic experiences. His example is Goethe:

> We thus create, out of nowhere, by the most obvious forms of artifice, a generality that has no root in reality. Goethe, neglecting the preparatory arts of drawing, accustoms himself to hold objects before his attention as mere opportunities for this emotional response. He seized them as a whole only 'in so far as they produced an effect'. For an artist, to know is to describe for feeling. Lyricism appears to us as a coherent system in which the mind is particularly agile and alive.[7]

This is an anomalous passage, breaking out in a work that is primarily concerned with articulating the pattern whereby scientific rationality progresses through different stages of approximation. Bachelard's motivation through *Intuition of the Instant* is to articulate a philosophy of time that is based on the kind of instantaneous seizure of experience and experience of seizure glimpsed in the remarks on Goethe.

Bachelard's life, I have suggested, was given its meaning from the experience of abrupt discontinuity. This is not just because the life that he would have wished to have was repeatedly interrupted, though that was certainly the case. It was, more fundamentally, because Bachelard built interruption into the central principle of his life. Bachelard saw the history of scientific thought as held together and given its shape through the repeated experience of rupture, as one way of viewing the world was forced unexpectedly to give way to another. The history of scientific thought formed a fabric woven of interruption, a continuity of discontinuities. It is only the continual fracture with the past that makes it possible for something like a continuous history of thought to be articulated, a word that connotes both joining and segmenting.

Bachelard found considerable support for this way of thinking in Roupnel's insistence on the importance of experiences of sudden revelation. More importantly, Roupnel provided the impetus for Bachelard to make a defining break with one of the most dominant philosophical frameworks of the 1920s and '30s, that associated with the work of Henri Bergson. Bergson's most influential claim was that most of the ways in which we think of the experience of time distort it, in that they chop time up into separable parts. The process and experience of the cinema seemed to Bergson like a perfect example of the denaturing dissection of time into snapshots. In reality, Bergson insisted, time was absolutely continuous, a matter not of a succession of discrete states, but of duration, or continuous change without distinction. Much of the energy of Bachelard's work from the early 1930s onwards comes from his aggressive denial of this idea, and the consensus established around it. It is from the moment of *Intuition of the Instant* that Bachelard develops what he would later characterize as his 'Philosophy of No'. The word 'sudden' is from Latin *subito*, *sub-* under + *-ire* to go. It therefore forms an unexpected alliance with the word *subject*, from *sub-* and *iacio*, literally that which is *thrown under*. Suddenness, especially the suddenness of dissidence, is what forms the subject.

Intuition of the Instant is a very gnarled read, but is really impelled throughout by the single intuition named in its title, that the most immediate experience of time is that of the instant, surging up constantly from, and standing out against, the background noise of continuous life. In a way, this is simply a reversal of the move made by Bergson, who argued that the idea of a single point in time is in fact the contrivance of geometry. In Bachelard's countermove, it is the idea of the continuity of time that is the construct of geometers, as a reification of the line rather than the point: 'if we establish that duration is a relative and secondary datum, always more or less artificial, how could our illusion of it contradict our immediate experience of the instant?'[8]

To read *Intuition of the Instant* biographically as well as philosophically is to wonder about the motivation for this 'consecration of the instant as time's primordial element' (*Instant*, 8). The real subject of Bachelard's assertion is in fact not concealed, but utterly manifest, for it concerns and performs its own power, its power of assertion. Just as the experience of the instant is of a snatching up of experience out of mere temporal subsisting, so the idea of the instant is itself, for Bachelard, a seizing of one's own seizure. Its motto is articulated in the book in the strange phrase '*every time we want to, we can experience the efficacy of our acts*' (*Instant*, 23). For Bachelard the experience of instantaneity comes not, as so often in religious discourse, and in the cult of momentariness in modernist writers such as Joyce and Woolf, as an epiphany, some unwilled revelation to which we are made subject, but as an act of self-willing, which Bachelard distinguishes from action, which must unfold in durational time:

> For Bergson, an action is always a continuous development that posits an underlying duration between a decision and its goal (each more or less schematic) – a duration that is always original and real. For a Roupnel supporter, an act is above all an instantaneous decision. (*Instant*, 11–12)

These themes of duration and instantaneity are intricately allied with Bachelard's own intellectual life. Just at the point at which, having laboriously constructed his own curriculum and intellectual life-course over so many years of remorselessly studious self-government, apprenticing every moment to his larger, longer purpose, he might have seemed ready to synchronize his life with the steady cadence of the work of institutional knowledge, Bachelard now finds himself overtaken by the desire to assert the force of desire, concentrated into pure decision, against duration. Having striven to build continuity in the face of interruption, Bachelard now turns against the idea of continuity at the very moment of seeming to attain it, recruiting interruption as the motive principle of his own striving rather than its antagonist. Strangely, this assertion of discontinuity will come itself to provide a principle of continuity in Bachelard's work. The principle of oscillation that was to the fore in the *Essai sur la connaissance approchée* is henceforth modulated by a new conception of a fractious rhythm of dissent that would allow for discontinuous events to be knitted together into history.

But, in simply inverting Bergson's doctrine of duration into a doctrine of instantaneity, Bachelard also gives himself a near-intractable problem. The problem arises not from the claim that there is an experience of discontinuity that should be taken as seriously as the experience of continuity, but from the promotion of that claim to generality, in the argument that time is all instantaneity and nothing beside. Such an absolute view inevitably poses two questions: first, the question of what kind of background such temporal instants might leap out from, and second, the question of what kind of continuity, and according to what principle, might arise from a sequence of such eruptions.

Bachelard attempts to find a solution to this problem through a musical metaphor. What we tend to think of as unbroken duration might be understood as the process formed through the concatenation of instrumental instants produced by an orchestra:

> While in the world's orchestra there are instruments that often fall silent, it is false to say there is always some instrument playing. The world is conducted in keeping with a musical measure imposed by the cadence of instants. (*Instant*, 25–6)

But what could this 'cadence of instants' be but some version of Bergson's frequently repeated comparison of the continuity of separate instants to the binding force of a melody, in which none of the component notes are completely discrete?[9]

Four years later, Bachelard would put these questions at the centre of an enlarged argument about the experience of time that he presented in *The Dialectic of Duration*. The argument now is no longer that time consists only and entirely of instants, with literally nothing occupying the space or time between them, but instead that 'the phenomena of duration are constructed by rhythms, rhythms that are by no means necessarily grounded on an entirely uniform and regular time.'[10] This allows the idea of the continuity of temporal experience to come back in and through the principle of rhythm: 'To have duration, we must entrust our lives to rhythms, that is to say to systems of instants' (*Duration*, 21). On this view, time is not fractured but syncopated, holding together, to be sure, by its edges and overlaps rather than by any continuous thread or undertone, but holding together nevertheless. In principle at least, this allows Bachelard to join together, or make continuous, continuity and discontinuity themselves – even if it seems to be at the cost of reinventing in the form of 'rhythm' the very Bergsonian duration that he is at such pains to refuse.

Rhythm reduces to an oscillation between two essential principles, that which produces newness through the negation of what has come before, and the opposite or remission of that striving antagonism. The new ingredient in this view of time is announced in the book's opening statement that it is 'intended to be an introduction to the teaching of a philosophy of repose' (*Duration*, 17). The rhythm of striving and repose will increasingly become not merely the subject of Bachelard's attention in his writing, but a way of dramatizing his own fraught relations to the ideas of thought and knowledge. Increasingly, we will be able to take all Bachelard's arguments as allegories of themselves, meditations on the force of their own formation and maintaining, which are driven by the effort to understand, and to live out, the work of thought as it is being undertaken.

Bachelard's thinking and argument in the books written in the middle years of the 1930s are not very hospitable to the reader. Their difficulty may well be the result of a new intellectual fertility and confidence on Bachelard's part. In *The Dialectic of Duration* in particular, new arguments press forward so thickly that it is extremely difficult for the reader to make any sustained headway through them. But if their difficulty is in part the effect of a supreme facility, and an unresting energy of objection and qualification, it seems in some ways also to be the effect of an inhibition. So intent is Bachelard on multiplying arguments and loading every rift with ore that it is as though he is denying himself the indulgence of any redundancy. It is as though Bachelard were disposed to react against the appearance of any continuity in his own arguments, in obedience to his stubborn opposition to every form of Bergsonian duration. As a result, nothing is allowed to stand for any period of time as a given, or to be taken for granted. The effect is often of a kind of inertia, of a mode of reasoning so pestled by internal dispute as to bring itself to an irritable standstill. Though endlessly declarative, Bachelard's writing in *Intuition of the Instant* and *The Dialectic of Duration* seems unwilling to settle into any declaration. A new word is to the fore in *The Dialectic of Duration*, a word that carries the force of the dialectic named in its title: more and more, discourse and debate are stiffened into *polemic*, from Greek πολεμικός, warlike, hostile: 'all effective judgements – that is to say all judgements that engage the consciousness – are for us negative judgements; they are the decisive arguments in a fierce polemic' (*Duration*, 32).

The new conviction that drives Bachelard's work is articulated into the self-certifying challenge: 'Is not knowledge essentially a polemic?' (*Duration*, 32). Pressed down into the grain of Bachelard's writing, this principle of unrelieved polemic can produce pages of tireless logic-chopping or, as exemplified in the theories that Bachelard unfolds about the therapeutic operations of vibrations in homeopathics, a kind of pseudoscientific fantasia, elaborating itself in rapturous midair:

> It is because doses are ultra-diluted that medical substances can propagate rhythms. In a massive form in fact, substance would in a way absorb its own rhythms; it would start resonating with itself, without fulfilling its role as a stimulus external to itself. It would escape indispensable destruction and fail to play with nothingness. It would reappropriate itself. Indeed, radiation physics does show that substances act above all through what is on the surface and that radiations from what lies deep are absorbed by radiant matter itself. (*Duration*, 141)

It may seem strange that the attainment of intellectual and professional security should have produced in Bachelard this kind of fractious exasperation rather than serenity, but such does seem to have been the case. This may be another example of the spirit of *après-coup*, as embodied in a peculiar side-comment about Galileo's famous recantation of his recantation:

> Back in his prison after having renounced his 'errors', Galileo murmurs 'yet it does move': He murmurs this in suffering, in the rancour of defeat, in a stifled polemic. But all his thought is a reaction against previous official denials. (*Duration*, 32)

In a sense, Bachelard's work might be said at this period to be inhabiting the mode of intense but empty disputation within logic itself that characterized late medieval Scholasticism. The psychoanalyst W. R. Bion developed a description of this attitude of corrosive doubt and denial that he called 'Attacks on Linking'. Such psychological actions are apparent in patients who cannot contain the tension of ambivalent impulses or values, and so seek to split off good from bad, to the point where even language, as the principal means of establishing links or continuities, comes under attack.[11] The paradoxical adherence to the principle of negation that Bachelard would later call the Philosophy of No may perhaps be read as an enactment of Bachelard's ambivalence towards the attainment of intellectual autonomy in knowledge, which is both insatiably desired and powerfully resented, as the very means of his exclusion. Bachelard's Philosophy of No constantly seeks vengeful mastery over the very knowledge that seems to offer him mastery.

Just as scientific enquiry found a new kind of definition and clarity of purpose in the work of observation and experiment – through the stabilizing intervention of objects into subjective querulousness – so, once freed to focus on external objects rather than gnawing inwardly at the texture of its own thought, Bachelard will find in the second half of the 1930s a new and more steadily sustained way of construing the history of scientific reasoning.

Bachelard in the 1930s.

4

Spirit of Science, 1934–40

In 1932 Bachelard was invited to give a lecture at a conference in the Netherlands organized by the Societas Spinozana to celebrate the three-hundredth anniversary of the birth of the philosopher Baruch Spinoza. Bachelard used his lecture, titled 'Physique et métaphysique', to build boldly on Spinoza's distinction between *natura naturans* – nature naturing (that is, expressing its own nature in its action) – and *natura naturata* – nature natured, or understood in terms of its necessary principles.[1] Bachelard introduced a third principle, to name the production by human reason of natural phenomena according to the realization of natural principles, which he called *natura constructa*: 'Human reason is therefore a *natura construans* which brings about a *natura constructa* which is much richer than all the structures found in nature.'[2] Bachelard unapologetically construed this re-engineering of nature as a new form of human self-engineering:

> In considering the success of experimentation one perceives that the destiny of clarity is an active destiny. Once we comprehend, we create; and, reciprocally, once we create, we comprehend. In accomplishing science, man accomplishes himself. In realizing science, man realizes himself.[3]

Building on such perspectives, Bachelard addressed himself ever more to the general question of what he called the 'ésprit scientifique', exploiting the leverage offered by that French word, which can mean both mind and, more capaciously and even romantically, 'spirit'.

We are given a glimpse of what will harden into the project of Bachelard's scientific epistemology in the extraordinary prediction delivered at the end of *The Dialectic of Duration* that 'intellectual life is to become the dominant form of life, physically speaking, with thought time prevailing over lived time.'[4] This grandiose sense of the 'intellectual life', which rhymes Bachelard's personal biography with the history of scientific thought, is developed most sharply and unmistakeably in three books of the later 1930s: *Le nouvel esprit scientifique* (1934), *La formation de l'esprit scientifique* (1938) and *La Philosophie du non* (1940). It will be maintained without serious revision through the remainder of Bachelard's writing about scientific epistemology. Though all these books remain focused around particular scientific controversies, they allow themselves to be nourished by the long view of the development of science itself. In these books, controversy about time is permitted to assume a narratable temporal shape in which the agonistic biography of science is the lengthened shadow of Bachelard's own struggle for, and simultaneously also against, knowledge.

Bachelard argues that twentieth-century science is revolutionary in that it embodies a decisive break with the realist understanding that has governed the understanding of the world and the place of humans in it. Where previous theories and practices of science had sought to know how nature worked, Bachelard's new science is driven by the impulse to know how science could work on nature. From this point onwards, Bachelard will insist on the essentially aggressive nature of scientific enquiry. This goes further than the well-known principle articulated by Francis Bacon in his *Novum Organon* of 1620, that 'the secrets of nature reveal themselves more readily under the vexations of art than when they go their own way.'[5] According to Carolyn Merchant (2012) there was a strong tendency over the course of the later seventeenth century and beyond to translate Bacon's original Latin 'vexationes artium' as 'tortures' or 'torments' of art.[6] The word 'polemical', which Bachelard will use increasingly of science, implies not so much aggression directed at nature as aggression directed at the opinions of others, or one's own opinions, previously held. 'Scientific observation is always polemical; it either confirms or denies a prior thesis, a preexistent model, an observational protocol.'[7] Scientific rationality therefore turns into itself through turning on itself. It might seem as though such a dynamism of dissent must tend to produce a turn away from nature and towards the introversion of debate and dialectic. But for Bachelard the work of negation in modern science tends always towards the displacement of passive realism as regards how things are, by active realization of how things might be made to be:

> once the step is taken from observation to experimentation, the polemical character of knowledge stands out even more sharply. Now phenomena must be selected, filtered, purified, shaped by instruments; indeed it may well be the instruments that produce the phenomenon in the first place. And instruments are nothing but theories materialized . . . A truly scientific phenomenology is therefore essentially a phenomeno-technology. Its purpose is to amplify what is revealed beyond appearance. It takes its instruction from construction. (*New Scientific Spirit*, 13)

Bachelard moves ever more emphatically and explicitly towards the evocation of something like a magical omnipotence, in which, by remaking nature and appropriating the powers of reproduction traditionally ascribed to it, man himself becomes miraculously self-making and self-transforming. The Cartesian vision of the world remade as thought expressed in *The New Scientific Spirit* is a kind of idealization of Bachelard's own autodidacticism:

> Wonderworking reason [raison thaumaturge] designs its own miracles. Science conjures up a world, by means not of magic immanent in reality but of rational impulse immanent in mind. The first achievement of the scientific spirit was to create reason in the image of the world; modern science has moved on to the project of constructing a world in the image of reason. Scientific reason makes rational entities real, in the full sense of the world. (*New Scientific Spirit*, 13)[8]

It is hard not to wonder why, at a time when many scientists were convinced of the necessity for socialist rationalization of economic and social life, Bachelard kept the cautious distance he did from this kind of extension into the real world of scientific rationalism. There is, however, just a flicker of this ambition in the final chapter of *The New Scientific Spirit*, in which, following from his statement that the new paradigms in physics and mathematics are 'historical dialectics that grew out of the correction of an error, the extension of a system, or the completion of an idea', Bachelard remarks that, 'in order for the new scientific spirit to take on the same formative value as a new economic policy, all that is needed is a little social life, a little human sympathy' (*New Scientific Spirit*, 172). The phrasing in Bachelard's original French makes unmistakeable the parallel between the new scientific spirit of his title and the Soviet economic episode of the 1920s known as the 'New Economic Policy': 'pour que le nouvel esprit, scientifique – le n.e.s. – prenne la même valeur formative qu'une nouvelle économie politique – la n.e.p.' 'such that the new, scientific spirit – the NSS – acquires the same formative value as a new political economy – the NEP'. 'NEP' was commonly employed in Russia and beyond as a shorthand for the New Economic Policy and its effects. The New Economic Policy introduced by Lenin in 1921 in fact involved the temporary relaxation of centralized economic control to revive Russia's sluggish economy. It was followed by return to collectivization under Stalin, the second of whose Five-Year Plans was well under way at the time Bachelard was writing.

It is difficult to know how seriously to take this allusion. Bachelard never went any further than this in considering the application of scientific rationality to social planning, so we are left to guess what he might have meant to suggest by the 'formative value' of scientific thinking. He certainly lived long enough to see the growth of the apprehension that pure rationality, as embodied in the subjection of social life to various kinds of large-scale calculation, was always at risk of degenerating into forms of abstract rationalization that come close to being irrationality itself.

A very great deal rides on the idea of 'formation', which appears in the title of the work of epistemology by which Bachelard would become most well-known during the 1930s, *La formation de l'esprit scientifique* of 1938. Having preoccupied himself in a series of books with the characterization of the revolutionary new dispensations of modern science, Bachelard again turned backwards in this book to consider 'pre-scientific' moments. English *formation* is less overlaid with ideas of social and psychological culture, especially through education, than French *formation*, which therefore has more of the connotations of German *Bildung*. The echo between *Le nouvel esprit scientifique* and *La formation de l'esprit scientifique* of four years later is also lost in the move from scientific 'spirit' to scientific 'mind' in the English titles. But it is clear from reading the text in either language that Bachelard saw the making of the scientific mind as something like soul-making, in a spiritualization of rationality, or even a kind of thaumaturgic thinking of thought.

This idea of the psychological striving involved in the effort to form scientific reason, which had never been far away in any of Bachelard's books, simultaneously receives a new inflection with a term that he introduced in the subtitle to *La formation de l'esprit scientifique: Contribution à une psychanalyse de la connaissance objective*. Bachelard's negotiations with psychoanalysis would be a constant feature of his thinking for the remainder of his life.

Psychoanalysis was slow to gain a foothold in French intellectual life. This was in marked contrast to England, where the London Psychoanalytic Society had been formed under the leadership of Ernest Jones in 1913, and reformed as the British Psychoanalytic Society in 1919. Much of its efforts were devoted to securing the authority of Freudian psychoanalysis following the disagreements between Freud and Jung that led to Jung breaking away in 1914, and the development of the more idealized, less clinical and more anthropological form of psychoanalysis that Jung called analytic psychology. Translations of Freud into English began to appear from 1909, and were given renewed impetus when Leonard and Virginia Woolf's Hogarth Press took over the responsibility of translating Freud, under the leadership of James Strachey.

As a result, psychoanalysis was much more well known in English public and intellectual life by the 1930s than in France. It was not until 1926 that the Société psychanalytique de Paris was formed under the leadership of René Laforgue. It would later benefit from the support of Princess Marie Bonaparte, Napoleon's great-grand-niece, who became an intimate and supporter of Freud, to the extent indeed of paying the very considerable ransom required to ensure his safe passage out of Vienna. A journal, the *Revue française de psychanalyse*, began publication in 1927. But with the occupation of Paris by Nazi Germany in 1940, French psychoanalysis almost ceased operations. Following the Second World War, it would experience a notable and influential revival, which would make France the centre of postwar psychoanalytic thinking, led by figures such as Jacques Lacan, Didier Anzieu, and Jean Laplanche and Jean-Bertrand Pontalis, whose *The Language of Psychoanalysis* (1967) was formative. But Bachelard had little or no contact with these later developments.

He seems first to have encountered psychoanalysis through Juliette Favez-Boutonier, a colleague teaching philosophy in the University of Dijon whom he met on joining the university in 1930. He may indeed have made her acquaintance earlier, since she studied for a doctorate in philosophy at the Sorbonne in 1926 with Léon Brunschvicg, who was at the time also Bachelard's supervisor. During the 1930s, she undertook medical training and was in contact with Daniel Lagache and René Laforgue, who were leading figures in the development of French psychoanalysis.

Juliette Favez-Boutonier in the 1950s.

She underwent psychoanalysis herself in Paris in 1935, and developed a specialist interest in child psychology.[9] She would work closely again with Bachelard in the 1940s, when he supervised her thesis on anxiety, which she submitted in 1945.[10]

Indeed, though Bachelard relied on and repeatedly referred to psychoanalysis for around a decade from 1940 onwards, his understanding of it was not based on very intimate or systematic acquaintance with psychoanalytic ideas or practice. References to psychology more generally are common in Bachelard's epistemological writings of the 1920s and '30s. In an essay on caprice published in 1934, Bachelard referred to the play of desire in the visual perception of the child, in ways that suggest a psychoanalytic receptivity to the work of desire in infantile sense experience:

> It is also in front of the distant image that we can grasp the true role of our caprice, the first form of the subject's intuition in his thaumaturgical action. The caprice is precisely the visual will, the will without subjective force, and without awareness either of the often unmasterable hostility of objective inertia. It is the sovereign power which rotates in play the kaleidoscope of distant miniatures. Thought governed by small muscles gets used to seeing the world moved by eye and finger. Before *homo faber*, the *puer lusor* possessed the World through its plaything. He acts out on his toy his own impulses and rather than learning the real hostility of objective force, he retains only the deceitful power of his caprice. All psychology would be modified if we could convince ourselves of the infantile character of our energetic experience.[11]

But up to around 1933, such insights were characterized as belonging to 'psychology', a field that was in fact highly developed and was closely associated with philosophy in France through writers such as Henri Bergson and Pierre Janet, to both of whom Bachelard makes frequent reference. The earliest use of the word 'psychoanalysis' in Bachelard's published writing is in *The New Scientific Spirit* in 1934, in referring to physicists 'liberating themselves from Euclidean presuppositions by engaging in what one might call a kind of psychoanalysis' (39). 'A kind of psychoanalysis' is a frisky translation of Bachelard's French original, in which he asserts more definitively that 'le physicien aborde un nouveau domaine en toute indépendance d'esprit, après une psychanalyse des entraînements euclidiens', which might be more obediently translated as 'the physicist approaches a new field with a complete independence of spirit, following a psychoanalysis of Euclidean habits' – with none of the provisionality of 'what one might call a kind of psychoanalysis'.[12]

Psychoanalysis gave a coherence to Bachelard's thinking and writing about science, and more particularly the psychology of scientific rationality, which had asserted itself continuously but unsystematically during ten years of writing. Cristina Chimisso is right to describe this, not just as a rational investigation of human psychology, but also as a 'psychology of reason' itself. As such it is not just a project to understand the workings of the mind, but also a project for the 'cure' of the mind' – almost, one might say, a project whereby the mind would cure itself of itself.[13] Psychoanalysis provided a kind of programme that pulled the various historical enquiries that Bachelard had undertaken into convergence, allowing them all to be seen as part of a process of unconscious self-analysis on the part of scientists, and therefore to programme the development of the future of science. But if psychoanalysis gave Bachelard's work coherence, it was a wilful kind of coherence, which sometimes approaches ferocity. Bachelard's psychoanalysis of knowledge is an aggressive turning of knowledge against itself, which very likely drew its energy from Bachelard's own experience, in which, having had to struggle so hard to break into the charmed and authoritative circle of accredited knowledge, he would continue to regard that world of knowledge with resentment and a fissile hostility. This ambivalent envenoming of desire with disdain would allow Bachelard to cling to his condition of exclusion even, and perhaps especially, as he was ever more comfortably accommodated within the official institutions and structures of knowledge.

Just as psychoanalysis provided a way for Bachelard to maintain his distance from institutional knowledge, so he also developed a wary, and sometimes potentially hostile, distance from psychoanalysis itself. Following the single evocation of psychoanalysis in *The New Scientific Spirit*, the term is used more freely in *The Dialectic of Duration* of 1936. Early in the book, Bachelard evokes psychoanalysis in support of the idea of 'the negating aspect of mental life', which opposes the spirit of curiosity and striving, remarking cryptically that 'psychoanalysis has recently given great importance to the death instinct, to necrophilia, and to the need to lose that gives a new and very dialectical meaning to the need to gamble.'[14] Elsewhere, in defence of the principle of homeopathy, Bachelard evokes a 'psychoanalysis of the feeling of having' that would help to dispel 'the obvious feeling of strength we get from possessing a substance, from cherishing our reserves and our capital' (*Duration*, 140). But psychoanalysis is mostly evoked negatively, and in particular in Bachelard's proposal for a rhythmanalysis that would both match and outdo psychoanalysis in its promotion of a 'philosophy of repose', which would 'introduce oscillation into the time of work' (*Duration*, 145).

Bachelard sees psychoanalysis wholly as a 'cathartic method', the phrase used repeatedly in reference to psychoanalysis and the rhythmanalysis that Bachelard hoped might rival and complete it (*Duration*, 147–8), which aims at dispelling conflicts by bringing repressed material to consciousness. But he is unpersuaded that such catharsis can be final or permanent. What is needed instead, and what rhythmanalysis can supply, is 'a clear system of inner forgiveness' (*Duration*, 147), the workings of which Bachelard evokes:

> The morality that deals with detail needs a more frequent and more flexible cathartic method. It is dependent on a rhythmanalysis better suited than is psychoanalysis to following the temptations that come like waves. Moreover, when we have to attain a positive life, inventing good and not just doing it, only rhythmanalysis can guide us. (*Duration*, 148)

One need not be a believer in the final and definitive types of cure in which psychoanalysts and their clients encourage each other to trust to find Bachelard's recommendation that 'a sick soul – especially one that suffers the pain of time and of despair – has to be cured by living and thinking rhythmically, by rhythmic attentiveness and rhythmic repose' (*Duration*, 21) epistemically impatient. What, one must wonder, and even more, who, is to distinguish 'ill-made durations' from the desired 'syntony of becoming' (*Duration*, 21)? Bachelard allows himself a romantic vision of a therapy aimed at the rediscovery of childhood, which seems wilfully, in fact voluntaristically, regressive: 'Rhythmanalysis is the complete antithesis of psychoanalysis in that it is a theory of childhood rediscovered, of childhood which remains a possibility for us always, always opening a limitless future to our dreams' (*Duration*, 153). From certain perspectives, such a condition of permanently available childhood might qualify as neurosis itself. Loving children means not wanting to be one.

Whenever Bachelard uses the word 'psychoanalysis' in a positive sense, he means by it purification. This requires him to subject psychoanalysis itself to a rather drastic cleaning up: there is very little in the work of Freud to support the idea that psychoanalysis is designed simply to drive out or get clean from unhealthy cognitive addictions, as opposed to building certain kinds of accommodation to them. There is nothing in what Bachelard has to say about psychoanalysis that reflects the kinds of compromise that are so important a feature of Freudian thought about psychological life. Most emphatically and systematically in *The Formation of the Scientific Mind*, by contrast, Bachelard maintains that the history of science only begins when human beings are able through psychoanalysis to disinfect their thought of delusions and infantile fixation.

Michel Serres, whose dissertation on Leibniz Bachelard supervised at the Sorbonne, was one of the earliest to point out the peculiar relationship that Bachelard had to psychoanalysis. In an essay of 1970 devoted to *The Formation of the Scientific Mind*, Serres notes that Bachelard 'hardly refers to Freud, and even then only from the outside'.[15] He argues that

> It is by the bending of the word psychoanalysis that the entire ethical heritage will impose itself. Quite frankly, there is not a word of psychoanalysis in *La Formation*. Just listen to the language it mobilizes: it connotes a morality.[16]

Serres objects in particular to the agonism of Bachelard's view of science, understood as emerging only and always from a purgation from science of what are in effect sins of the flesh. Serres observes that this obsession with purgation, far from allowing science to be born from the growth away from the pre-scientific fixations of alchemy, in fact re-enacts just the obsession with purgation that drives alchemical thinking:

> *Mutatis mutandis*, Bachelard is confronted with the same adventure as the alchemists in the chemistry of the object: his lexicon is seized by the dominant language, his psychoanalysis returns to the state of alchemy, it veers toward moralizing initiation. It no longer translates anything, because the libido remains lust, sadism wrath, and anality avarice. This venture is ordinary: just as the soil has remained the same, the puritan ethics is always well suited to the psychoanalytic project and its practitioner is seen as a confessor. Instead of devoting himself to a psychoanalysis of the pre-sciences, Bachelard ends up treating the former as one of them.[17]

Bizarrely, one might say that Bachelard only begins to defeat the fantasy of purification that drives alchemy when he ceases to see the development of scientific consciousness as a project of purgative driving out. He does this finally through the idea, developed in his later epistemological writing, of phenomenotechnique, or the knowledge that comes through making, and through synthesis rather than analysis. Bachelard points out that chemical purification is not a process of subtraction, since it can only occur through processes that involve the energetic commingling of the human and the natural. It seems singular that Bachelard should not in fact have made another connection here with alchemy, which was similarly focused on the production of matter, in ways that might merit the application of the term 'rational materialism', though, as Bernadette Bensaude-Vincent and Jonathan Simon point out, 'he himself, under the influence of Carl Jung's interpretation of alchemy as a spiritual quest articulated around images and symbols rather than as a laboratory practice, refused to apply this term to alchemy.'[18] In fact, though, Bachelard's understanding in *Le matérialisme rationnel*, of the process he called 'facticité', implying the artificial making of factual conditions, means that the chemist must 'give existence to [faire exister] bodies that do not exist', which does seem to open up the possibility of some continuity between the alchemical enterprise and modern synthetic chemistry:

> The old concept of the alchemical wedding, suitably freed of its innate materialism, suitably psychoanalyzed, solemnized the union of innumerable bodies. This creativity is a fundamental characteristic of educated materialism, it is the very mark of what we call ordered materialism. Here human activity increases the order of nature, creates order, effaces natural disorder.[19]

It is true, however, that Bachelard recoils later in the same book against the very suggestion that there can be any continuity between alchemical fantasy and chemical synthesis, such as is suggested in popular expositions: 'why evoke such a legendary background? What impurity of thought!'[20] He is as dogmatic as he can be about the fundamental gulf between alchemy and modern chemistry:

> For nothing, absolutely nothing, legitimates the line of descent from alchemical to nuclear transmutations. To allow such a line of descent is to confuse values, and to fail in the philosophical duty to institute essentially scientific values, establishing them in their proper autonomy.[21]

Like many of Bachelard's books, *The Formation of the Scientific Mind* has as a powerful undertow a concern with education. Here, Bachelard is able to make good his argument against what had been the governing principle of French scientific education. As Cristina Chimisso explains, the reforms that took place in secondary education, especially in the increased emphasis on the teaching of science, were based upon the principle of steady and continuous intellectual progression, in which acquaintance with and reflection on concrete experience were confidently expected to build towards abstract thought.[22] The fact that Bachelard had ten years of experience teaching at secondary-school level makes his conviction, maintained throughout his life, that immediate experience is a barrier to be overcome rather than a royal road to scientific understanding, remarkable. But he is unresting in his insistence that no simple transition is possible from indwelling conceptions of the material world and our relations to it to rational understanding of it. Where his first book argued that the transition from the real to the rational could be achieved through a process of rectification that, though austerely self-inspecting, nevertheless preserved the possibility of a route to the rational that passed through the real, Bachelard moved during the 1930s more and more emphatically to the idea that rational understanding could only arise through aggressive abjuration. More emphatically, and immovably than ever before, Bachelard proclaimed that

> the task of the philosophy of science is very clear: it is to psychoanalyse interest, to destroy all utilitarianism, however disguised its form and lofty the status it claims, and to turn the mind from the real to the artificial, from the natural to the human, from representation to abstraction.[23]

One side of this is a dynamic commitment to the desire and power of the mind to overcome its own limits. For Bachelard, the history of thought is not one of steady and patient progress, but nothing less than permanent revolution – more Nietzsche than Hegel. 'Through the mental revolutions that scientific invention requires,' Bachelard insists, 'humankind becomes a mutating species, or to put it better still, a species that needs to mutate, that suffers if it does not change. Mentally, humans need to need' (*Formation*, 26). The assertion that 'we must replace closed, static knowledge with knowledge that is open and dynamic' would not be difficult to accept for an adherent of liberal ideas of the formative function of education, designed to create critical individuals rather than servile functionaries (*Formation* 29). But one must wonder quite how it is that

Bachelard thinks that the movement beyond naive or simplistic understandings of the physical world is ever to be achieved if there is to be no continuity at all between common first approximations and the refined kind of understanding that comes from rational analysis. There is an important difference between preferring one thing to another, which may imply but not require absolute rejection of the less preferred (a preference for brown bread need not imply any particular revulsion from white) and a preference that is defined by its absolute negation of an earlier preference. The latter, which is characteristic of the arguments of *The Formation of the Scientific Mind*, is a phobic preference for purgation over preference. What Bachelard called the Philosophy of No says an unconditional no not just to the affirmative philosophy of Yes, but also to the more qualified philosophy of Yes, but or No, but. One might wonder how a teacher of such long experience could possibly maintain such a view, or, while maintaining it, actually entertain it, in the face of what must have been his experience year after year of leading students gradually to better understanding. Perhaps, though, one might allow oneself the suspicion that only a teacher habituated to this process of gradual growth could hatch and cling to the implausibly aristocratic ideal of a knowledge formed, not through steady and sustained heuristic, but by Archimedean Eureka, out of the intuitive blue.

Bachelard had provided examples in earlier books of the impediments to understanding represented by various forms of realism. *Le Pluralisme cohérent de la chimie moderne* has as its centrepiece the replacement of the idea of atomic weight, or the estimated mass of the atom, by atomic number, which refers specifically to the number of protons the atom has. This is a move away from a conception that seems continuous with a realistic understanding of the world, in which different substances may be distinguished and grouped in part by their weight, to one based on mathematical relations. Bachelard sees this move away from realism as crucial to the development of a complete and consistent ordering of chemical elements in the Periodic Table. Drawing on the fact that protons have a force of attraction, Bachelard teasingly characterizes the principle of number rather than weight (what would you weigh an atom *on*?) with the formula '*attraction [allure] is order*', using a French word that, more than English attraction, can apply both to physics and to physicality, thereby emphasizing the sirenic seduction of realistic feeling.[24]

Bachelard had followed through the movement from realistic to rational understanding more systematically in *Atomistic Intuitions* of

1933, which outlines the process whereby naive understandings of the atom as an incompressible and indivisible bead of primal stuff (*a-tom* meaning 'without a cut') must similarly give way to abstract understandings of calculable functions and relations. If we insist on being told what an atom actually and in itself *is*, when it is at home and we are safely away, the only coherent response is to replace the noun 'atom' with the adjective 'atomic'. This allows one

> to translate what belongs to *method* while leaving aside any reference to a quality that belongs to *being*. Thus, the chemical atom, for this philosophy, is nothing more than 'atomic' phenomena studied by the chemical method . . . Thus does the science of the atom complete chemistry through geometry. Intuitions of the senses must give way to rational intuitions.[25]

In this and other books, especially those that concern the ways of understanding subatomic physics (which he tends to call 'microphysics'), Bachelard anticipates the remark famously made by the physicist N. David Mermin in 1989 about the indeterminate state of matter proposed in the 'Copenhagen interpretation': 'If I were forced to sum up in one sentence what the Copenhagen interpretation says to me, it would be "Shut up and calculate!"'[26] This is why Bachelard almost always uses the word 'rational' not in the sense of sane, sensible or intelligent, but in the more restricted sense of subject to calculative measure (*ratio*).

The Formation of the Scientific Mind offers a toothsome album of the pathologies of thought represented by what is called common sense. Like Thomas Browne before him, Bachelard assembles a *Pseudodoxia Epidemica*, examining in turn, if in no discernible order, the intoxication with the idea of substance, the fascinating power of the metaphor of the sponge, the will to power in explosions, the craziness of incautious generalization, the fantasy of thinking as a kind of digestion, and the dangerous allure of knowing as a kind of avarice.

Bachelard's interest in the history of chemistry had given him the advantage of an acquaintance with the long and colourful history of pre-scientific thinking represented by alchemy. A similar story might have been told about the colourful pre-scientific history of cosmology or biology, but alchemy had produced a much more sustained and excitable delirium. The continuing tenacity of the material imagination exercised in alchemical tradition made it easier to demonstrate the intimate haunting of the cognitive obstacles it represented. Indeed, there is a hint of the Gothic in the way in which Bachelard sometimes summons pre-scientific thinking: 'Even in a clear mind there are dark areas, caverns still haunted by shades, and traces of the old remain in our new ways of thinking. The eighteenth century still lives secretly within us and may – alas – return' (*Formation*, 19). And yet what must be disavowed for Bachelard are not midnight shivers and shrieks, but rather the everyday institutions that seem most immediate and instinctive in our encounters with the material world.

There is something crude and unsupervised in the mockery into which *The Formation of the Scientific Mind* often descends: it sometimes seems to amount to a kind of calenture of rationality. Charles Rabiqueau's eccentric speculations about astronomical optics are introduced with the words: 'The contemporary scientific community is so homogeneous and so closely guarded that the works of mad or disturbed authors are hard to publish. This was not the case a hundred and fifty years ago' (*Formation* 37). For all the evocation of painful ordeals of psychocognitive laundering, Bachelard often prefers the snort or sneer to explanation. The pre-scientific mind is drawn to curiosity, wonder and the picturesque. Like the child in search of distraction '*it does not seek variation but variety*' (*Formation* 40). Like most teachers of chemistry, Bachelard is thoroughly acquainted with the histrionic power of the classroom explosion, and advises the teacher 'to keep moving from the laboratory bench to the blackboard in order to extract the abstract from the concrete as soon as possible' (*Formation* 48–9). Out of nowhere, Bachelard produces a psychoanalytic explanation (admittedly rather a tempting one) of the source of the excitement in explosions, in their enactment of the will to power:

> It seems that for adolescents, any explosion suggests the vague intention of harming, of frightening, and of destroying. I have questioned many people about their memories of school. In about fifty per cent of cases, I found the memory of explosions in chemistry lessons. Most of the time, the objective causes of these had been forgotten and what was remembered was the look on the teacher's face and the fright of the shy child nearby: there was never any mention of the narrator's fright. All these memories suggested, by the very alacrity with which they were recalled, the repressed will to power, anarchic and satanic tendencies, and the

> need to have control over things in order to be able to oppress people. (*Formation* 48)

There may perhaps be something to be said for this view, and one can imagine and excuse the irritation of one who had come straight from four years' exposure to actual howitzers to the meretricious whizzbangs of a secondary school science laboratory, but the casualness of the explanation, pulled as it seems out of Bachelard's back pocket, has the appearance itself of a party trick, and certainly does not do much to exemplify the cool and careful abstraction of the scientific intelligence.

The formation of rational intelligence has to overcome not only the obstacle of ignorance, but the obstacle provided by the fixed will of

> the teacherly soul, proud of its dogmatism and fixed in its first abstraction, resting throughout its life on the laurels of its schooldays, its knowledge spoken out loud every year, imposing its proofs on others and wholly devoted to that deduction which so conveniently bolsters authority, teaching its servant as Descartes did or middle-class youngsters as do the proud holders of university degrees. (*Formation*, 12)

Bachelard refers approvingly in a footnote to passages from H. G. Wells's *The Open Conspiracy* (1928), which similarly assumes the privileged view of the autodidact who has stormed the citadel of intellectual life, and prides himself on seeing through the purblindness of formal education. Wells recommends the move towards a 'world commonweal', overseen by a world directorate, which would establish universal forms of collective ownership and maintain a stable system of money by means of a 'socialised world banking organisation'.[27] The enemies of this movement towards a scientific world consciousness include, in the passages to which Bachelard makes apparently approving allusion, the institutions of formal education, which Wells sees as largely conservative in their effects:

> The schoolteacher tends therefore to accept and standardise and stereotype, even in the living, progressive fields of science and philosophy. Even there he is a brake on the forward movement. It is clear that the Open Conspiracy must either continually disturb and revivify him or else frankly antagonise him. Universities also struggle between the honourable past

> on which their prestige rests, and the need of adaptation to a world of enquiry, experiment and change. It is an open question whether these particular organisations of intellectual prestige are of any value in the living world. A modern world planned de novo would probably produce nothing like a contemporary University.[28]

Wells saw a programme of world education, based on science, as the indispensable means of creating his rationalized world state.[29] Bachelard never commits himself to any such explicitly political programme, but the way in which he evokes psychoanalysis as a kind of clearing away of maladies and maladjustments of thought may have disposed him to approve also of Wells's recommendations of a programme of 'mental sanitation', to disperse the kind of 'mental infection' constituted by 'Emotion and sentimentality [which] are evoked in the cause of disciplines and co-operations that could quite easily be sustained by rational conviction'.[30]

Bachelard's evocation of scientific rationality is a contradictory mixture of humility and imperiousness. He moves in the course of a single paragraph from the evocation of 'a suffering scientific consciousness, given over to ever imperfect inductive interests and playing the dangerous game of thought that has no stable experimental support' to the final aim of '*the soul desperate to abstract and reach the quintessential*', which is sure of 'the duty of scientists, at last refining and possessing the world's thought' (*Formation*, 21). In Bachelard's rapt French, 'la possession enfin épurée de la pensée du monde!', it is the possession, and not the thought itself, that is purified.[31]

Bachelard plainly enjoys himself far too much in *The Formation of the Scientific Spirit* in his work of scorning the 'arrant nonsense' (*Formation*, 46) that he finds in such abundance in seventeenth- and eighteenth-century natural philosophy. He cannot always be blamed for this self-indulgence. What is more, amid all the haughty disdain, and stern injunctions, perhaps to himself in part, to tarry no longer amid alchemical fatuities, a new strain begins to be perceptible in the analysis. For Bachelard also shows himself increasingly absorbed in making out the intricate forms of logic that animate the fantasies he sets out to lay waste. An example is the brief outlining of the inversive logic that suggests that power can be concentrated through sacrificial destruction:

> Pearls and precious stones are so greatly esteemed that there is some merit in grinding them in a golden mortar and dissolving them in a potion. So great is the sacrifice of an objective possession that there is the fervent hope that from this a subjective possession will come. (*Formation*, 142)

Bachelard exercises his newly discovered facility in spelling out the unconscious logic of metaphor with a gusto that redeems the disgust we feel we should be being made to feel:

> Indeed, digestion corresponds to taking possession of a fact that is more obvious than any other and whose certainty cannot be questioned. Digestion is the origin of the strongest kind of realism and of avarice at its most acquisitive. It is indeed the function of animist avarice. Its entire coenaesthesia lies at the root of the myth of inwardness. This 'interiorisation' helps us to postulate an 'interiority'. Realists are eaters. (*Formation*, 172)

Slowly, the sense begins to grow that Bachelard is beginning to appreciate the poetic force of the 'as-if', or the 'let it be that' or the world of the 'would-that-it-were', that is enacted through the fecund imagination of matter in previous centuries. This may be associated with what I. A. Richards defined as the 'pseudo-statement' characteristic of poetry, which is 'justified entirely by its effect in releasing or organizing our impulses and attitudes', as opposed to an objective statement, which is 'justified by its truth, *i.e.* its correspondence, in a highly technical sense, with the fact to which it points'.[32] Magical thinking may depend on objects, forces and values that are wholly imaginary, but the force exercised by magical thinking itself, most highly developed for Bachelard in the very idea, at once humdrum and metaphysical, of *substance*, is very far from being insubstantial. The kinds of matter dreamt of by the material imagination may have no existence but, increasingly for Bachelard, there will be no denying the actuality and power of the 'realization' they effect.

Religious belief as a subject is almost entirely absent from Bachelard's writing, but a kind of religiosity nevertheless thrums through Bachelard's ways of evoking scientific knowledge, work and belief. In 'Idéalisme discursif', an essay of 1934 that serves as a kind of rehearsal for *The Formation of the Scientific Mind*, Bachelard represents the Cartesian spirit of inhabitation of 'doubt as a method' as a 'veritable rational conversion', which allows one to 'assist at the birth of a new psychism – *ortho-psychism*'.[33] 'Whenever we look back and see the errors of our past', Bachelard lamented in *The Formation of the Scientific Mind*, 'we discover truth through a real intellectual repentance [repentir intellectuel]' (*Formation*, 24).[34] A religious register is employed again in the complaint that 'Where intellectual culture is concerned, the more recent the fault, the more grievous is the sin' (*Formation*, 160).

Psychoanalytic purification is seen explicitly and repeatedly as exorcism: 'we will allow a kind of *unconscious of the scientific mind* to be constituted, which will then require slow and difficult psychoanalysis if it is to be exorcised' (*Formation*, 49); 'the *myth of interiority* is one of those fundamental processes of unconscious thought that are the hardest to exorcise' (*Formation*, 107); 'substantial origin is very hard to exorcise' (*Formation*, 112); 'Value is the most insidious of hidden qualities. It is the last to be exorcised' (*Formation*, 148); 'what is vaguest is what is most powerful where the libido is concerned. The precise is already an exorcism' (*Formation*, 186). But there can be no more tenacious believer in ghosts, or the malign power of belief in them, than the one who exerts himself to evict them. Bachelard is alert to the many unconscious myths and previously unnamed 'complexes' that are obstinately cemented in everyday thinking, but he does not seem to have recognized the workings in himself of one of the most pervasive myths of all; namely, that health essentially depends upon the forcible expulsion of corrupting admixtures. That he should have been so aware in his writing on the history of chemistry of the impossibility of absolute purity makes the stubborn persistence in his own writing of what in another he might have diagnosed as a Purgatory Complex all the more singular. When writing of scientific rationality, Bachelard cannot rid himself of the idea that knowledge is fundamentally a process of aggressively getting rid of error, a process requiring a painful work of formation through self-undoing, thereby giving birth to the new being of the converted soul. 'L'acte de connaître doit être saisi dans son état naissant', Bachelard had written in his first book – 'the activity of knowing must be grasped in its state of nativity'.[35] In fact the rhyme between *connaître* and *naître* is without etymological warrant: *connaître*, frequently written historically as *connoître*, derives from Latin *cognoscere*, while *naître* derives from Latin *nasci*.

There are occasional hints that Bachelard sees the parallels between his view of the need to purify chemistry of alchemy and alchemy's own primal myth of purification: 'alchemy is only conceivable if substances develop in one direction only, in that of a completion, a purification, and a conquest of value,' he writes (*Formation*, 94). At the end of *The Formation of the Scientific Mind*, we come on a passage in which he reflects upon the myth of renewal in alchemy, a passage that allows us to see Bachelard identifying his own kind of alchemy, in which intellectual lustration is the work of reversing time to preserve the sexual vigour of youth:

> Usually, the alchemist is the Old Man, the Old One. This is why the theme of rejuvenation is one of alchemy's dominant themes . . . It is the hope of growing young again that keeps them going in the long watches of the night, in the long hours at the furnace, and that makes light of a fortune lost, the hope of finding themselves in the morning with once again a gracious countenance and smouldering eyes. The perspective from which alchemy can be understood is that of the psychology of fifty-somethings, the psychology of a man who has just felt a first threat to sexual worth. Who will not spare any effort to drive this shadow away, to erase this ill omen, and defend what is supremely valued? (*Formation*, 197)

'Why should not old men be mad?', demanded W. B. Yeats, in elderly irascibility.[36] Here, the professor who had himself just turned fifty, the writer who was already beginning to become identical with his bibliography, could teasingly hold out to his readers the doctrine that

> It is by interpreting occupations in terms of preoccupations that we can understand their real, inward meaning. Once it has really been accepted that alchemists are always fifty-year-old men, then the subjective, psychoanalytical interpretations we are proposing here become very clear. (*Formation*, 197)

5

Fission, 1938–40

On the point of entering the period of his celebrity, Bachelard began to give signs of the intellectual fission that would characterize the final two decades of his life. Thereafter, the one thing that Bachelard would be known for was the fact of there being two Bachelards. The process begins with *The Formation of the Scientific Mind*, in which the absorption in the psychological intricacies of alchemy begins to pull away from the official 'curative' narrative to which Bachelard is set on subordinating them. *The Formation of the Scientific Mind* would be the last book in which Bachelard would trust himself to put the two sides of his intellectual nature in such close proximity. Thereafter, the two Bachelards, one devoted to the wide-awake world of scientific rationalism, and the other to the spellbound gloaming of magical thinking, would not be permitted to coexist in the same work.

However, the book that comes closest to engineering this encounter between knowledge and imagination was *The Psychoanalysis of Fire* (1938). Bachelard writes in his introduction that its discussion of 'the subjective convictions related to the knowledge of fire phenomena' should be thought of as 'an illustration of the general theses put forward in our recent book, *The Formation of the Scientific Mind*'.[1] It thereby represents itself as an expansion of what might easily have been an episode of the history of pre-scientific thinking provided in the earlier book. Bachelard also makes an explicit connection through contrast to his doctoral dissertation on the history of ideas about the propagation of heat, in which he 'attempted to describe, in connection with heat phenomena, a clearly-defined axis of scientific objectivization' (*Fire*, 3). Now, he tells us, it is 'no longer the axis of objectivization but that of subjectivity' (*Fire*, 3) that will be his orientation.

Bachelard's method, applied rather more systematically than the glances and gleams in earlier books, is to work through a series of what he calls 'complexes' involved in attitudes towards fire, though, in his introduction to the English translation of 1964, Northrop Frye aptly remarks that they might better be called 'myths', a usage to which Bachelard himself will increasingly turn (*Fire*, viii). Bachelard begins with what he calls the Prometheus complex, which he characterizes as 'the Oedipus complex of the life of the intellect' (*Fire*, 12). This is because, as he argues, the infant experience of fire is one simultaneously of instruction and prohibition – the child is taught a kind of fearful obedience to the prohibition on getting too close to fire. With brilliant, swift lucidity, Bachelard represents fire as igniting in the child a '*clever disobedience*' and proceeds to sketch a portrait of the intellectual artist, as involved in a struggle, to topple the father not sexually, but intellectually. The Prometheus complex therefore gives rise to

> all those tendencies which impel us *to know* as much as our fathers, more than our fathers, as much as our teachers, more than our teachers. Now it is by handling the object, it is by perfecting our objective knowledge, that we can best hope to prove decisively that we have attained the intellectual level that we have so admired in our parents and in our teachers. The acquiring of supremacy through the drive of more powerful instincts naturally will appeal to a much greater number of individuals, but minds of a rarer stamp also must be examined by the psychologist. If pure intellectuality is exceptional, it is nonetheless very characteristic of a specifically human evolution. (*Fire*, 11)

A passage like this gives the sense of Bachelard catching sight of himself in the mirror. The Prometheus complex is not just one aspect of the psychology of fire, it is also the myth of the knowledge of fire, which governs the process undertaken throughout the book. It is part of the psychoanalysis of fire, but the intellectual exercise of psychoanalysing fire is also part of it, so that fire is in fact both the object of knowledge, and the image of the desire exercised in knowledge. The knowledge of fire is knowledge about knowledge itself: 'among all phenomena, fire alone is sufficiently prized by prehistoric man to wake in him the desire for knowledge, and this mainly because it accompanies the desire for love'

(*Fire*, 55). The thought of fire leads Bachelard irresistibly to the thought of the ardency of thought:

> What better proof is there that the contemplation of fire brings us back to the very origins of philosophic thought? If fire, which, after all, is quite an exceptional and rare phenomenon, was taken to be a constituent element of the Universe, is it not because it is an element of human thought, the prime element of reverie? (*Fire*, 18)

In one sense, Bachelard also sees the purification of thought he relies on his idiosyncratic idea of 'psychoanalysis' to supply as a kind of alchemical refinement, a cauterizing of inessential encumbrances and sensory impediments. His chapter on the 'Novalis complex' is focused on the sexual associations of fire, both in terms of its generative capacity and in terms of the specifically sexual movements of frication required to produce it. This extends even to 'the joy of rubbing, cleaning, furbishing, and polishing that could not be adequately explained by the meticulous care taken by certain housewives', and earns the judgement that 'Psychoanalytically speaking, cleanliness is really a form of uncleanliness' (*Fire*, 30). Chapter Five, on the chemistry of fire, reprises the programme enacted in *The Formation of the Scientific Mind*, and repeats its article of faith that it is necessary 'to psychoanalyze the scientific mind, to bind it to a discursive thought which, far from *continuing* the reverie, will halt it, break it down and prohibit it' (*Fire*, 59–60).

In his conclusion to *The Psychoanalysis of Fire*, Bachelard attempts a rapprochement of scientific analysis and psychological experience. For a moment, he can represent the workings of the imagination, not as a muddying adulteration of sane reflection on objects, but as an object of scientific analysis in itself or, as he puts it, 'a basis for a physics or a chemistry of reverie, as the outline of a method of determining the objective conditions of reverie' (*Fire*, 109). Hints of this kind have encouraged some who seek to build a bridge between the scientific Bachelard and the poetic Bachelard, through the view that 'Bachelard's aesthetic philosophy is the complementary counterpoint to his scientific philosophy rather than its antithesis.'[2] But by this point in the book, the idea of fire, and the kind of thought it both encourages and epitomizes, has begun to put up a kind of resistance to analytic procedure. This is because it has become an image of the very kind of thinking required to make sense of itself:

'fire is, among the makers of images, the one that is most dialectized. It alone is *subject and object*' (*Fire*, 111). Reverie resists being reduced to an object because reverie is the work of cooking objects up.

One might even characterize Bachelard's hostility to what he regards as the force of the unconscious, leading him throughout his career to characterize scientific thought as the Philosophy of No, as something of a neurotic fixation. This is especially the case in the light of the books that celebrate the work of the imagination that Bachelard produced from 1940 to his death. The oscillation between striving and repose, rational work and irresponsible imaginative play, might itself be thought of as inviting psychoanalytic investigation. Why, one must ask, should Bachelard hold so sedulously to two outlooks so obviously contradictory without ever trying to draw them into conversation with each other, or resolve their contradictions? Despite his frequent recourse to the word 'dialectic', Bachelard's understanding of dialectic seems oddly to preclude any form of the interaction of opposites that is commonly assumed to be part of it.

One of the influences that one might have expected to impel such interaction was the affinity that Bachelard developed with surrealism in the late 1930s, and never abandoned. Bachelard's interest seems to have been sparked by a meeting with Roger Caillois at a scientific congress in Prague in 1934. In the following year, Tristan Tzara formed a discussion circle, the Group d'Etudes pour la Phénoménologie Humaine, who aimed to produce a journal out of their discussions: the editorial group consisted of Tzara, Louis Aragon, Caillois and Jules Monnerot. When Caillois persuaded Bachelard to write for the new journal *Inquisitions*, having, in Bachelard's words, recognized his ambitions for science 'from certain glints dispersed through my books', he opened up an intellectual possibility that would be fully realized only from 1940 onwards.[3] In a letter of December 1935 to Caillois concerning the piece he had agreed to write for *Inquisitions* (only a single issue of which was ever published), Bachelard had written, a little enigmatically, 'for me, youth is an effort and no longer a nature' ('pour moi, la jeunesse est un effort et non plus une nature').[4] In his remark to Caillois, Bachelard seems to anticipate the prospect with which the short essay 'Surrationalisme' ends:

> closed rationalism gives way to open rationalism. Reason happily incomplete can no longer fall asleep in a tradition; it can no longer count on memory to recite its tautologies. It must ceaselessly

> prove and put itself to a test. It struggles with others, but first of all with itself. This time, there is some guarantee that it will be incisive and young.[5]

Given the obvious and intended parentage of the term 'surrationalism' in 'surrealism', one might have expected to find what, in his preface to a collection of Bachelard's shorter writings, Georges Canguilhem calls 'the contestation of a euphoriant rationalism . . . a reason systematically divided against itself'. This would imply some effort to escape the restrictions of 'scientific superstition' that might in its turn open up, on the model of surrealism, some expansion or greater inclusiveness of view, to overcome the seclusion of science from art and imagination.[6] But, though Caillois would call 'Surrationalisme' a 'manifesto', Bachelard's work never does more than intimate such an opening up.[7] In this respect, it may be that Bachelard did rather more for surrealism than surrealism did for him.

The interest of the surrealists in Bachelard's work seems to have been concentrated on his *The New Scientific Spirit*, which Gavin Parkinson describes as 'a pivot for debates among the Surrealists and their friends (and enemies) on science, epistemology, politics, the object and art, as well as a bridge between Surrealism and postwar French philosophy'.[8] If it is really true, as Parkinson suggests, that Bachelard's *New Scientific Spirit* was 'read by every individual in the Surrealist group and its orbit', then it cannot have been read very attentively;[9] for, though it reviews developments in modern scientific thinking, some of them almost half a century old, it offers little in the way of general prospects for the revolutionary transformation of society and thought of the kind feverishly dreamt of by many of the surrealists.

As Gavin Parkinson observes, André Breton drew strongly on Bachelard's arguments in 'Surrationalisme', explaining that 'In Bachelard, he discovered a learned figure in sympathy with some of the aims of Surrealism, whose academic status promised to strengthen its standing and its claim to historical authority in circles beyond those of poetry and art.'[10] Despite the 'polemical swagger' of 'Surrationalism', the evidence of Bachelard's writing does not really bear out the idea that, reciprocally, he 'saw in Surrealism a mode of address and a set of theoretical precepts unencumbered by the drier language of academia, useful to the conscription of geometry and physics into his *révolution spirituelle*'.[11] Bachelard's scientific rationalism would remain almost entirely unperturbed by his writing on the imagination. Where surrealism breaks down barriers of purity, Bachelard's surrationalism in fact strives for ever greater purification. Instead, the liberation of the mind to which Bachelard looked forward in 1935 would be unfolded in relation to the project of a systematic study of poetry and imagination, developed in isolation from studies of the practice of science, rather than in any kind of surrealist renewal of scientific thinking. When Bachelard's philosophical colleague at the Sorbonne, Jean Wahl, wrote that 'Bachelard unites the conclusions of the most recent sciences with the profound resonances of the images of matter,' he was articulating what many, looking mostly at the titles of Bachelard's works rather than their contents, wanted to be true of his work, or assumed must be true, rather than what actually was.[12]

Perhaps the most attentive reader of Bachelard among the surrealists was Roger Caillois. His developing interest in play and games, which would lead in 1958 to the appearance of the book by which he is most well known outside France, *Man, Play and Games*, in which he emphasizes the importance of rule, rationality and number in competitive game-playing, may be seen as a development of the possibilities of rational play articulated in Bachelard's 'Surrationalism'. Before Bachelard embarked in earnest on the sequence of books on the elemental imagination that would occupy him throughout the years of the war and beyond, he produced two books that dramatized the two poles of his thought. The first, a short study of the poet known as Lautréamont, was stimulated by long conversations that Bachelard had had with Roger Caillois at the Prague scientific congress in 1934, who had urged Bachelard to read Lautréamont, who had become a kind of patron saint of surrealist writing, and a copy of whose *Chants de Maldoror* he later sent to him.[13]

Bachelard had published an extract from a book he was writing on Lautréamont in the *Nouvelle revue française* in November 1939.[14] The *Nouvelle revue française* was published by Gallimard, which had in fact grown out of the magazine and established itself as one of France's leading literary publishers, with Valéry, Proust, Malraux, Saint-Exupéry, Simenon and Sartre on its list, and a catalogue of works in translation that included Pirandello, Faulkner, Kafka, Steinbeck, Nabokov and Freud. Bachelard had offered the complete book, of which 'La bestiaire de Lautréamont' was an extract, to Gallimard, but they had shown no interest in it. This was especially disappointing given that Gallimard had published Bachelard's *La psychanalyse du feu* in the previous year.[15] He conveyed his disappointment to Albert Béguin, who was a professor of

French literature at the University of Basel, and had published in 1937 a very successful book, *L'Âme romantique et le rêve*, with the publisher José Corti, who specialized in works of and related to surrealism. Corti had recently published Lautréamont's *Oeuvres complètes*, and, following an introduction by Béguin, signed up Bachelard's book, inaugurating an association and friendship that would last for four books and nine years.[16]

As a sustained study of the work of a single author, *Lautréamont* is the only work of recognizable literary criticism that Bachelard ever wrote. Published in 1939 and probably written closely in time to *The Formation of the Scientific Mind* and *The Psychoanalysis of Fire*, *Lautréamont* is one of a cluster of works that embody the turn from rationality to imagination in Bachelard. More precisely, perhaps, it is a sudden convulsion of Bachelard's thinking, for in it he turns on thought itself, finding in the displaced subject of Isidore Ducasse an opportunity to give free rein to an intense aggression exercised both through thought, and against it.

Bachelard reads in the few facts known for sure about Ducasse's life an assertion of life breaking free from biography.

> Nothing in his life is *strange*. He comes from Montevideo. He moves to France to study in a lycée. He goes to Paris to do mathematics. He writes a poem. He has trouble getting it published. He prepares another work that more prudently takes into account the publishers' timidity. He dies. There is not an incident and especially not a single action that reveals anything strange. One must therefore return to the work itself, enter it completely – for it has an inspired insanity – and then the test of originality can begin.[17]

These lines assert an ideal of self-making in and through the act of writing that in some ways corresponds to the ideal enacted through Bachelard's own life of writing. 'There are minds for which *expression* is more than life, other than life' (*Lautréamont*, 55), Bachelard asserts.

And yet, Bachelard has recourse to speculative biography of Ducasse to locate the origins of this rupture between life and writing, even if it is a biography that must be read out backwards from the very writing that erupts out of it. *Lautréamont* is governed by '[a] psychoanalysis of learning', which aims to 'identify specific complexes at their sedimentary level – cultural complexes above the lower levels of Freudian psychoanalysis that are the result of premature fossilization' (*Lautréamont*, 34). The relation of life and thought is embodied in the relation to mathematics, which is the area of Ducasse's biography on which Bachelard dwells in the chapter titled 'The Biographical Problem'. The primal scene that programmes the violent destructiveness of Ducasse's writing is that of a teacher exercising domineering violence over an adolescent. It is a scene that 'must always be reawakened when mathematical training is recalled' (*Lautréamont*, 52). The 'cold and rational violence' (*Lautréamont*, 52) with which Bachelard summons up this scene is as aggressively calculated as what it describes:

> There is no mathematical learning without a certain spitefulness of Reason. Is there a more fixed, swift, icy irony than that of the mathematics teacher? Squatting in the corner of the classroom like a spider in his crevice, he waits. Who has not known that horrid silence, those deadly hours, the exquisite retardation of torture in which the best of students suddenly loses, along with his self-confidence, the dynamics of his locked-up thoughts? (*Lautréamont*, 52)

The result is a kind of Oedipal/Satanic rebellion that frees itself through a perpetuating reduplication of the very inaugural violence that calls it into being: 'The creatured creature will, through violence, become a creator' (*Lautréamont*, 40).

In writing of Ducasse that 'in putting aside the fundamental habits of life he eludes the very principles of biographical study' (*Lautréamont*, 56), Bachelard finds a mirror for the anti-biographical supremacy of writing over life that he attempted to maintain in his own life. Bachelard seems never to have alluded to Freud's idea of omnipotence of thoughts involved in magical thinking, but he identifies, and amplifies, something like this omnipotence in Ducasse: 'an adoration of thought is part and parcel of an execration of life in Ducasse. But why did God make life when he could have made thought directly?' (*Lautréamont*, 54). Bachelard puts in play here a strange idea, though it is one with precedents in Gnostic mysticism – that the creation of life might be thought of as a kind of aberration, entailing the slow work through history, and indeed as history itself, of ever-closer approximation of life to pure thought, or reality to reason.

Lautréamont is also the work in which Bachelard speaks most directly about the relation between life and the act of writing, which here bursts away for the first time away from supervision and precaution. In *Lautréamont*, Bachelard writes an oblique, yet searingly stripped autobiography, which seems to reveal the source of the 'schoolroom atmosphere' (*Lautréamont*, 42) that pervades his own work as much as that of Ducasse. At times, the directness of the will-to-identification is almost painfully palpable:

> when schools dominate and aesthetics is taught, the metamorphosing powers are arrested. Only a few solitary poets are allowed to live in a state of permanent metamorphosis. For loyal readers they are models of tangible metamorphosis. Certain direct poets bring about a sort of induction, a rhythm of the nerves in our feelings that is different from linguistic rhythm. They must be read as examples of vigorous life, as examples of an original will-to-live. And so I have attempted to relive the inductive force that runs throughout *Maldoror*. I have devoted lengthy months of docile and sympathetic experience to the study of this poem in attempting to recover the specific ferment of a life quite different from ours. (*Lautréamont*, 60)

Bachelard inserts an even more playful identification between himself and Ducasse:

> When reading *Maldoror* one cannot fail to be struck by the number of references to the dignity of hair. At a time when Sarcey's letter on beards destroyed the career of a holder of a degree, what must have been the severity of the school censor who enforced the official propriety of hairstyle on pupils? During schooltime did not Isidore Ducasse suffer from 'inability to express oneself in a hairstyle'? 'Do I not remember how I myself was scalped, even though only for five years (the exact period of time escapes me)?' Five years is, more or less, exactly the time that Ducasse was locked up in the prisons of a Pyrenees university. From then on if one considers seriously that the least disturbance can have a very great impact on an adolescent, one would acknowledge without hesitation a *scalp complex* that is a metaphorical form of *castration complex*. (*Lautréamont*, 36–7)

Bachelard in the 1950s.

Bachelard's allusion at the beginning of this passage is to Francisque Sarcey, who in 1851, when he was still a schoolteacher, wrote a letter to the rector of his college to protest against a government edict prohibiting the wearing of beards and moustaches, because it was believed they tended to the fomenting of political subversion.[18] Though Cristina Chimisso reads Bachelard's beard as an icon of magisterial sagacity, believing that it 'played an important part in the legitimisation of his work and his presentation as an authoritative figure', she notes that he also takes an unrazored condition as the expression of delinquent defiance of established opinion.[19]

Bachelard finds in Ducasse's work 'a genuine phenomenology of aggression', which he links to 'pure aggression in the same sense as one speaks of "pure poetry"' (*Lautréamont*, 2). This is a somewhat puzzling analogy. Pure poetry is usually thought of as poetry that is concerned exclusively with its own formal quality and occasion, rather than with objects of external reference. But Bachelard seems more concerned with the kind of purity of intent one finds in animal violence, which is wholly directed at its object, without awareness of itself. Here, Bachelard is drawn into the adolescent fascination with the assertion of cruelty to be found in the work of Donatien Alphonse François de Sade. Where, in the works of de Sade, the desire for excess produces an absurd accountancy of cruelties, intensifying through aggregation, Bachelard is eager to find in Ducasse an aggression that is so intense it scorches through its own method and medium. Ducasse's language is pure cry:

> We shall find new evidence of the primitiveness of Ducasse's poetry in the prominence given to *cries*. Those who desert this perspective on the primeval as a hierarchy of energies find cries to be only accidents, fragments or archaic survivals. On the contrary energetic primitiveness demonstrates that cries are not rallying calls or even reflexes. They are essentially direct. A cry does not call – it exults. (*Lautréamont*, 64)

In his conclusion to *Lautréamont*, Bachelard repays Caillois for introducing him to the work of Ducasse with some approving references to his recently appeared book *Le myth et l'homme* in which Caillois had declared that 'mythology is beyond (or beneath, if you prefer) the force which impels being towards perseverance in being.'[20] That perseverance in going beyond itself will survive in Bachelard's strange insistence that poetry is language exercising an 'attack on linking', which is to say, on language itself. *Lautréamont* leaves its reader with the antagonism unresolved between the pure antagonism of force and 'the idea that a pure act must desire a form, a coherence' (*Lautréamont*, 85).

There is a strange discordance between the efforts that Bachelard makes to reassure his reader of his patiently attentive scholarship, in his reference to 'lengthy months of docile and sympathetic experience', consorting with his eager appropriation of the 'rhythm of the nerves', 'vigorous life' and 'original will-to-live' (*Lautréamont*, 60). There is a kind of unsupervised wildness in Bachelard's writing in *Lautréamont*, a wildness that doubles, and is indemnified by, the wildness of his subject.

That discordance persists, though shifted into a very different stylistic register, in *The Philosophy of No*, the book that followed so closely upon *Lautréamont* that its writing may even have been interleaved with it. Having characterized a new spirit in scientific thinking in his work of the 1930s, Bachelard seemed to feel the need to define a new kind of philosophy of science to underwrite it, and so attempts to substantiate in an explanatory fashion the ideas he had introduced in the exclamatory mode of 'Surrationalisme'. In a series of densely argued chapters, Bachelard retraces many of the argumentative paths found in previous books, showing how, with respect to concepts such as mass – a notion that, he offhandedly remarks, in its primitive beginnings 'concretizes the very desire to eat' – substance, linearity and logic, 'the philosophy of science goes in the direction of a growing rationalism, eliminating, with respect to all notions, the initial realism.'[21]

Bachelard comes close to implying that this would no longer resemble what is usually thought of as a philosophy at all:

> the philosophy of physics is perhaps the only philosophy which is applicable even when it decides to overstep its own principles. In short it is the only *open-ended* philosophy. All other philosophies posit their principles as intangible, their primary truths as total and complete. All other philosophies glory in their *closedness*.[22]

On the one hand, the willingness to say no has been a part of philosophy, conceived as the exercise of dialogue and dialectic, from the very beginning. Bachelard sometimes offers this reassuring sense of negation as a progressive revision:

> we must recognize the fact that new experience says *no* to old experience, otherwise we are quite evidently not up against a new experience at all. But, for a mind which can turn principle into dialectic, which can accommodate new kinds of evidence, which can enrich its body of explanation without partiality to some supposedly natural organon designed to explain away everything this 'no' is never final.[23]

But lifting this adaptive willingness into a more absolute will-to-negation, as Bachelard attempts in the lyric mode of *Lautréamont* and discursive mode of *The Philosophy of No*, pushes a philosophy that says no towards the condition of saying no to philosophy itself. The difficulty of establishing a principle of fusion out of the fission itself is in a sense the paradox of Bachelard's own intellectual life. For the next decade, Bachelard would withdraw from this paradox.

6

Occupation, 1940–42

By 1938, having published a book almost every year following the award of his doctorate, Bachelard had built up an impressive, even intimidating, publication profile. He had shown himself not only to be an erudite commentator on many different problems and periods in the history of science, but a vigorous proponent of what he characterized as the 'new spirit' of science, over which philosophy would have to surrender its accustomed superiority, in order to make studious accommodation. It was this polemical streak that confirmed his reputation. In 1934 he was the French representative at the 8th International Congress of Philosophy in Prague, at which he made the acquaintance of a young philosopher of logic named Jean Cavaillès, with whom he established an immediate and lasting rapport. In 1936 he attended the Décades in the Cistercian Abbey at Pontigny, an annual series of discussions on literature, religion and philosophy run by Paul Desjardins, and wrote from there, 'My presentation on Sunday was quite successful. It split the Décade in two, and there were interminable discussions between Bachelardians and non-Bachelardians. All very courteous.'[1]

If he was not quite yet, in W. H. Auden's words on the death of Sigmund Freud in 1939, 'no more a person/now but a whole climate of opinion', he was in a fair way to becoming it.[2] In early 1937 he received an approach from the Sorbonne enquiring if he would be willing to consider election to the Chair of Logic, which was due to become vacant on the retirement of Professor André Lalande. The invitation plunged him into an agony of indecision. He wrote to the wife of his friend Daniel Giroux:

> I feel that the question of a nomination in Paris will arise and do not believe I will be able to decide one way or the other without

> heartache. I had a little discussion about it with Suzanne and I was physically very upset. Since then, I have made the decision not to talk about it any more with her, but I am all the more unhappy. I have never felt so alone: I have never seen so close up the hardness of my life . . . It may appear logical that I would want to accept what, for intellectual workers, must count among the most illustrious of positions. On the other hand, I no longer feel I have the energy to set myself up in a new life. (quoted Parinaud, 233)

Suzanne was by now seventeen, so in principle able to be left alone, and indeed seems to have wished him to accept the position (Parinaud, 235), but Bachelard, who was now 53 years of age, and had rarely been parted from his daughter for more than a few days at a time since her birth, found the thought of prolonged separation difficult to contemplate. By May letters were beginning to arrive urging Bachelard not to let slip an opportunity that might vanish were he to delay further, but, a month or so later, he finally put an end to his agony by declining the nomination.

However, from that time onwards, Bachelard began to feel less settled in Dijon, and the declaration on 1 September 1939 by Britain and France of war on Germany, following the invasion of Poland, created a state of growing anxiety, despondency and ill health in Bachelard. He wrote:

> My whole life has been a constant effort. If I had worked less, I would be peacefully at home eating the fruits of my orchard, and I would sit on the hillside quietly, chatting with my friends and sleeping quietly at night. Now, I am deprived of everything, of the silent and cool night, of the trees and the plain. (Parinaud, 237–8)

He wondered apprehensively 'what kind of life will we be living a few years from now? We are in the midst of a world in ferment' (Parinaud, 238). The privations of wartime and the disruption to his university environment meant that the rural contentment that he had chosen over the opportunities of Paris seemed to have been taken from him. He wrote in February 1940, 'I take less and less pleasure in the university. I no longer find there an atmosphere in which to work or the necessary sources of information. More and more I live in solitude' (Parinaud, 238). He refused the position of dean when it was offered to him in March 1940. On 10 May German forces invaded France, which formally signed an Armistice dividing France into an occupied and an unoccupied zone governed from the spa town of Vichy on 22 June 1940.

All these circumstances changed the equation for Bachelard, who accepted a new offer from the Sorbonne in November 1940 to succeed his dissertation supervisor Abel Rey as professor of the history and philosophy of science and director of the Institute of the History of Science that Rey had set up. Accompanied now by Suzanne, he found an apartment in rue de la Montagne-Sainte-Genevieve and, like other residents of Paris during the Occupation, embarked on the long struggle against the cold, the power cuts and the endless queuing for vegetables.

Under the nominal control of the puppet government installed by the Germans, universities were able to continue their work: Bachelard gave his first lectures in January 1941. The most conspicuous area of interference was in the constraints applied to Jewish students and faculty under the two Statuts des Juifs, the French equivalent of the Nuremberg Laws, enacted in October 1940 and in July 1941. Rather than being directly

Jean Cavaillès in the 1930s.

imposed by the German authorities, these measures came 'entirely from within', with the general population being indirectly enlisted in the work of applying them:

> The Germans had put no pressure at all upon Vichy to begin organised anti-Semitism. Persecution of Jews was therefore a matter of voluntary propitiation of Hitlerism, an early offering of goodwill, one of those favours which it was hoped would be one day recompensed.[3]

Quotas were applied to student admissions to universities and Jewish faculty members lost their jobs. There was little sign of opposition. Only one public demonstration occurred, when students in Paris gathered on 11 November 1940, nominally to commemorate the Armistice of 1918: a hundred students were detained, and there were no other such demonstrations during the four years of German occupation.[4] Only one academic, Gustave Monod, at the University of Paris, seems to have refused to apply the law, and was removed from his position as a result.[5] But, in general, the anti-Jewish measures were resisted as little in universities as elsewhere: Gilles Maigron writes that 'the authorities mistrusted the university world, and its silence reassured them.'[6] Two chairs in racial ideology were imposed on the Sorbonne, one on the history of Judaism, held by Henri Labroue in the Faculty of Letters, and another on racial ethnology, held by René Martial in the Faculty of Medicine.[7]

The heroic resistance that became so much a part of the mythology of French experience under the Occupation would come later. When the young Irish writer Samuel Beckett, who had spurned the safety of neutral Ireland to rejoin his friends in Paris at the outbreak of war, joined a Resistance cell in September 1941, it was a very unusual act. According to Barbara Will:

> the number of individuals who joined the Resistance at its inception, in 1940–41, was a minuscule fraction of all *résistants*. Furthermore, most writers and intellectuals at the time shied away from joining the Resistance until it became politically unpalatable not to do so.[8]

Simone de Beauvoir wrote later that 'in that occupied France, it was enough to breathe to consent to the oppression.'[9] The hyperbole here might be seen as defensive, pointing at once to the helplessness of the collaborator and to the ubiquity of collaboration. Jean-Paul Sartre articulated a similar sense in an essay published five years after the liberation of Paris, in writing that 'Every one of our heartbeats plunged us deeper into a culpability which horrified us.'[10] For Sartre, the keynote of the period was the sense of the emptying out of reality, of a horror that was the more penetrating for the fact that there seemed not to be a way of exactly feeling it:

> Paris was fading away and yawned hungrily under the empty sky. Withdrawn from the world, fed out of pity or on a calculated basis, it possessed no more than an abstract and symbolic existence . . . Everything was hollow and empty: the Louvre without paintings, Parliament without deputies, the Senate without senators, the lycée Montaigne without students. The artificial existence that the Germans still maintained in it: the theatrical presentations, the races, the gloomy and dreary feasts only had as goal to show the world that France was intact because Paris was still alive.[11]

Sartre writes of what seemed like the strange collaboration between the Germans, who wished to maintain Paris as the legendary city of light and leisure, and the Allies, who refrained from bombing it:

> the English bombed Lorient, Rouen and Nantes, but had decided to spare Paris. As a result, we enjoyed in this city in agony a deathly and symbolic calm. All around this island, it rained iron and steel: but just as we weren't allowed to share in the provinces' labors, we no longer had the right to share in their suffering. A symbol: this hardworking and irascible city was no more a symbol. We looked in each others' eyes and wondered if we too hadn't become symbols.[12]

A central experience for Sartre was that of temporal dislocation. 'All our acts were provisional, their meaning was limited to the very day when they were accomplished.'[13] Elizabeth Bowen registers a similar suspensiveness in the experience of wartime London, in evoking 'that "time being" which war had made the very being of time'.[14] Bachelard's setting aside of his epistemological writing was, if not prompted, then prolonged during the period of tense suspension of the Occupation, the experience of time evoked by Sartre and perhaps aptly characterized by Samuel Beckett in one of the works he wrote after the War as a life that, 'at the same time it is over and it goes on, and is there any tense for that?'[15]

What may have begun as a short diversion, allowable in one who had built up such an impressive philosophical CV, turned into an extended vacation. It was a turn away from what in English is referred to as the 'day job', the expectations and responsibilities of one in his newly exalted academic position, to allow for a return to the feelings of childhood. Sartre evokes too a kind of nostalgia for a lost happiness, a 'memory cult that we practiced for four years and which had as its objective, through our distant friends, a lost sweetness of life and pride in living'.[16] Still, in the watchful, phoney peace of the Occupation, small and subliminal gestures could count for much. When Daniel Giroux visited Bachelard in Paris, who told him he was due to lecture on Schopenhauer, he was swiftly reassured 'Don't worry! He is not one of theirs!' (Parinaud, 240).

Already, in *The Psychoanalysis of Fire*, Bachelard had been forming the idea for the sequence of books that would occupy him almost exclusively over the first decade of his professorship at the Sorbonne. Building out from his suggestion that fire is 'the prime element of reverie', Bachelard suggested that there were temperaments that could find themselves otherwise 'in their element', as we say both in French and in English.[17] Distinguishing the meanings of alcohol for Edgar Allan Poe as opposed to E.T.A. Hoffmann, Bachelard affirms of the former that 'the element to which his imagination has become polarized is water or lifeless earth on which no fire grows; it is not fire.'[18] This provides a bookmark for the sequence of four books that would appear between 1942 and 1948, completing the study of fire with studies of the mustering power on particular writers of water, air and (in two volumes) earth:

> If our present work serves any useful purpose, it should suggest a classification of objective themes which would prepare the way for a classification of poetic temperaments. We have not yet been able to perfect an over-all doctrine, but it seems quite clear to us that there is some relation between the doctrine of the four physical elements and the doctrine of the four temperaments.[19]

The first of these volumes was *L'eau et les rêves: essai sur l'imagination de la matière* (1942), devoted to poetic reveries centred on water. It was published by the small literary publisher José Corti, himself a poet, who had published Bachelard's short study *Lautréamont* in 1939. We can measure the gap between the way of proceeding that Bachelard evolved during the 1940s and a more conventional kind of literary psychoanalysis, through his approving reference to the study of Poe published in two volumes by Marie Bonaparte in 1933. Where classical psychoanalysis, both in its Freudian and Jungian versions, had depended on the principle that dreams were, according to Freud in *The Interpretation of Dreams*, 'the royal road to a knowledge of the unconscious activities of the mind', Bachelard is interested in a form of mental action that, while belonging to waking life, lies halfway between dream and fully present-to-itself consciousness, which from this period onwards he would call 'reverie'.[20] For Bachelard, the reverie is a kind of directed waking dream that combines looseness and lucidity. For all the respect that he pays to Marie Bonaparte's biographical analysis of Poe's writing, Bachelard is always concerned to generalize and impersonalize her arguments, turning what Bonaparte presented as biographical symptoms into a kind of archetypal apotheosis of the material imagination as such. It is almost as though, in moving from the specific meanings of water, as embodying Poe's melancholy mourning for his dead mother, to 'the *element* itself, substantial water, dreamed about as a substance', Bachelard were pointing to an anonymous process, at once below and beyond the imaginative processes of an individual, in which the elements dream themselves through the material imagination to which they give rise.[21]

Bachelard saw the process of reverie at work in particular in the exploratory play of children with matter, especially the indeterminately clayey substance he called *pâte*, which covers more in French than the English equivalent 'paste' does:

> Since in this book I am analyzing only the more highly developed psychic conditions, those more directly adapted to objective experiences and poetic works, I must describe the work of moulding in its purely active elements, disengaging them from their psychoanalytic taint. Work in these substances has an orderly childhood. (*Water and Dreams*, 109)

In contrast to the puritanical sternness with which Bachelard viewed the intoxications with substance in his scientific epistemology, there is a kind of loving attentiveness in Bachelard's writing on the material imagination to the similarly loving attentiveness that he found in it. Where Bachelard had inveighed against the cloying effect on scientific reasoning of the belief in substance, here he celebrates the fact that '*water*, in Poe's imagination, is a superlative, a kind of substance of substance, a true mother substance' (*Water and Dreams*, 46). The cleansing psychoanalysis in which Bachelard had reposed such confidence is now itself recoiled from as a 'psychoanalytic taint' (*Water and Dreams*, 148) – 'tare psychanalytique'.[22] It is not clear whether the taint belongs to psychoanalysis itself or 'the interest in their own excrement shown by children and some of the mentally ill' (*Water and Dreams*, 109) of which Bachelard reminds us that Marie Bonaparte reminds her readers. French 'tare' is broader in its reference than English 'tare', which is restricted, mostly through the influence of its New Testament usage in the parable of the sower in Matthew 13.25, to weeds. French 'tare' can also mean a blot, stain or blemish more generally; for example, of illegitimacy, or, in 'tainte héréditaire' as the taint of hereditary insanity. Whether it is the child or the analyst who is supposed to have their fingers in the pie, Bachelard is now intent on elevating this from polluting play to a 'purely active' status – 'purement actifs' – in the 'more highly developed psychic conditions' (*Water and Dreams*, 109) of a primal kind of sculpture.[23]

Bachelard's earlier understanding of psychoanalysis as a purification begins in *Water and Dreams* to be conceived, not as a purgative preliminary to the work of real science in abstract or mathematical process, but as a protoscientific process in itself:

> If we admit that an obvious – though quite generally accepted – biological error can correspond to a profound oneiric truth, then we are ready to interpret dreams materially. Therefore, along with the psychoanalysis of dreams there should be a psychophysics and a psychochemistry of dreams. This intensely materialistic psychoanalysis should return to the old precepts that held elemental diseases to be curable by elemental medicines. The material element is the determining factor in the disease, as in the cure. We suffer through dreams and are cured by dreams. (*Water and Dreams*, 4)

Later in the book, Bachelard will reaffirm this faith in 'imaginary medicine', or the self-healing placebo of the imagination: 'material images, soft and hot, warm and humid, cure us. They belong to that imaginary medicine, so oneirically true and forcefully dreamed that it retains a considerable influence over our unconscious life' (*Water and Dreams*, 128).

An important part of Bachelard's own 'psychochemistry' (*Water and Dreams*, 4) is the intensified work he gives to the Freudian concept of sublimation. Bachelard might have been particularly attracted to this term by its origin in chemistry, to refer to the process whereby a solid becomes a vapour without passing through the intermediary stage of a liquid. Building on the metaphorical use of the word in the condition described from the eighteenth century onwards as 'the sublime', sublimation indicates in Freudian psychoanalysis the process whereby the energy of an instinctual drive is displaced upwards into something more socially valued, often involving artistic, religious or intellectual activity. Like many Freudian concepts, sublimation has an ironic cast, for a kind of repression or imposture always remains in it. By contrast, Bachelard seems determined to take the aim of sublimation as its achievement, thereby as it were sublimating the idea of sublimation itself. Bachelard had already urged in *The Dialectic of Duration* that 'Sublimation is not some deep drive; it is a call. Art is not a poor substitute for sexuality. On the contrary, sexuality is already an aesthetic tendency.'[24] In the final chapter of *The Psychoanalysis of Fire*, 'Idealized Fire: Fire and Purity', Bachelard drew on Max Scheler's denunciation, in the 1923 French translation of *Zur Phänomenologie und Theorie der Sympathiegefühle und von Liebe und Hass* (1913), of psychoanalytic theories of sublimation, as a '"feeding from the roots" theory, which would deny man any chance of an existence on a higher plane'.[25] *Water and Dreams* begins where *The Psychoanalysis of Fire* had, somewhat tentatively, ended, with an emphatic and unconstrained assertion of the self-transcending powers of imagination:

> The imagination is not, as its etymology suggests, the faculty for forming images of reality; it is the faculty for forming images which go beyond reality, which *sing* reality. It is a superhuman faculty. A man is a man to the extent that he is a superman.
> A man should be defined by the sum of those tendencies which impel him to surpass the *human condition*. (*Water and Dreams*, 16)

Where Freud saw sublimation as a kind of compromise, consisting of a nearly good-enough balance between thwarted and realized desire, Bachelard had a much more Romantic understanding of sublimation as a kind of realization through self-levitation – a more Nietzschean identification of the human with the superhuman. Freud's narcissism is a forgiving concession to reality: Bachelard seems to favour the more imperative assertion of the narcissist by conviction and vocation, in which 'Narcissus no longer says: "I love myself as I am"; he says: "I am the way I love myself." I live exuberantly because I love myself fervently' (*Water and Dreams*, 23).

Simone de Beauvoir saw Bachelard's *Water and Dreams* as an exception to the general condition of 'vegetation' that descended on literature in France during the Occupation, writing of it that he 'applied to the imagination a method very close to existential psychoanalysis: hardly anyone had yet risked this kind of exploration and the book interested us'.[26] In *Being and Nothingness*, while applauding the 'real discovery' of Bachelard's 'material imagination' in *Water and Dreams*, which had appeared in the previous year, Sartre uses the book to focus the ways in which an existential psychoanalysis might be distinguished from Freudian psychoanalysis.

The period of abeyance in French psychoanalysis that was a result of the Occupation no doubt left the field clearer for this kind of critique than it might otherwise have been. Sartre's criticisms amount to the view that Bachelard's analysis of images is too dependent upon the mechanics of Freudian explanations, and so insufficiently attentive to the way in which neurotic 'symptoms' are not detachable from the entire world of meanings both built and inhabited by a human subject. He accuses Bachelard of reproducing the habit common among psychoanalysts of bringing to bear external concepts like the sexual libido, the will to power or the trauma of birth, when what is required is an account of the ways in which humans make their choice of being, meaning that 'we should establish the goal of psychoanalysis strictly from the standpoint of ontology.'[27] Sartre goes on to characterize what he means by ontology:

> human reality, far from being capable of being described as libido or will to power, is a choice of being, either directly or through appropriation of the world. And we have seen – when the choice is expressed through appropriation – that each thing is chosen in the last analysis, not for its sexual potential but depending on the mode in which it renders being, depending on the manner in which being springs forth from its surface. A psychoanalysis of things and of their matter ought above all to be concerned with establishing the way in which each thing

> is the objective symbol of being and of the relation of human reality to this being.[28]

The odd thing about this criticism is that it so closely resembles the criticism that Bachelard himself will from this point on increasingly make of psychoanalysis. Bachelard does not foreground the question of choice of being as firmly and formally as Sartre does, but his emphasis increasingly is on the ways in which particular beings actively and purposively, if not entirely self-consciously, make their imaginative worlds. Indeed, in *Air and Dreams*, published shortly after *Water and Dreams*, though not referred to by Sartre, Bachelard criticizes psychoanalysis for just the same kind of mechanical application of a method as Sartre does:

> psychoanalytic symbols are the fundamental concepts of psychoanalytic inquiry. Once a symbol has been interpreted, that is, once its 'unconscious' meaning has been found, it becomes a mere instrument of analysis, and one no longer thinks that he need study it in its context or in its variations.[29]

The idea that psychoanalysis was essentially a theory underpinning a clinical practice employed to treat individual illness had never been very much to the fore in Bachelard's thinking, and he showed even less interest in the process of psychoanalyis or its attendant dramaturgy in the talking cure, according to which the patient must come to curative awareness through transferential acting-out in the scene of the analysis. Bachelard alluded in *Water and Dreams* to the work of Charles Baudouin (*Water and Dreams*, 17–18), a Swiss psychoanalyst who associated psychoanalysis with the exercise of 'inner discipline' and the training of the will characteristic of religious traditions: he founded an International Institute of Psychagogy and Psychotherapy in 1924, alluding to the tradition of psychagogy as the spiritual direction of souls. He wrote that 'It is in the guidance of sublimation that the analyst does the finest work and incurs the greatest responsibility. It is in this field that he becomes a veritable educationist and a spiritual director.'[30] But, for all his interest in pedagogy, and the testaments to his sympathetic generosity during his many years as a teacher, Bachelard seems to have been powerfully motivated by an indwelling and self-impelling exercise of self-making.

7

Tension of Relaxation, 1943–8

Bachelard's appointment to the Sorbonne in 1940 marked his achievement of the status of public intellectual, doubtless made more satisfactory by the fact that he stepped into the position occupied by his own supervisor, Abel Rey, a kind of Oedipal-apostolic succession that still often characterizes academic life. Bachelard might have felt able, at the age of 56, to settle into a life of admired celebrity. In a sense, this was exactly the course that his final years took. At the same time, such a settling left the striving energy of self-formation that had propelled Bachelard into this position of eminence with no more work to do. What was to be done when the world seemed to have said Yes to The Philosophy of No, the title of the book that Bachelard published in the year in which he took up his position at the Sorbonne? While not exactly qualifying as one of those 'wrecked by success', according to Freud's 1916 essay 'Some Character Types Met With in Psycho-Analytic Work', Bachelard's apparent success did not seem to encourage him to the serene surcease it might have been expected to, and indeed seemed to provoke a kind of aggressive assault, in the form of the sequence of four books to which Bachelard devoted himself through the war and beyond, until his return to the epistemology of science in *Le Rationalisme appliqué* in 1949.[1] One may add to this the fact of the Occupation itself, which provoked the sense that withdrawal might in itself constitute a kind of resistance: Bachelard wrote to Daniel Giroux's mother on 20 August 1942, 'We must also drive out the war from our brains.'[2]

Sartre makes extensive use in his *Being and Nothingness* of a phrase that Bachelard introduces in the final chapter of *Water of Dreams*, in which he articulated the idea that '*reality* can never be well founded in men's eyes until human activity is sufficiently and intelligently aggressive. Then all the objects in the world receive their true *coefficient of adversity*.'[3] Sartre was sufficiently struck by the phrase 'coefficient of adversity' to employ it more than twenty times in the course of *Being and Nothingness*. Sartre's reflections in that book on the nature of the *visqueux*, the slimy-sticky, are much more famous than Bachelard's, though one cannot but be struck by the parallels between Sartre's intense, almost phobic arguments, and Bachelard's discussions of what he calls 'mesomorphic imagination – that is, of an imagination intermediate between the formal and the material' (*Water and Dreams*, 106). Indeed, the parallels between Bachelard and Sartre are so close, making it seem that they are in some strange way taking turns at writing the same book, that one can for this very reason almost certainly rule out influence, since much more care will typically be taken to disguise actual influence of this kind. Bachelard's idea of the mesomorphic is self-characterizing, for the term is applied not to the kind of material imagined, but the imagination itself, which seems to be thought of as having the same intermediate condition as the matter with which it is taken up. The mesomorphic imagination inhabits both meanings of the word 'form', as raw materiality, and formed material. Bachelard's evocation of the capacity of water to create different grades of paste, between the solid and the liquid, is metamorphic as well as mesomorphic, for it identifies the essential oscillation, which is played out in different modes throughout Bachelard's life and writing, between the assertion of the subject over the material object, and the indolent assimilation of the subject to matter as mere mass:

> The objects of mesomorphic dream take form only with great difficulty, and then they lose it; they collapse like soft clay (*pâte*). To the sticky, pliable, lazy, sometimes phosphorescent – but not luminous – object corresponds, I believe, the greatest ontological density of the oneiric life. Those dreams in which we dream of clay are by turns struggle or defeat in the effort to create, form, deform, or mould. (*Water and Dreams*, 106)

One might say that the intermediacy of the mesomorphic imagination is most strikingly embodied in the work of writing itself, which works to transform mere life into shape and meaning, and yet, in becoming identical with life, threatens to collapse into the 'ontological density' of formless dreaming on display here. The imagination of paste becomes the essential image of the mediation between life and work that writing

Bachelard in his study in Paris, 17 December 1960.

enacts. Manual, digital, the making of paste is an image of the writing that images it.

The final chapter of *Water and Dreams* offers another example of the coefficient of adversity. For Bachelard, always alert to the possibility of something to oppose, the dominant principle of water, its power to dissolve forms and overflow limits, is the very thing that seems to summon up the will, in the actions of plunging and swimming, in a pure combat that '*is seen before the combatants*' (*Water and Dreams*, 167). The only way for a human to float, like the only way to hover for a bird, is to work at it. Immersion enjoins urgency.

As often in Bachelard's writing, the evocation of what he continues to call 'images' aims to go beyond vision, or retreat away from it, into kinetic sensation, in a distinctive mixture of the abstract and the dynamic, form and force:

> Even though visual images arise from the imagination and give a form 'to the adversary's limbs,' we should certainly recognize that these visual images come second and in a subordinate position because of the necessity of conveying to the reader an essentially dynamic image that is itself primary and direct and which, therefore, has its origin in dynamic imagination, in the imagination of courageous movement. This fundamental dynamic image is, then, a kind of struggle in itself. More than anyone else, the swimmer can say: the world is my will; the world is my provocation. It is I who stir up the sea. (*Water and Dreams*, 167)

In a certain sense, the repose that Bachelard allowed himself in his alchemicopoetic reveries, just as he allowed himself his regular retreats back to rural ease in Burgundy from his demanding work in the metropolis, was more than a mere relaxation. For it comes at times to constitute a kind of assault mounted on the work of scientific knowledge, and perhaps even on the idea of work itself. As Bachelard remarks in *Water and Dreams*, 'What is true human calm? It is calm acquired by self-control; it is not natural calm. It is calm gained by defeating violence and anger' (*Water and Dreams*, 177). Far from being a simple remission from striving, repose is, in Bachelard's fecund phrase, the coefficient of adversity, a way for striving to strive against itself, and therefore become its collaborator. It is the storm within the calm, or, in the phrase that Bachelard archly permitted himself in the book that followed, 'tension of relaxation' (*Water and Dreams*, 121). After dreamy, drawn-out dalliances with lament, melancholy and submissive enervation, *Water and Dreams* ends with conjurings of the bracing Byronic muscularity of the swimmer.

Bachelard picks up these dynamic themes straight away in what would be the next book in his elemental series, *L'Air et les songes*, as though it issued from the same unbroken spate of writing. *Air and Dreams* begins as *Water and Dreams* ended, with an assertion of the dynamism of matter. It restates the proposition found at the beginning of *Water and Dreams* that 'The imagination is not, as its etymology suggests, the faculty for forming images of reality; it is the faculty for forming images which go beyond reality, which *sing* reality' (*Water and Dreams*, 16). In *Air and Dreams*, this becomes: 'We always think of the imagination as the faculty that *forms* images. On the contrary, it *deforms* what we perceive; it is, above all, the faculty that frees us from immediate images and *changes* them.'[4] The unifying force of *Air and Dreams* is provided by the idea of force itself, always going beyond static and closed forms, in 'the supremacy of dynamic over formal imagination' (*Air and Dreams*, 82). Air, however, offers a difficulty in the very fact of its apparent immateriality, for 'air is very thin matter' (*Air and Dreams*, 18). It is not surprising that mapping the material imagination of air should require Bachelard to focus on what moves through, or by, the air, like clouds and trees. But where Bachelard is responsive to the omnidirectional impetus of water, expressed both in the flow of a river, and the turbulent maelstrom of a stormy sea, *Air and Dreams* is concentrated around a single vector, in the uplift of an '*ascensional psychology*' (*Air and Dreams*, 9).

Bachelard is clear about the ironic problem that aerial dreams seem to present for him; namely, that they seem to involve much less of the coefficient of striving. Almost comically, his desire to find dynamic desire, or, where it does not seem to exist, to incite it, sets his analysis irritably at odds with the thematics of ease and peacefulness that are characteristic of airy dreams. Confessing that he has not been able to find many examples of wrathfully buffeting winds, he concludes: 'violence, then, remains a characteristic that does not fit well into an aerial psychology' (*Air and Dreams*, 16).

Bachelard seems in this book to have settled on his method, which is a reading of the dynamics of imagination established specifically through the analysis of poetry. It is clear from his remarks along the way that this method of research involves a rather elementary process of inductive scanning across large numbers of poetic texts, mostly Romantic and modern, and with a strong preference for poets associated with or responsive to surrealism. Though Bachelard has a perfect right to restrict his focus to poetry, the reliance on poetry to reveal the logic of imagination as such does mean that that there are large areas of inattention. He admits that one of the most conspicuous of these omissions is the experiences of religious ecstasy, which, oddly, he says are not to be encompassed in the kind of 'discursive sublimation' he aims to study, in which experiences of air play 'between impression and expression' (*Air and Dreams*, 13). Though Bachelard says that this 'places problems of religious ecstasy out of reach' (*Air and Dreams*, 13), religious poetry and mystical writing are powerfully, one might almost say overwhelmingly, energized by just this ambivalence. In the end, Bachelard pads such experiences away with the mock-modest excuse, 'I am not qualified to deal with them' (*Air and Dreams*, 13). In dismissing religious writing in favour of a conscious attention to poetry, Bachelard rules out for himself the attention to a broader understanding of poetics that his work in fact makes available for future writers.

The principal reason for Bachelard's lack of excitement by religious forms of imagination may be that religious experiences seemed to him to mandate passivity rather than passion (he seems not to have been familiar with the work of John Donne). Bachelard's effort throughout *Air and Dreams* is to avoid the two forms of 'ineffective' air (*Air and Dreams*, 12), images of inertness and volatility, by constituting the imagination of air as a kind of ballistics, this in line with his view of the elements as 'the hormones of the imagination' (*Air and Dreams*, 11). The biochemical word *hormone* was introduced by Ernest Henry Starling, in the first of his Croonian Lectures on the Chemical Correlation of the Functions of the Body, on 20 June 1905 at the Royal College of Physicians in London, in a reference to 'these chemical messengers . . . or "hormones" (from ὁρμάω, I excite or arouse) as we might call them'.[5]

Where *Water and Dreams* had been given both tension and thrust by Bachelard's politely polemical response to Marie Bonaparte's reading of Edgar Allan Poe, enlarging upon it in ways that set it at naught, Bachelard finds a cohering centre for *Air and Dreams* in the work of a more marginal writer. Though Bachelard refers frequently to psychoanalytic writers, the little-known work of Robert Desoille is discussed at greater length than any other.[6] Bachelard may have encountered Desoille's work via Juliette Favez-Boutonier, whose doctoral thesis on anxiety he was supervising during the 1940s: Favez-Boutonier had experience of waking dream therapy with Desoille, and her thesis itself devotes a chapter to Desoille.[7]

Bachelard may have been drawn to Desoille's work in part by the striking resemblance between his life and that of Desoille, who himself began training as an engineer that was interrupted by his service in the First World War. One can imagine Bachelard being struck by the remarks about Desoille's lack of professional or academic training made in the preface by Charles Baudouin to Desoille's first book, *Exploration de l'affectivité subconsciente par la méthode du rêve éveillé dirigé* (1938):

> The author of this book is not a professional. This condition could be disadvantageous in one who lacked prudence and, what is more, had not had a scientific education. This is not the case for M. Desoille, who has an acute awareness – possibly too acute – of the lacunae in his personal education and who has devoted himself to overcoming them.[8]

Though he found a following, Desoille, unlike Bachelard, never found a secure institutional home, or reputation, but remained part of the Kuiper Belt of divergent analysts distantly orbiting the Freudian sun.

One of the most striking features of the material imagination is that, for all of the dynamism on which Bachelard insists, it never forms anything that might be called narrative, for that would be for force to ossify into form. Dynamic states may be sustained, but they never seem to build or develop. But this, in turn, means that dynamism can never go anywhere, or lead to anything. The work of Desoille provides Bachelard with a way of understanding this dynamism as both directive and directed. In a sense it represents the fulfilment of the desire that is apparent throughout Bachelard's evocations of psychoanalysis, that it should be seen as, more than a form of therapy, a pedagogy, or purposive project of self-formation. Indeed, Bachelard associates Desoille explicitly with this aim, suggesting that his technique should be seen as 'one of the most effective procedures in this *Psychagogy* of which Charles Baudouin is one of the principal movers' (*Air and Dreams*, 111).

Bachelard seems by the 1940s to have become impatient with what he saw as the abstract dogmatism of Freudian psychoanalysis, which he associated with the institutional kind of knowledge against which he reacted so vigorously throughout his life. Bachelard finds in the self-directed dreaming of reverie an autodidacticism of the imagination that matches his own deep investment in the fantasy of self-education (for nobody can educate themselves). Bachelard imagines imagination to be a pure exercise of will: 'Imagination and Will are aspects of a single profound force. Anyone who can imagine can will. To the imagination that informs our will is coupled a will to imagine, a will to live what is imagined' (*Air and Dreams*, 111–12). There is still a role for psychoanalysis – now with the proviso that it 'might be more aptly termed psychosynthesis' – in 'determining what conditions of synthesis are necessary for developing a *new* personality' (*Air and Dreams*, 113), but Bachelard is now attracted strongly by the idea that the patient who is experiencing blockage might be able to dream his or her way out of it, with only minimal direction from outside. In her discussion of Desoille's practice of the directed waking dream in her book *L'angoisse*, Juliette Favez-Boutonier evoked 'the therapeutic effect of the waking dream, which in fact appears independent from the conscious interpretations one might give it'.[9] Bachelard largely relies in *Air and Dreams* on Desoille's first book, published in 1938, but refers in a footnote to a future work, presumably Desoille's *Le rêve éveillé en psychothérapie*, which would appear in 1945, which he says will contain 'a complete account of waking dreams directed by patients with virtually no psychoanalysis simply by re-establishing the function of sublimation' (*Air and Dreams*, 113 n. 2).

Perhaps the concept and practice of the directed waking dream, devised by a writer who had experienced, like Bachelard, an interruption to his dream of becoming an engineer, acted out the idea of a psychic engineering, which operated on the matter of consciousness in a more immediate and quasi-physiological way than that offered by the highly mediated and discursively rather than practically focused work of interpretation in Freudian psychoanalysis. Desoille commonly employed the technique of asking his patient to imagine a place containing an object, which the patient was then encouraged to take hold of and then move with through the place.[10] After the Second World War Desoille tried to blend his therapeutic system with the ideas of Ivan Pavlov, moving even further away from the idea of the interpretative talking cure towards a conception of therapy as a kind of psychophysical orthopaedics of impulse, and retraining of conditioned reflexes.[11] Such a practice may have recommended itself to Bachelard as the 'material form of psychoanalysis' that he found in Virginia Woolf's *Orlando*, and as a psychological version of the phénoménotechnique he applauded in the industrial applications of physics and chemistry.[12] Bachelard does not seem himself to have had any experience in practice of directed waking dream but he did have close personal contact with Desoille. In writing that 'Desoille shows that it is possible to put to work intuitions like those of Bachelard . . . and derive benefit from them in therapy,' Marta Ples-Bęben instructively presents Desoille's work as an example of the 'applied rationalism' that provided the title of the first book that Bachelard produced on his return to scientific epistemology in 1949 after his wartime immersion in the imagination.[13]

If, in some ways, Bachelard's purging of the ambivalence in Freudian sublimation can be seen as a sublimation of sublimation, its literalization allows it to be seen as what, in 1964, Herbert Marcuse would influentially (though perhaps, looking about us, we might think not influentially enough) call 'repressive desublimation'. Marcuse in fact uses a quotation from Bachelard's *Le materialisme rationnel* (1953) to sum up the repressive tendency of desublimation in the conclusion to his *One-Dimensional Man*:

> An entire psychoanalysis of matter can help us to cure us of our images or at least help us to limit the hold of our images on us. One may then hope *to be able to render imagination happy*, to give it good conscience in allowing it fully all its means of expression, all material images which emerge in *natural dreams*, in normal dream activity. To render imagination happy, to allow it all its exuberance, means precisely to grant imagination its true function as psychological impulse and force.[14]

Marcuse comments that

> 'to give to the imagination all the means of expression' would be regression. The mutilated individuals (mutilated also in their faculty of imagination) would organize and destroy even more than they are now permitted to do. Such release would be the unmitigated horror – not the catastrophe of culture, but the free sweep of its most repressive tendencies.[15]

For the most part Bachelard has little interest in the clinical aspects of psychoanalysis, which accounts in part for the haziness, even, unkindly, the laziness of his view of psychoanalysis. At the same time, he seems to have been drawn to an expansive view of the function of psychotherapy that tends towards a kind of mysticism. More and more, Bachelard surrenders to a sense of the omnipotent power of thought, not only to elevate, but, through the operations of sublimation, to exalt itself. This becomes much more than a way of overcoming emotional blockage: it is, Bachelard affirms, a kind of morality. In *Air and Dreams*, the 'synthesis of purification and reward' is always 'both moral and physical' (*Air and Dreams*, 52). Literary evocations of exaltation provide us, he says, with 'lessons in a physics of morality, an ethics whose symbolic life already exists in the material elements' (*Air and Dreams*, 57). Repeatedly, Bachelard insists on the 'moral' force of this levitation: 'A moralist working on the documents

I have given here would have to acknowledge, I think, that in certain respects height is not only moralizing, but is in itself physically moral, so to speak' (*Air and Dreams*, 61). In the end, 'a pride is born in our sense of morality, in our sublimation, and in our life's story' (*Air and Dreams*, 123).

One of the reasons that Bachelard may have become increasingly unsatisfied by Freudian psychoanalysis, and, in truth, did not go out of his way to seek it, is that it offers so little in the way of moral authority. According to Samuel Beckett, on being reminded of Kant's remark that our sense of the sublime is irresistibly stirred both by the starry heavens above and by the moral law beneath, Freud's dry-eyed reaction was: 'The stars are undoubtedly superb.'[16] It is hard to know what Bachelard might mean by the morality of elevation he affirmed, beyond the mystical elevation of morality. The tendency towards mystical thinking, which, counterintuitively, is sometimes more likely in mathematicians and physicists than in others, was allowed the light of day in the enthusiasm for homeopathy already noted in *The Dialectic of Duration*, which concludes triumphantly with the prospect of an art of 'micro-nutrition', which would account for the fact that, as Bachelard alleges, 'the more delicate and rare are the aromas and bouquets of food and wine, the more effectively they act on our digestion . . . With a micro-foodstuff, we take in duration and rhythms rather than substance.'[17] The mystical impulse is increasingly given release in *Air and Dreams*. Interestingly, the single reference that Bachelard provides to accompany his admission that he will not be dealing with 'problems of religious ecstasy' is to a book on the history of levitation.[18] 'Breathing exercises, as we know, take on a moral value,' Bachelard assures us (*Air and Dreams*, 236–7). Desoille had first developed his ideas about the suggestive force of guided dream in early work with Eugène Caslant, a military historian who became director of the Laboratoire de la Physiologie des Sensations, and moved from study of the history of aeronautics to investigation of supernormal abilities.[19] Bachelard takes serious note of the consideration given in Desoille's work to telepathy and clairvoyance (*Air and Dreams*, 120–21).

It should be no surprise that, alongside Desoille, the other guiding spirit of *Air and Dreams* is Nietzsche, 'the prototype of the *vertical poet*, the *poet of the summits*, the *ascensional poet*' (*Air and Dreams*, 127), whose images, Bachelard tells us, provide 'an experimental physics of the moral life' (*Air and Dreams*, 149). This moralization of will could be seen in an opposite sense in terms of the arguments in Nietzsche's *Genealogy of Morals* that morality has its origin in the exercise of will. In the absence of any kind of arguments relating to morality, beyond the sense of the abstract pressure of the ought and the must, Bachelard's certainty that the material imagination is a moral imagination seems to be vulnerable to a Nietzschean critique as the moralization of pure force:

> I would not be unfaithful to Desoille's thought if I said that there is in his method a transformation from oneiric energy to moral energy, in the same way that a diffused heat can become motion. Moralists like to talk about discovery in morality, as though moral life were the work of the mind! Instead they should talk about the primordial power of the *moral imagination*. (*Air and Dreams*, 112)

We must surely take leave to wonder why this power should be thought of as primordial, wondering too whether it might not at least in part be because of the updraft provided by the idea of the 'primordial' itself. Bachelard finds in Desoille's work an occasion for the simultaneous denunciation of intellectuality and its omnipotent reassertion:

> Psychologists want *understanding*, when they really should be imagining. They need to experience the power of the *imagination*, the supreme power of completed sublimation, willed and adumbrated throughout all of its 'correspondences.' In the intellectual life, instead of living the imagining being, do we not instead suppress its sublimations? (*Air and Dreams*, 124)

8

Overcoming, 1947–53

If air does not seem solid or substantial enough really to count as 'material', then the last two books in Bachelard's sequence of books on the four elements centre on the element that seems to embody the idea of materiality as such. But, if the sublimation for which air stands risks evaporating it into pure subjectivity, then the risk of earth, the element that comprehends all the others, is that it comes to seem all substance. In fact, it seems to be in recognition of this duality that Bachelard found himself having to write two volumes about the imagination of the earth: the first devoted to aggressive exercise of will, the second to the 'philosophy of repose' he had anticipated in *The Dialectic of Duration*.

These two books on earth, which are almost as long as the rest of the sequence of books on the elements put together, represent the summation and the summit of the mode of analysis that Bachelard made distinctively his own in filling out his idea of the material imagination. Just as water means liquid for early natural philosophers, and air, in the absence of any understanding of its components, means gas, so, for Bachelard, earth is the synecdoche for solidity. Just as the word *heat* encompasses the complete range of temperatures, from incandescent to freezing to cold, so solidity encompasses every gradation of hardness, up to and including the liquid, gaseous and plasmatic states of matter. Earth is underfoot, but the sky similarly teems with worlds. The other 'elements' allow for the thought that they might be rendered pure, through the reduction of every admixture, to arrive at 'bodies incapable of decomposition', in Humphry Davy's characterization.[1] But earth allows for no such condition of purity, for it exists only and always as a 'mixed body', in and as some kind of composition. It is the least elementary of the so-called elements, meaning that there can be no 'as such' in the idea of earth as such. Any effort to imagine earth in an essential or ultimate form – as stone, say, or rock – gives one only an exotic variant on the essentially inultimate idea of earth. Earth constitutes what in the science of dynamic systems is called a 'phase-space', an abstract representation of all the possible states of the system. The two volumes of Bachelard's work on earth could really be simplified into studies of earth in its hard and soft forms, with the reservation that, just as cold is a degree of heat, so softness is a grade of hardness. There will always be some mode of consistency, which is precisely what makes the element of earth essentially inconsistent. And, most of all, earth is mixed with us, through what the subtitle of Bachelard's first book on the earth calls the 'reveries of the will': the dream of the will is both more and less than the exercise of it.

The turn to the earth produces a new focus on the idea of work, understood in terms of a concentration into a single affective condition. For Bachelard, work is not duty, or fatigue, or tedium, or absorption, or self-expression: work is essentially anger, identified with the principle of concentration, anger being the concentration of being, and being as concentration: 'Anger of this sort is not only expressed by the strength of one's hands but pours through one's entire being concentrated in dynamic unity.'[2] The opening chapters of *Earth and the Reveries of Will* give us the encounter of hard matter and soft imagination in one, monotonously repeated form: *matter makes us angry*. This might be regarded as a passionate condensation of the single organizing principle of the whole of Bachelard's life and work, whether it is called will, polemic, striving or the philosophy of no. Bachelard represents the relation between subject and object as primordially one of hostility, of an 'anger which pits the worker against the eternal primordial recalcitrance of matter . . . Hard matter is conquered by the angry hardness of the worker' (*Reveries of Will*, 16, 44). If anger may be seen as a kind of desublimation, or assertion of force over form – the concentration and release of energies in such a way as to overcome the impediment of form by sheer force – then Bachelard finds in work a sublimation of this force: 'the anger involved in labor destroys nothing. It remains intelligent' (*Reveries of Will*, 44–5). Bachelard wants us to believe that anger 'even forms a metaphysics, for always anger is a revelation of being. In anger one feels reborn, renewed, called to new life . . . In this way matter, work, and anger unite' (*Reveries of Will*, 45). Again and again, Bachelard insists that 'the human being becomes a centre of hostility . . . the *human* being is revealed as the being *opposed* to things, not siding *with* things but standing *up* to them' (*Reveries of Will*, 90).

Bachelard really seems to be exercising his own kind of force here. Anger may very well be an important correlative or constituent of the exercise of force, but the assertion that force – and perhaps therefore the force of assertion itself – is nothing but and no more than anger, seems curiously fixated. Over and over again, Bachelard insists that 'the provocation of matter is immediate and that it engenders an immediate anger directed at an object. Resistance and anger are connected in this objective sense' (*Reveries of Will*, 45). The principle of overdoing in *Air and Dreams* modulates in *Earth and Reveries of Will* into the principle of overcoming.

Ordinarily, because anger is the gathering of energies for discharge, it is dissipated by it. One of the singular features of Bachelard's working material imagination is that it struggles against the emptying into completion that its own consummation as a 'work' would bring:

> In fact, the material imagination is, as we might say, always in action. It is never satisfied with realized work. The imagination of form reposes in its objects. Form, once achieved, is so rich with objective, negotiable social value that the high drama of associations relaxes. By contrast, the dream of modeling is one which holds on to its possibilities. (*Reveries of Will*, 76)

The exercise of will defeats all clinging indeterminacy. Where Sartre sees the principle that he calls the 'viscous' as a jeopardy of selfhood, Bachelard emphasizes triumph over matter. Even though 'Women create no images of smithing or the forge' (*Reveries of Will*, 82 n. 5), the victory over indeterminate matter can be found as much in the kitchen as in the virile heroics of the forge: 'We can domesticate the viscous through an indirect attack with dry matter. At the mixing bowl we are demiurges. We determine the destiny of matter' (*Reveries of Will*, 88). Bachelard makes clear that Sartrean existentialism is in his sights in his exclamation that 'The defeated existence of this viscosity, overwhelmed and transformed by the powerful imperialism of the human subject, is yet one more example of a superexistentialism' (*Reveries of Will*, 92).

The focus on the work of wrath makes for the most astonishing omission of the whole of *Earth and the Reveries of Will*, of which, ironically and winningly enough, Bachelard makes open admission at the end of his preface:

> In a work devoted to earth, I have left out images of agriculture [labourage]. Certainly this is not due to any lack of love for the soil. In fact, it seemed to me a betrayal of the orchard and the garden to speak of them in only one short chapter. It would require an entire book to unearth the agriculture of the imagination, the joys of spade and rake. Besides, cliches of the plough have masked the real powers in such imagery so well that extensive psychoanalysis would be necessary to free literature from its false cultivators [faux laboureurs]. (*Reveries of Will*, 11)[3]

It is a perplexing passage. In one sense, agriculture represents just the kind of labour from which Bachelard had apparently toiled so hard and long to escape, into the cultivated world of the scientist and intellectual. Having engineered through heroic and self-sacrificing toil his escape from existence in traditional, rural, agricultural France into modern, metropolitan French life, Bachelard found himself free to idealize the 'agriculture of the imagination'. But it is precisely the false labour of intellectual cultivation, in the images of agriculture projected in literature, that writing about agriculture would commit Bachelard to having to desublimate, through the rather grim process that he calls 'extensive psychoanalysis', in a return to the old idea of psychoanalysis as penitentiary re-education that these books on the imagination seemed otherwise to have moved beyond.

The most distinctive and surprising feature of Bachelard's rapturous absorption in work is the fact that it is understood as absolutely solitary. In this, Bachelard sets aside the single principle that characterizes human work (and indeed the action of work in other species too); namely, that it is organized in, and itself organizes, human groups. For Bachelard, work is reduced to a primal encounter between an individual subject, typified in the heroic figure of the blacksmith, and the world of matter, always considered, no matter what particular form it might take, rock, wood, metal, clay, as materiality as such. Bachelard's idealization of the activity of work is therefore, in the literal sense, a reification of it, reducing it to the direct and immediate encounter between subject and object.

One of the most memorable passages in *Earth and Reveries of Will* focuses on chapter 94 of Melville's *Moby-Dick*, 'A Squeeze of the Hand', in which Ishmael describes the 'sweet and unctuous duty' of squeezing the spermaceti derived from the whale's head, in order to keep it in its liquid state.[4] Bachelard at once simplifies and exalts this work into the transfusing encounter of matter and 'the hand': 'A cosmic sweetness fills, then surrounds the hand that kneads. A perfumed spring is born in the gratified hand' (*Reveries of Will*, 62). Ishmael's narrative moves from his own individual trance to the 'strange sort of insanity' of the mingling of hands in the bath, evoking a sentimental feeling of universal fellowship. Bachelard quotes the climax of Ishmael's narration: 'let us squeeze ourselves universally into the very milk and sperm of kindness.'[5] The editors of the 2002 English translation note that Bachelard in fact misquotes this passage in his text, rendering 'lait de bonté' as 'lait de beauté' (*Reveries of Will*, 318).[6] Though scarcely a criminal error, it is perhaps a symptomatic one, for Bachelard's emphasis on beauty rather than bounty prizes an abstract idea of immediacy over the social mediation of collective labour. Though he recognizes that 'Earthen stuff worked in tandem makes us brothers at work,' Bachelard is perhaps encouraged by his misreading to move from social relations to an aesthetic ideal: 'Human tenderness is a legitimate metaphor for its beautiful material images. As we will see time and again, the pancalism of matter allows it to offer its images to the full range of human ideals' (*Reveries of Will*, 63). Bachelard's offhand 'pancalism of matter' is a reference to a philosophical theory developed by the American philosopher James Mark Baldwin, nowadays rarely discussed. In the third, culminating volume of his *Thought and Things*, Baldwin announces that 'The theory which justifies this procedure and issues in the reasoned view that in aesthetic contemplation we have the fullest revelation of what reality means, I shall venture to call Pancalism.'[7] Baldwin proposed 'Aesthetic Immediatism' as an alternative form for the idea that aesthetic contemplation is the most complete and absolute of the ways in which objects may be known.[8] Bachelard uses the word 'pancalism' repeatedly in *Air and Dreams* and *Water and Dreams*, explaining in a footnote in *Air and Dreams* that, according to Baldwin, 'pancalistic activity tends to transform any contemplation of the universe into an affirmation of universal beauty.'[9]

The volume that Bachelard paired with *Earth and the Reveries of Will* is intended to form a clear counterpart to it. Where *Earth and the Reveries of Will* is held together tightly, and even rather compulsively, by the idea that dreaming is a kind of willing, *Earth and the Reveries of Repose* seems to surrender this impetus, or perhaps redirect it. The theory is clear enough: where the first book comes to a climax with the discussion of the psychology of gravity, in the resistance to it of various kinds of exertion and the assertion of vertical velocity, the second will be centred around descent to the earth and the peculiar kind of intensification of descent represented by burrowing into it. Analysing the images of 'repose, refuge and rootedness' involved Bachelard in the study of what he called in his subtitle 'images of interiority'. This is not quite the opposite of the 'imagination of movement':

> Where humans are concerned, repose is inevitably ruled by an *involutive* psyche. Turning in on oneself cannot always remain an abstraction. It can resemble the *curling up* on itself of a body that becomes an object for itself, that touches itself.[10]

The books come to be 'ruled by an *involutive* psyche' (*Reveries of Repose*, 4), with involution becoming an image of Bachelard's own intellectual posture. The most remarkable feature of the elemental sequence of books that he produced in the decade between 1938 and 1948 is its gradual movement away from historicity. In place of the development of scientific thinking through the progressive rectification of error, and the valorization of the principle of innovation through active refusal of the past, Bachelard's focus, reaching its culmination in *Earth and the Reveries of Repose*, is on cosmic archetypes, which can be recalled but never forgotten, and can deepen but never develop in any direction but inwards. Bachelard's personal past, from which his own work of writing had distanced him unreturnably, is able to be brought back through its fusion with an impersonal past:

> There is, in fact, no past that does not let us taste our own past, that does not soon become a more distant, more uncertain past within us, an immense past where dates no longer exist, where the dates of our personal history are no longer known. (*Reveries of Repose*, 90)

The relentless calling up of the words 'cosmic' and 'archetype' evidences a new passion in Bachelard for persistence and immutability. The force of will persists but is now detached from any sense of temporal thrust. As Bachelard writes in his introduction to *Earth and Reveries of Repose*, 'My first study of earthen imagination, marked as it was by the preposition *against*, must therefore now be supplemented by a study of images that are marked by the preposition *in*' (*Reveries of Repose*, 2). The centrifugal movements of the will, asserting itself ubiquitously in Bachelard's works from the very beginning of his career, now give way to a centripetal movement inwards:

> despite their great variety and their considerable differences in both appearance and form, all these images are if not isomorphic then at the very least isotropic, isotropic in the sense that they all counsel us to make the same movement toward the sources of repose. (*Reveries of Repose*, 4)

Indeed, the governing idea of the book is no longer the earth, as an external element, but the idea of a labyrinthine self-assimilation, which is epitomized in the nonsensical story that Bachelard reproduces from a collection by André Bay of stories told by children to their class members:[11]

> Another story goes like this: 'One day when a pig was very hungry, it swallowed a whole tortoise. The tortoise rearranged all the pig's insides and made itself a house out of them.' The two images of interiority interchange their values here. This story is particularly curious because of how it develops. Since the pig is in a lot of pain, it makes 'a big hole in its belly in order to get the tortoise out. After that, it felt a lot better. It also pulled the house out.' Yet images of sweet repose are not readily abandoned. As it is so cozy in the 'belly's house,' the child calmly adds that the pig went into its own belly where it felt really comfortable. 'Ah!' it said, 'I'm cozy and warm!' To my mind, a storytelling image such as this justifies my description of it – and of images like it – as an auto-Jonah, as the dream of really living 'in your own place,' 'at the center of your own being,' and 'in your own belly.' (*Reveries of Repose*, 96)

The French subtitle of the last work in Bachelard's elemental sequence refers to '*images de l'intimité*', the full force of which is not really captured by '*Images of Interiority*'. This makes more sense of the antithesis that appears early in Bachelard's preface to *Earth and Reveries of Repose* between 'l'intimité de la matière' and 'l'hostilité de la matière', which is a contrast between intimacy and antagonism, rather than simply between interiority and exteriority.[12]

Bachelard is always tempted by the ambition of generalization, and here that impulse indulges itself without any sense of impediment, though the reader can sometimes feel an interrogative itch. 'The interior that is dreamed is warm, and never burning' (*Reveries of Repose*, 39): what of volcanoes? 'In dreams, beehives are often subterranean' (*Reveries of Repose*, 162): really – how often? Amid a number of arresting reflections on the psychology of cleaning, we are suavely assured that 'Housekeepers prefer cleaning up stains rather than just rings left on things' (*Reveries of Repose*, 32). This could easily be true, and no doubt sometimes is, but mostly, I would say, is not. In fact, one could all-too-easily imagine an argument of Bachelardian subtlety being developed to prove that the 'gleaming victories' (*Reveries of Repose*, 32) derived from the removal of minor blemishes ('Yet here's a spot') in fact perversely outweigh the psychic yield from the purging of pollutions on an Augean scale.

But in this case and in many others in which Bachelard offers himself as infallible guide, one's reservation seems rather beside the point. For the most distinctive feature of Bachelard's writing in his works on the elemental imagination is its intellectual inventiveness. Bachelard gives himself licence not just to risk extravagant generalizations, but also to improvise, sometimes whimsically, new objects of thought and modes of argument. Central to this is the idea of reverie, as a development of the directed daydream Bachelard found described in the work of Robert Desoille. The term conjoined the unsupervised association and unrestricted possibilities contained in the idea of the dream and the idea of an analysis conducted upon it. For Bachelard, a reverie was a more or less conscious working out of the logic of a dream, which nevertheless remained suspended within an oneiric frame. Bachelard's work was a dreamwork, both in the sense that it performs work on dreams and in the sense it gives of a self-amusing dream of what intellectual work could be.

Although the vector of *Earth and the Reveries of Repose* is inward, it is not backward, for it obeys a principle of inward expansion. Like Bachelard's other books on the imagination, it is full of intimations of the nested inexhaustibility of his material and the unfinishability of his task, as it continually registers new projects and prospects:

> A comprehensive study of the material images of interiority ought to give lengthy consideration to all the values of hidden warmth. Were I to undertake such a study, I would have to revise the whole of my book on fire . . . In most of the chapters in this book, I have given preliminary sketches of what could be a series of monographs studying isolated images . . . Were my task just to summarize the role of serpents in the myths of India, I would need to devote a book to it . . . The ring has such a wealth of

> images that it would take a whole book to classify them ... A psychologist conducting a lengthy study of the different images of the root would explore the human soul in its entirety. A whole book could be written on this theme. (*Reveries of Repose*, 38, 187, 191, 204, 212)

Bachelard ends the preface to *Earth and the Reveries of Repose* with the teasing words: 'A metaphysics of repose being beyond the scope of this present work, elementary as it is [Faute de faire, dans un livre élémentaire, la métaphysique du repos], my aim here has been to try to characterize the most constant psychological tendencies of repose' (*Reveries of Repose*, 4).[13] Bachelard's 'élémentaire' has the same ambivalence in French as in English, for it means both simple and, as 'elemental', universal. In writing about the infinite reach of intimate space, Bachelard is characterizing his own enterprise in this book: 'In short, all interior richness extends the inner space in which it is condensed, making it boundless. Dreams retire into this place and develop there in the most paradoxical of pleasures, in the most ineffable bliss' (*Reveries of Repose*, 39).

In repeatedly glimpsing these fractal expansion points within itself, Bachelard hints at the huge expansion of knowledge in subatomic physics, meaning that 'what we are dealing with here is in fact an Ultra-Cosmos and an Ultra-Microcosm' (*Reveries of Repose*, 3). Bachelard relates this both to the history of alchemy and to the eighteenth-century theory of *emboîtement* or 'encapsulated preformationism', according to which the ova in Eve's womb already contained within them ova and ova within ova, which would be unfolded to form the history of humanity. Bachelard remarks that 'The theory of the *emboitement* [*sic*] or encasement of seeds – of seeds within seeds – may be a learned kind of Jonah complex' (*Reveries of Repose*, 116).

Throughout Bachelard's writing about the material imagination, the material objects of thought are made to participate in their thinking. This process is particularly to the fore in *Earth and Reveries of Repose*, a book in which the focus on participation rather than antagonism engenders subject–object exchanges. Late in the book, for instance, Bachelard turns the thought of a tree into an arboreal image of thought itself:

> The imagination is a tree. It has the tree's integrating virtues. It is both root and bough, living between earth and sky, in the earth and in the wind. Little by little, the imagined tree

> is the cosmological tree, the tree that sums up a universe, that makes a universe . . . We need to appreciate the power of the imagination here, which turns a peaceful tree into an *insatiable being*, a being dynamized by relentless hunger. (*Reveries of Repose*, 219, 225)

Just as Bachelard never performed experimental work on matter though writing at length about the importance of experiment in physics and chemistry, so, equivalently, his studies of the material imagination are, with only a few exceptions, conducted indirectly through literary rather than more 'material' forms like the visual or plastic arts. But this is because literary art is 'discursive', that is, it moves (*dis-course* , from *dis-* + *currere*, is, etymologically, what runs about) rather than being arrested in form, so is actually close to the motion with which, for Bachelard, matter is mined. Accordingly, 'the serpent is first and foremost a pure literary image. It needs the discursiveness of a literary image for all its contradictions to be actualized' (*Reveries of Repose*, 194), and, similarly, 'in literature, the serpent lives by expressing itself: it is a long, morbid discourse' (*Reveries of Repose*, 200).

Bachelard's evocations of linguistic effects tend to emphasize the principle of what he calls 'psychosynthesis' ('psychosynthèse'), in contrast to 'psychoanalysis', pointing to effects of induction or seduction.[14] Thus the word root 'is an inductive word, a word that makes us dream, a word that comes to dream in us' (*Reveries of Repose*, 214). Serpents are like the labyrinths in which, in dreams at least, one tends to come upon them. This is the reason for, or the imaginative dividend of, Bachelard's fascination in the book with the labyrinthine analogues of coiling animals like snakes:

> Some animals – and the snake is among these – also give us tuition in the will, leading us to take on the likeness of animal will. In this statue, Laocoon is entwined and his contortions correspond to the coils of the entwining being. (*Reveries of Repose*, 207)

The labyrinth is an indeterminate structure in movement: 'the oneiric labyrinth has no corners; it only has bends, deep bends that draw dreamers forward as though they were *dreaming matter*' (*Reveries of Repose*, 157) – 'il n'a que des inflexions et des inflexions profondes qui engagent le rêveur comme s'il était une matière rêvante'.[15] Both the French and the English here leave it deliberately unclear whether the matter is dreaming or being dreamt. Bachelard draws the physical action of his writing into this labyrinthine self-procreation: 'Everything becomes animate when our pens dream, be it festoon, creeper, or serpent, or even life that is intertwined, twisted, and coiled up' (*Reveries of Repose*, 199).

Firmly established in his institutional position, Bachelard was building himself his own cave or burrow of busy repose. More and more, he tended to be photographed or painted in his tiny Paris apartment, the magus in his self-made igloo, scooped out by his own intellectual rotations, like an animal swirling out its place of sleep. At the same time, Bachelard was becoming ever more celebrated, constantly in demand for radio and TV interviews. His very withdrawal invited efforts to draw him out, into public utterance.

Paul de Man suggested that many texts may be understood as 'allegories of reading', dramatizations of the very process to which they are subjected in order to be understood.[16] We may perhaps conceive Bachelard's images and reveries similarly as allegories of writing, images of the very process that claims to unfold them. This might help interpret Bachelard's repeated claim that literary images are more dynamic than visual images. The movements, of striving, soaring, curling, are the movements of writing itself, struggling with and against its material. The act of writing is material in two senses: it is imaged as a coefficient of adversity, with and against matter; but it is also the matter of Bachelard's life, enacted through the acts of writing that consumed and consummated it.

> When we dream depth, we dream our own depth. When we dream of the secret virtue of substances, we are dreaming of our secret being. The greatest secrets of our being are hidden from us, however: they lie in the secrecy of our depths. (*Reveries of Repose*, 38)

In his early works Bachelard served his painful, belligerent apprenticeship to a knowledge that needed to be conquered – both broken into and, in revenge for its obdurate exclusiveness, broken down. In his works of worked-over reverie, Bachelard makes an object and a habitat of his own writing. But such writing, though offering a kind of narcissistic repose, also risks losing definition, leaving its writer without form or orientation. Repeatedly, there is the sense that Bachelard is struggling, not against obstruction, but against the dissolution of it, and the energizing resistance that it might supply:

> images grow blurred and disappear along this path of the imagination. The interiority which, when dreamed in substances, called forth so very many images, is now wholly *intensity*. Here, this interiority gives us primary values, values so long and deeply rooted in the unconscious that they go beyond familiar images and meet the most archaic of archetypes. (*Reveries of Repose*, 42–3)

Bachelard in his study in Paris, 17 December 1960.

There are moments in which Bachelard's writing resembles that of Samuel Beckett, writing at almost the same moment, in his novel *Molloy*, a few streets away in Paris, of his confinement within writing itself. At such moments, Bachelard reflects on the autological enclosure that results from writing a life that has been nothing more than a life of writing:

> For one who is just a philosopher writing and reading from day to day, his book is an irreversible life, and just as he would wish to relive life in order to think it better – which is the only philosophical method of living life better – so he could also wish that, having finished the book, he had to start it all over again. How useful to this new book would the finished book be! I have the melancholy impression that through writing, I have learned how I ought to have read. And having read so much, I would like to read it all again. (*Reveries of Repose*, 44)

Partly as a result of the works he had been publishing on the imagination since 1940, Bachelard began to enquire into the phenomenologically orientated psychology that was beginning to be known as existential psychoanalysis. As we have seen, Sartre, though not himself involved in psychoanalysis as a clinical practice, had already offered influential formulations of existential psychoanalysis in his *Being and Nothingness*, and associated Bachelard with it. But the most prominent figure in the development of existential psychoanalysis was the Swiss psychologist Ludwig Binswanger, who developed from the 1930s onwards a blending of psychoanalysis with the phenomenology of Husserl and Heidegger that he called Daseinsanalyse. Binswanger had been a member of the Freud group set up by Jung in Zürich, and remained on friendly terms with Freud, even as he developed a mode of analysis that broke with Freudian theory and practice in a number of respects.

Bachelard seems first to have encountered existential psychoanalysis, especially as exemplified by the work of Swiss psychoanalysts, in 1947. Bachelard was in contact with Binswanger's associate Roland Kuhn, whom he had met in 1947, when he travelled to Paris to meet with the couple Georges and Jacqueline Verdeaux, who were working in an Electro-Encephalogram (EEG) laboratory in the Sainte-Anne Hospital in Paris. Kuhn himself was interested in the psychiatric possibilities of the psycho-diagnostic inkblot test developed by Hermann Rorschach prior to his early death in 1922. Bachelard mentions to Kuhn his reading of the work of Binswanger's junior colleague Medard Boss, who had made reference to Bachelard's *Psychoanalysis of Fire* in support of his suggestion in 1947 that the symbolic intent of a patient's sado-masochistic fantasy of setting fire to a woman's bed is 'to resolve the earthbound rigidity of objects, to lift up their secret insides and to impart an impressive movement to the originally stationary, unalterable things'.[17] It may have been Kuhn who informed Bachelard of the work of Binswanger, for Bachelard wrote to Kuhn on 28 December 1947 that he had 'read and reread' Kuhn's 'Daseinsanalyse eines Falles von Schizophrenie', mentioning also that he was reading, 'with growing enthusiasm', Binswanger's *Ausgewählte Vorträge und Aufsätze* (1947).[18]

Bachelard then himself wrote to Binswanger on 26 January 1948 to thank him for his *Ausgewählte Vorträge und Aufsätze*, along with two case studies of schizophrenic patients, Ellen West and Jürg Zünd. He explained that he was caught 'between enthusiasm and regret' at reading Binswanger: 'What a pity for me not to have known of your thinking, but also what excitement I feel at the thought of the task I wish to pursue!'[19] The texts Binswanger seems to have sent him were ones in which Bachelard's own work is mentioned approvingly. Binswanger had been particularly impressed in his 'The Existential Analysis School of Thought' by Bachelard's account of the 'existential-analytical significance of the fundamental metaphors *de la hauteur, de l'élévation, de la profondeur, de l'abaissement, de la chute*'.[20] He was particularly struck by the opposition between aerial ascent and earthly descent in Bachelard's writing. Binswanger would repeat his praise of Bachelard in his study of extravagance (Verstiegenheit), in his *Drei Formen missglückten Daseins*, underwriting his view that the psychology of the will cannot be understood without reference to the idea of imaginary flight.[21] However, Binswanger also offered a mild reproof in observing that Bachelard 'speaks of a psychology – we would call it an anthropology – *ascensionelle*' ('Existential Analysis', 211), and amplifies his qualification in a footnote regarding Bachelard's *The Psychoanalysis of Fire*, *Lautréamont*, *Water and Dreams* and *Air and Dreams*: 'Bachelard's investigations are still based on imagination . . . What is still missing in them is an anthropological, and even more, an ontological, basis for B.'s studies' ('Existential Analysis', 212 n. 37).

This is a surprising objection, one that we might expect to have been made to psychiatry by literary criticism, rather than the other way around. Binswanger repeats, however, that '[b]y "existential analysis" we understand an anthropological type of scientific investigation – that is, one which is aimed at the essence of being human' ('Existential Analysis', 191). It is hard to repress the sense that the interest of existential psychoanalysis in general lies much more in the philosophical ambition of the knowledge to which it aspires, than in practical utility in terms of diagnosis, therapy or cure.

Binswanger's criticism seems nevertheless to have gone home, for, in his letter to Roland Kuhn, Bachelard had written, 'I am going to write a new work in which I would like to benefit from everything your new school offers.'[22] Bachelard closed the letter with a rather pitiable request, which one could imagine coming from the isolated provincial schoolteacher he had once been rather than the eminent Sorbonne professor he had become, for Kuhn's help in mugging up on Daseinsanalyse:

> I would like to be instructed about your school of Daseinsanalyse only from the anthropological point of view. In short, we have lived in isolation in France for 5 years and it is not easy for us to get up to date. Books are difficult to obtain. As regards myself, I have had to work alone. Because I also have to study mathematical physics, I have to deal with very different kinds of reading. In addition, my task would be made easier if you were able to give me the titles of essential works – I wish in fact to concentrate my efforts on a book on a cosmology combined with an anthropology.[23]

In Binswanger's 'The Case of Ellen West', first published in 1944, Bachelard would have found echoed back to him his own elemental cosmology of polarized verticality and descent, in the constantly reiterated oscillation in the psychophysical world of the anorexic Ellen West between the two 'existential directions' in which 'its standing-on-earth is constantly opposed by a swaying and flying in the air and a being-confined in and under the earth'.[24] Binswanger not only gave admiring approval to the sublimatory structures he found in Bachelard's *The Psychoanalysis of Fire*, he also anticipated the duality of spiritual ascent and descent marked out in the two volumes devoted to the imagination of earth that Bachelard had yet to publish, and in the page proofs of which Bachelard was immersed when he received Binswanger's texts:

> We are particularly happy to find in Bachelard insight into the fact that those forms of being which are characterized by dropping and

Ludwig Binswanger in the 1950s.

> falling, those of a descending life in general, invariably lead to an *imagination terrestre*, a turning into earth, or a bogging down of the existence. ('Existential Analysis', 212)

There is therefore again something of the 'sign of the latecomer' in Bachelard's determination to instruct himself in existential psychoanalysis, which was perhaps motivated by the desire to deserve the praise he had already been given. Accordingly, he took the opportunity to introduce into the proofs he was correcting a brief reference to Binswanger in the first volume, *Earth and the Reveries of Will*, and a longer reference in the second volume, *Earth and the Reveries of Repose*, accompanied by the apology that he had 'got to know all too late the fine work done by Ludwig Binswanger and Roland Kuhn on both Dasein analysis and the Rorschach tests and shall only be able to make use of this elsewhere' (*Reveries of Repose*, 56). Though he drew regularly on psychiatric case-histories, Bachelard recorded his regret at having to access this kind of material at second hand:

> I have very often envied, as I worked away in solitude at my books, those psychiatrists to whom life brings new 'cases' every day, 'subjects' who come to them with a complete psyche. My 'cases' are very small images found by chance as I read, found in the isolation of an unexpected phrase and not caught up in any description of reality. (*Reveries of Repose*, 56)

And yet Bachelard's reliance on such quasi-psychiatric evidence also seemed to him to allow for the possibility of 'examining the psychology of subjects who are expressing themselves or, to put it better, of subjects who are *imagining their expression*, who direct their responsibility into the very poetry of their expression' (*Reveries of Repose*, 56–7). In fact, this judgement points up the poetic project that lies latent within Daseinsanalyse, in its efforts to understand the striving for expression in patients' being-in-the-world. If Bachelard aspired to a kind of literary psychiatry in his writing, this mirrored the aspiration in the practitioners of Daseinsanalyse to become literary critics of psychic material, to the point sometimes at which the disorders of patients seem to be being plundered for the dramatizations they offer of general existential principles. Binswanger's study of Ellen West moves progressively away from a biographical account of its subject to an account of 'the existence of Ellen West', this tendency being crystallized in the oddly stiff reference by the essay's translators to 'the existence called Ellen West'.[25] When he came to develop his own form of psychological analysis in his final years, Bachelard would be driven by this sense of personal experience heightened into a kind of impersonality.

Bachelard would later write a preface to the 1957 edition of Jacqueline Verdeaux's translation of Roland Kuhn's book on the phenomenology of the mask, which had first appeared in 1949.[26] Bachelard found in the discerning of mask-like forms in Rorschach inkblots the evidence of a will to expression for which he found support in in Daseinsanalyse. The mask embodies the 'right we grant ourselves to have a double', and to reach into the futurity of a self remade:

> If we pass through all the intermediate stages to uncover the phenomenological roots of dressing up, of disguise, and essentially of the desire to wear a mask, we find that the mask represents the will to a fresh future, the will not only to control one's face but to reshape one's face, to have henceforth a new face.[27]

The idea of the mask therefore asserts the kind of will to formation through self-expression that is so unquenchable and insatiable throughout Bachelard's life of writing:

> There is occasion to wonder whether the radical conscious act underlying all phenomenology can reveal itself in 'madness,' in other words whether the mentally disturbed person is in possession of the being of his disturbance . . . Are we . . . to see in the darkest depths of the disturbed mind that will to be which so clings to man, to this creature who never loses his need to show himself forth?[28]

Bachelard seems to have been impressed by the emphasis in existential psychoanalysis on the need to understand psychiatric conditions not, as in Freudian psychoanalysis, as local disorders or deviations from normal psychological functioning, but rather as expressions of the entire 'world' of the patient. It is this world that needs understanding, rather than isolated symptoms. One needs to understand the whole form of life of a patient in something of the way in which one attempts to understand a culture anthropologically: the volume of selected essays that Binswanger sent to Bachelard in 1948 is subtitled *Zur phänomenologischen Anthropologie* (Toward a Phenomenological Anthropology) and contains an essay that Binswanger wrote in 1936, titled 'Freud's Conception of Man in the Light of Anthropology'.

In 1936, Freud, with whom Binswanger maintained cordial relations to the end of Freud's life, wrote politely to Binswanger in response to this essay, taking the opportunity to characterize the difference between the idealistic conceptions of Binswanger and his own. The metaphor Freud uses aligns with the way in which Bachelard would conceive the sublimation he sought from psychoanalysis, in terms of a willed ascent to the upstairs of existence rather than the guided descent into the cellar of unconscious instinct:

> I have always confined myself to the ground floor and basement of the edifice. –You maintain that by changing one's point of view, one can also see an upper story, in which dwell such distinguished guests as religion, art, etc. You are not the only one to say this; most cultured specimens of *homo natura* think the same thing. In this you are conservative, and I am revolutionary. If I still had

> a lifetime of work ahead of me, I would be confident of my ability to make room in my humble little house for those lofty things. I have already found a place for religion, by putting it under the category of the 'neurosis of mankind'. But probably we are speaking at cross purposes, and our differences will be ironed out only after centuries.[29]

Bachelard also took from existential psychoanalysis the view that patients should be regarded as not merely suffering the effects of their disorders, but as actively and formatively giving them existence. Tellingly, Binswanger wrote, not of disease or disorder, but in terms of more or less successful projects of existence, referring in the title of one of his books to *Formen missglückten Daseins*, forms of failed or unfortunate existence.[30] In the essay 'Über die daseinsanalytischer Forschungsrichtung in der Psychiatrie' included in the volume of essays he sent to Bachelard, Binswanger wrote:

> we do not say: mental illnesses are diseases of the brain (which, of course, they remain from a medical-clinical viewpoint). But we say: in the mental diseases we face modifications of the fundamental or essential structure and of the structural links of being-in-the-world as transcendence. ('Existential Analysis', 194)

Bachelard stayed in intermittent contact with Binswanger at least until 1955, and reassured him in 1949 that he had been making frequent reference to 'the Heideggerian direction of the psychiatric enterprise' in his Sorbonne lectures: 'It is rare for your name not to be mentioned in a class.'[31] Though he read widely and with abiding interest about psychiatric illness and in particular the psychology of children, Bachelard never showed much interest in the clinical details of psychoanalytic treatment, being more interested in the general philosophical and anthropological perspectives that might be developed from them. And, as had been clear from his enthusiastic embrace of the ideas of Robert Desoille, Bachelard was strongly inclined to the Romantic idea of the imagination as an actively formative force and attracted to the more holistic perspectives of existential forms of psychoanalysis, which might act as a kind of therapeutic philosophy of imagination rather than through medical technique.

9

City of Science, 1948–53

The traditional autonomy accorded to professors in the Sorbonne allowed Bachelard to forge his own intellectual path largely unrestricted, and there is little sign that Bachelard came under any institutional pressure to return to publication in the areas identified in the name of the Institute for the History of Science and Technology of which he was director. Among his students in the years following the Second World War was the young Michel Butor, later to become a celebrated novelist. Butor completed a diploma thesis, roughly equivalent to an MA thesis, under Bachelard's supervision, titled 'Mathematics and the Idea of Necessity'.[1] He singled out Bachelard from the other professors in the Faculté des Lettres as an extraordinary teacher, and recalled Bachelard's remarkable force and presence in the lecture hall: 'Physically, he displayed a generous belly. When he spoke, with his ruffled hair and long patriarchal beard, he looked like a river in spate. He had an extraordinary gift for improvisation.'[2]

When *La terre et les rêveries du repos* appeared in 1948, Bachelard was 64, and six years away from the official retirement age of seventy. Even without any inducement from his colleagues or institution, he might perhaps have felt that, not having produced any substantial research in the area of his professorial speciality since his appointment eight years earlier, he owed his institution and his reputation some new work in scientific epistemology.

There are some signs of his ten-year sabbatical among poets, just as there are frequent reminders in his elemental studies of his expertise as a historian of science. Aware of the ever-growing gap between his writing about the imagination and his writing about science, Bachelard seems conscious that he might be expected to find some bridge between them.

He returned at the beginning of *Earth and Reveries of Repose* to his old theme of the inattention of philosophers to the developments of science.[3] Bachelard observes that

> By learning from one kind of experience, philosophers render themselves inert with regard to experience of other kinds. And sometimes very lucid minds shut themselves away like this in their lucidity, denying all the light – and all the enlightenment – which comes from darker areas of our psyche. Thus, where the problem under discussion is concerned, a theory of the knowledge of reality that takes no interest in oneiric values can indeed be felt to cut itself off from some of the interests that encourage the attainment of knowledge. I shall be dealing with this problem in another book.[4]

Bachelard never succeeded in writing that book, nor ever really tried to, though few would have been more qualified. The most remarkable feature of the three studies in the philosophy of science that he published after the end of the Second World War, and prior to his retirement in 1954, *Le rationalisme appliqué* (1949), *L'activité rationaliste de la physique contemporaine* (1951) and *Le matérialisme rationnel* (1953), is that they seemed to pick up the epistemological thread where it was snapped in 1940, as though nothing else had happened. Having devoted – and prodigiously indulged – himself in the monumental enterprise of his elemental sequence, Bachelard put himself back into school with a sequence of works that exhibit the same kind of sustained seriality as the earlier books on the imagination. *Le rationalisme appliqué* looks forward repeatedly to the book that would appear as *L'activité rationaliste de la physique contemporaine*, and *Le matérialisme rationnel* represents a recapitulation of the whole series, with 'rational materialism' seeming like a chiasmatic restatement of 'applied rationalism'.

In 1947 Bachelard founded the scientific journal *Dialectica* alongside Ferdinand Gonseth and Paul Bernays. The short editorial for the inaugural issue identified the principal challenge that it aimed to meet, of the incursion of science into all areas of human life:

> In all branches of learning, the specialist's knowledge has overstepped the frontier of general evidence and his powers are always beyond the reach of our natural resources. As the

> serpents wind themselves round the caduceus, so do many evils envelope [*sic*] the forces that Science discovers and liberates. What do we do to be equal to this knowledge? What do we do to keep it on the horizon of human values? If it is not to escape us or overwhelm our minds, a very decided and sustained philosophical effort is necessary on our part.[5]

The opening essay of the journal, 'La philosophie dialoguée', came from Bachelard himself, and would later be reprinted as the introduction to his book *Le rationalisme appliqué*. Bachelard announces in his opening sentences the relationship that has preoccupied him since his doctoral thesis, between theory and experiment. Indeed, the very words that Bachelard employs here might have served perfectly well as an introductory framing of *Essai sur la connaissance approchée*:

> If we follow with attention, that is, with passionate interest, the activity of contemporary physics, we see the development of a philosophical dialogue which has the merit of being exceptionally precise: the dialogue between the experimenter provided with precise instruments and the mathematician who aspires to closely inform the experiment.[6]

The new emphasis, though it is an amplification of an old theme for Bachelard, is on the question of the application of reason. Part of the answer that Bachelard gives to the question of how rationality should be put to work is that rationality can only ever come about *by* being put to work. For Bachelard, science always consists in work. This may be why his emphasis is not usually on the joy, curiosity, achievement or wonder of science, but on its practical accomplishments, on what it takes and what it makes, the work it requires and is able to do. In *Le Rationalisme appliqué* and *Le matérialisme rationnel*, Bachelard enlarged the demand implicit in the concept of *phénoménotechnique* that he had introduced in 'Noumenon and Microphysics' in 1932, making engineering not just the useful byproduct of scientific rationality, but the principal means by which it makes progress. Rather than science producing technology, technology produces science. 'A lever', Bachelard maintains in *Le Rationalisme appliqué*, 'is a theorem'.[7] Similarly, 'rationalist philosophy is essentially a philosophy which works, a philosophy of work [une philosophie qui travaille, une philosophie au travail]'.[8] Writing in praise of the Parisian museum of science the Palais de la Découverte at a conference on 20 October 1951, Bachelard sternly laid down the law for visitors:

> The Palace of Discovery is not a museum for gawpers. You do not wander into it on a rainy day, to pass the time, or kill time. You go there to work. You go there to put your mind to work. You go there to form a new mind, by understanding the newness of science.[9]

As Bachelard had argued in *Le Pluralisme cohérent de la chimie moderne* (1932), one understands what an element is, not by analysing it, but by synthesizing new elements. Science can only purify itself by being applied, with the risk that comes with it of impurity. Bachelard never comes near to wondering how the forms in which science is applied might be subject to deliberation, or who is to do the deliberation, or how. His concern is entirely with science's government of itself, in the progressive rectification of purely scientific understanding. Science, for Bachelard, is a self-governing polity:

> What tacit agreement reigns in the *city of physics*! In what manner the unrepentant dreamers wanting to 'theorize' far from mathematical methods are dismissed! The theoretician must actually possess all the mathematical past of physics, that is to say, all the rationalist tradition of experience. The experimenter, on his side, must know entirely the present of technique. We would be surprised if a physicist used the old vacuum air pump, even if it was provided with the Babinet tap. Modernism of the technical reality and rationalist tradition of every mathematical theory: this is the double cultural ideal that should permeate all the themes of scientific thought.[10]

Bachelard's faith in the self-corrective powers of the scientific community seems absolute and unshakeable, with the magic word 'rectification' being as prominent as it was in his very first book. Nor does he show any awareness of the possibility that 'tacit agreement' might at any given time serve or be sustained by external social or economic pressures, such that scientific consensus might itself sometimes form an impediment to pure thought rather than assisting it, despite his previous insistence that it always in fact does form such an impediment. Bachelard's understanding of science is resolutely internalist, with the development and purification of science being regarded as self-evidently a matter for scientists themselves – with the question of who is to provide the financial resources to make that work possible being a matter for others. In a review of *Le materialisme rationnel*, Raymond Ruyer noted astutely that Bachelard's City of Science resembles Augustine's City of God:

> This scientific City has its discipline, its laws, its regulated movements and pathways. From it emerge new bodies in organic or nuclear chemistry. In the terrestrial City of ordinary knowledge, water is an element. In the City of Science – we almost wrote in the celestial City – in the order of technical realities, Technetium, Promethium, Astatine, or even element 99, which still has no identified material existence [subsequently named Einsteinium], have as much reality as iron or copper, and are more elementary than water.[11]

Bachelard can perhaps be forgiven for not anticipating the ways in which contemporary scientific enquiry is distorted by the institutional pressures to focus in certain ways on certain areas of enquiry, but he cannot have been ignorant of the grotesque distortions of scientific enquiry effected by the totalitarian regimes in Germany and the USSR: the Stalinist condemnation of 'bourgeois physics', for example, or the authority given to the condemnation of genetics by Trofim Lysenko.

The question that this characterization of scientific rationality raises, irresistibly and yet unapproachably, is that of the relation that it might have with the other kinds of rationality with which Bachelard had been fervently tarrying for the previous decade. That the question certainly occurred to Bachelard's associates and contemporaries is evident from an essay published in the second number of *Dialectica* in May 1947, by Bachelard's associate and co-editor Ferdinand Gonseth and his son Jean-Paul. The essay begins with an account of two lectures given by Bachelard on 19 and 20 February of that year in Zürich, one concerned with rationalism and technology, the other with the imagination of material force in the lyricism of the blacksmith's forge. The essay records Bachelard's apparent equanimity at lecturing on 'two subjects so astonishingly distant from each other, and treated with a striking difference of tone and inspiration'. 'I am not', he said, 'a man with only one desk [Je ne suis pas, dit-il, l'homme d'un seul tablier].' But for some, write the essay's authors, this duality presents a 'disturbing mobility'.[12]

The essay that follows is an attempt to enlarge on this disquiet. The majority of their essay repeats the account offered so insistently through Bachelard's scientific writings of the necessary move away from realist intuitions of the nature of objects towards the more inclusive, but also paradoxical perspectives offered by the sciences of relativity and quantum physics. The essay turns from objective knowledge to poetic knowledge only in its final pages. Just as the new science does not sweep away the old Euclidean or Newtonian convictions, but reveals that they operate only at certain scales and under certain conditions, so, the authors propose, the magic character of primitive thinking persists in such a way that there is a need to '*render justice* to the thought we have characterized as anterior'.[13] There is, they write, no reason to deny Bachelard his interest in 'the desires, aspirations and even the profound necessities of the human being in its relations with the world'. And yet, this kind of 'magical divination' must necessarily fail to do justice to the dialectical progress of objective thought.[14] So the essay ends up merely restating the terms of the dichotomy with which it began. The two forms of rationality can both be allowed, it seems, and indeed, in justice, must be, but cannot do so without reciprocal injustice being done. This seems to mimic the détente that Bachelard himself enforced between the two modes of thought, which can and must coexist, but can never cohabit.

There is no stronger evidence of the strange relapse that seems to have taken place in Bachelard's thinking about scientific epistemology than the way in which the idea of psychoanalysis is again drawn on to secure it. In the works from *Lautréamont* onwards, Bachelard had become ever more critical of orthodox Freudian psychoanalysis, centred, as he saw it, on a large and inflexible body of theoretical precepts and a practice of analysis in which the abstract power of discourse is paramount. In his poetic elementalism, the name of Freud, never evoked with very much interest or respect, yields place increasingly to the name of Jung. At the same time, Bachelard is drawn increasingly away from the idea of psychoanalysis towards what he instead calls 'psychosynthesis', which is focused not on the cheerfully pessimistic aim that is often attributed to Freud, of helping the neurotically unwell to become, like everybody else, merely unhappy, but on an ideal of growth and the development of a fuller and more intense kind of being. Bachelard imagines this being achieved not through the translation of impulses into abstract discourse, but through a kind of psychic engineering, which works as directly on the psychic matter of dreams as physics and chemistry work on physical matter.

However, when Bachelard returned during the 1950s to questions of scientific epistemology, this idea of a positive work performed on psychic material is definitively retracted. Now, in writing of science, Bachelard reverts to the idea of psychoanalysis as a kind of purification, precisely of the psychic from rationality itself, a purification that must be absolute and therefore interminable: 'a psychoanalysis of objective and rational knowledge would never be definitive: one will never definitively conquer psychologism' (*Rationalisme appliqué*, 15). It will include not only an evacuation of affect, but a 'minute psychoanalysis of empirical memory in pursuit of a rational memory' (*Rationalisme appliqué*, 50). Where Bachelard elsewhere proposes a sublimated form of sublimation, here he proposes a generalized, rectified form of the persecutory super-ego. First of all, he accuses psychoanalysis of installing itself in the place of the super-ego:

> completely taken up with the sufferings of the observed, it has not been able to see the sadistic pleasures, within the same subject, of the one observing. Psychoanalysis itself assumes the sadistic pleasures of the observer, identifying itself with the *observational* activity which the observed subject ought to possess if it were in a state of happy division. The fairly common dogmatism of psychoanalysts is very instructive in this regard. (*Rationalisme appliqué*, 71)

But then, in contrast to the Freudian idea that the super-ego is an internal condensation of all the persons who sit in judgement upon us, Bachelard proposes that 'the cultural psychoanalysis which we will try to develop will come down to the *depersonalization* of the powers of the super-ego, or, what will come to the same thing, the intellectualization of the rules of culture' (*Rationalisme appliqué*, 71). This resulting 'intellectualized surveillance, based on a super-ego psychoanalyzed as a super-ego' will allow for the refinement of the 'psychic controls' (*Rationalisme appliqué*, 71) on which culture, by which Bachelard means a thoroughly rationalized culture, depends. So the sublimation of the process of sublimation is accompanied by a generalization of the empire of the super-ego, into a kind of sur-superiority.

One might say that Bachelard maintains, in place of psychoanalysis, a wish-fulfilling fantasy of what psychoanalysis might be and do to secure the purity of scientific rationality. Moreover, as Michel Serres sharply observes, one might make out strong parallels between the psychological work of self-purification that is an essential part of the work of rationalized materialism and the range of lustrations and ablutions that are so central a part of the Great Work of alchemy. As Serres concludes: 'It turns out that no gap whatsoever exists between Bachelard's psychoanalysis and pre-scientific morality. And the initiation to the scientific mind is indeed the same catharsis as the initiation of the alchemist: *quod erat demonstrandum*.'[15] The effort to purge chemistry of all its lingering alchemical dreams resurrects the dreamwork of alchemy itself. Bachelard's account of the purification of reason reads at times like the spiritual discipline required of the alchemical practitioner – a kind of psychological battle against psychology itself. Bachelard is right to call it 'the psychology of depsychologization' (*Rationalisme appliqué*, 27), but perhaps not necessarily in the way he means, for his phrase hints that the apparent depsychologization of science may be, whatever else it is, a thoroughly psychological phenomenon. The idea that the applied rationalization of chemistry will give rise to the synthesis of new substances and compounds might also be taken as a triumphant fulfilment of the dreams of mastering matter entertained by alchemists, with the immoderate will to power concealed but not subdued in the abstraction of mathematics. As in alchemy, the perfecting of the work is dependent on the perfecting of the soul – and indeed that perfecting may be what the Magnum Opus allegorically signifies. As Bachelard gives himself leave to announce in *Le materialisme rationale*, 'only really wishing to make chemistry, Nature has finally created the chemist.'[16] Bachelard unveils an astonishingly uninhibited vision of the power of science, making the connections with nuclear physics completely explicit:

> Through chemistry and nuclear physics, man is granted unexpected means of power, positive means which surpass all the philosophical reveries of power. Instructed materialism, which is not solely a speculative philosophy, equips [arme] a will to power, a will which stimulates itself through the very power of the means offered. It seems that there too, in the psychological dimension, the will-to-power knows a chain reaction. The more one has, the more one wants [Plus on peut, plus en veut]. (*Matérialisme rationnel*, 5)

Contemplating the literalness of the power opened up in prospect, Bachelard first distinguishes it from the impotent omnipotence of the philosophical dreams of the past, and then himself instantly reverts to the psychology of magic:

> While the will to power was naive, while it was philosophical, while it was Nietzschean, it was only effective – for good or for ill – at the level of the individual. Nietzsche acted on his readers: a reader of Nietzsche who turns author has only a derisory effect. But once man effectively appropriates the power of matter, once he no longer dreams of intangible elements and hooked atoms, but actually organizes new bodies and manages real forces, he attains to a will-to-power provided with objective verification. He becomes a veritable magician, a positive demon. (*Matérialisme rationnel*, 5)

The paradox here is that the wilful forms of desire that are purged in order to make objective knowledge possible continue to blaze in the incendiary will to purgative rationality itself. Rationalism here seems to be a kind of poesis, a form of material imagination. The counterpart of the knowledge of the imagination is not the knowledge of materiality, but the material imagination of knowledge.

Like many of the self-taught, or those who have struggled against exclusion from education, Bachelard had a profound ambivalence towards knowledge. This ambivalence is much stronger in one who achieves epistemic success against the odds, but who can never forget the envious resentment of the outsider even as they achieve entry into the realm of knowledge.

On the one hand, Bachelard had an exaggerated sense of the power and value of knowledge. Again and again, he stressed that knowledge was not a mere acquisition: rather, it required and was itself a means of self-production and self-transformation. This is nothing less than the truth for humans, for whom the process of socialization will inevitably mean the acquisition of different skills and capacities – the performative knowledge of how to sing, dance, fight, run, draw, as well as the declarative knowledge of the things of the world. But it appears that, for Bachelard, knowledge was being itself. It was the product of struggle, and perhaps, indeed, was nothing without it. Given that the quest for alchemical knowledge is a quest for universal knowledge, and requires an arduous discipline and exercise of the will, it is not surprising that Bachelard should have been so drawn to alchemy and, what is even more striking, should have found it so hard to draw away from. Alchemy, a discipline above all of purgation, could never itself be finally or sufficiently purged. Like sin, it seems, alchemy lurked everywhere, and had to be brought to light and thereby put to flight by the thing that Bachelard persisted in calling 'psychoanalysis'. He would not have needed telling by C. G. Jung of the 'psychic nature of the alchemical work', and would surely have approved of what he read in Jung's *Psychology and Alchemy* in 1944:

> the real nature of matter was unknown to the alchemist: he knew it only in hints. In seeking to explore it he projected the unconscious into the darkness of matter in order to illuminate it. In order to explain the mystery of matter he projected yet another mystery – his own unknown psychic background – into what was to be explained: *Obscurum per obscurius, ignotum per ignotius*. This procedure was not, of course, intentional: it was an involuntary occurrence . . . while working on his chemical experiments the operator had certain psychic experiences which appeared to him as the particular behaviour of the chemical process . . . Such projections repeat themselves whenever man tries to explore an empty darkness and involuntarily fills it with living form.[17]

Bachelard may have had this particular passage in mind when considering the nature of alchemical mystery in *Le materialisme rationnel*:

> The lessons of the alchemist are immediately the lessons of intimate psychology. The objective mystery refers to the subjective mystery and vice versa. The mysterious planes of material substance reveal the hidden planes of the human unconscious. The two grand shadows correspond as though they were object and image in a mirror. (*Matérialisme rationnel*, 25)

Bachelard maintains that, by contrast with that of the alchemist, the world of the chemist is only partially unknown, rather than wholly mysterious. What is scientifically unknown is relative, rather than absolute, meaning that 'scientific thought follows a path of progressive clarity, while the alchemist awaited a revelation' (*Matérialisme rationnel*, 26). This is not entirely true, for it leaves out of account the strong emphasis within alchemy of pathways to be diligently followed, the progressive unfolding of secrets, and the perfecting by painful degrees of the questing spirit, even if the progress was indeed largely imaginary. This argument therefore does not quite defend as successfully as Bachelard might have wished against the intense psychic investment in progressive knowledge that the modern physicist might share with the alchemist. Bachelard returns so insistently to alchemy, being drawn back into the routines of denunciation of the pre-scientific even in his last epistemological work, *Le materialisme rationnel*, not because he comes to regard it with fond forgiveness, but precisely because he can never forget and forgive his own inextinguishable fondness for it.

The distinctive new stress in Bachelard's late epistemology of the 1950s was the modulation of the adolescent idea of the surrational into the idea of the corrational. In place of the individual refusing the conformity demanded by institutional education, Bachelard's later work tempers individual aberration with the authority of consensus, in the holy city of science. The principle of endless rectification with which Bachelard had concluded his inaugural work on approximate knowledge in 1928 persists, but is now expressed by and on behalf of a collectivity. Nevertheless, scientific knowledge is still to be clearly distinguished from all the forms of common knowledge, which reproduces the historical relation between the pre-scientific and the scientific.

Running alongside his devotion to knowledge, Bachelard maintains, from the beginning to the end of his life, a strangely intense and unabating contempt for any knowledge that is merely inherited, and a deep antagonism to the pedagogy of mere transmission, to a teaching that is itself untutored. It is as if every kind of knowledge that was not self-born, or born from the refusal of what has been inherited from the past, were a snare and a delusion. So the forming of knowledge was always also a deforming, in which one must continuously discharge whatever one has merely assimilated. What results from this is a simultaneously exorbitant veneration of knowledge, and a hostile rejection of knowledge as impurity and impediment.

If the trilogy of books on the epistemology of science Bachelard produced after the Second World War represents a kind of *summa* of the arguments that he had been developing since the late 1920s, deepened and diversified with a range of different examples from physics and chemistry, the last of them, *Le materialisme rationnel*, is remarkable for being the only place in which Bachelard attempts to bring his work on the elemental material imagination into any kind of extended communication with his scientific epistemology. Bachelard opens this book with a statement about the intertwining of psychology and matter that seems closely in accord with the Jungian perspectives of the final book of his elemental series: 'all thoughts bear the sign of the thinking being and a chemical analysis is also an analysis of thought . . . A complex psychology necessarily accompanies a complex science' (*Matérialisme rationnel*, 3). His introduction to *Le matérialisme rationnel* makes explicit reference to his own decade-long sojourn with the material imagination:

> To come right out with it, and speaking personally, I have just lived out for a dozen years all the circumstances of a division of materialism between imagination and experiment. Little by little, this division evident in the facts was imposed upon me as a methodological principle. It leads to an awareness of the radical opposition between an imaginary materialism and an instructed materialism. In other words, there is great advantage, it seems to me, in distinguishing, in two tables, the elements of human conviction: the conviction by dreams and images; and the conviction by reason and experiment. (*Matérialisme rationnel*, 17)

Like the book to which it is a prelude, this statement simply, fixedly, unrepentantly restates the division between the two modes of human conviction. Bachelard may demonstrate in his work that there is nothing human that he thinks alien to him, but he is not prepared to do anything but point to the absolute alienation within human experience between the two modes of thought and existence. We must recognize in the case of Bachelard what Sartre describes as a 'being which is what it is not and which is not what it is'.[18]

Bachelard was attracted by Jung's ideas of archetypes perhaps because he was inclined to see the work of imagination as essentially timeless, or nonhistorical, as contrasted with the progressive work of science. This may be allied to his own tendency to think of his own personal history, or at least to represent it to himself and others in his writings, as a kind of time out of time. And yet, in a strange sense, it is science that is timeless for Bachelard, precisely because he persisted in seeing science as always breaking with history, in a paradoxically permanent condition of revulsion or revolution. As we have seen, Bachelard was always deeply opposed to the pedagogical principle that children should be encouraged to move from their own practical experience to more advanced kinds of scientific understanding, and, against the grain of thinking among historians of science, saw no possibility of growth from the practices of alchemy to modern chemistry: 'Let me repeat: alchemy in no way prepares for chemistry: it blocks it' (*Matérialisme rationnel*, 57). This is a surpassingly absolute thing to write for one who so cherishes the word 'dialectic'. It is hard to know quite how Bachelard thought chemical knowledge might ever have arisen, apart from some kind of special revelation.

In this respect, it is striking that Bachelard was so unresponsive to the area of science that, as Jacob Bronowski observed, had begun to displace physics, which had previously been dominant both in science and in the public imagination of it. Bronowski remarks that, from 1945 onwards, 'the pre-occupation of science has been moving from physics to biology.' For Bronowski, the importance of biology is that it enabled and required humans to understand themselves and other species historically:

> biology is distinguished from other sciences in being a historical subject, the study of evolution that has shaped each animal to take its own path, behavior and species-specific form. Above all, what has made man take a different path from the other animals – has made him, for example, adapt his environments to himself instead of the other way about?[19]

Bachelard's inattention to biology, which, just at the moment he was celebrating the achievements of physics, would be transformed by the discovery of DNA in 1953, was of a piece with the antagonism to historical thinking that so strangely characterized the Chair of History and Philosophy of Science that Bachelard occupied. It also lies at the heart of the parting of ways between him and his most distinguished successor in the philosophy of science, his student Michel Serres, for whom the sciences of information, never alluded to by Bachelard, would provide the bridge between the 'hard' order of physics and the 'soft' order of signs, between which Bachelard could see no possibility of communication. Indeed, Bachelard insists more emphatically than ever in *Le materialisme rationnel* that the break made by the new science, and the 'psychoanalysis' required to make that break, must be, in a word deployed repeatedly through the book, 'brutal' (*Matérialisme rationnel*, 19, 41, 58).

10

Retirement, 1954–7

In the year after the appearance of *Le matérialisme rationnel*, Bachelard reached the age of seventy, the official retirement age at the Sorbonne. He applied for and was granted a further year as an honorary professor, though he remarked in a letter of 27 November 1954, having received confirmation of his appointment, that 'it does not rejuvenate me.'[1] The year passed quickly, and on 7 July 1955 he recorded, 'Yesterday I conducted the last licentiate examination of my career. From today, I am now retired. I have just been for an hour's walk, which I have not done for a fortnight.'[2] Bachelard's celebrity was undiminished, and he was subject to many invitations.

The stubbornest of the illusions against which the new science heralded and explicated by Bachelard over 25 years of writing struggled had to do with localization: with the conviction that real objects exist in real space. This is essentially a projection into the world of the relation of containment by means of which all humans must experience their own being, or at least represent it to themselves: that they exist *in* a body, which itself is placed exclusively *in* a space. The thematic oscillation between reason and imagination in Bachelard's writings is shadowed by the alternation between Paris and Dijon, which he evoked at the beginning of the chapter titled 'The House of Our Birth and the Oneiric House' in *Earth and Reveries of Repose*:

> Yes indeed, which of these is the more real: the house where we are sleeping or the house where, when we sleep, we regularly go and dream? I cannot dream in Paris, in this geometric cube, this cement cell, this bedroom with its iron shutters that are so hostile to nocturnal matter. When dreams are kind to me, I go away, away

to a house in Champagne or to just a few houses in which the mysteries of happiness are condensed.[3]

Bachelard reported in a letter of 1951 a development in his Paris apartment that seemed to create an interior space of dreaming repose within it: 'I have had a bathtub installed in our little apartment. Of course, getting in and out of the tub requires gymnastics, but the bath gives us repose.'[4] In Bachelard's writing, scientific rationality always implied movement outwards and away, while writing about poetry or imagination meant movement inwards. Bachelard had anticipated this movement of recoil at the end of a remarkable essay titled 'The World as Caprice and Miniature' published in 1934, and not reprinted until after his death:

> One will delude oneself if one gives to intellectual activity a positive and formative action in the domain of experience as primitive as vision. No matter what our degree of spiritual freedom in the realm of abstract conceptions, it is no less true that we imagine with the retina. One cannot transcend the retinal conditions of the imagination. The mind can burst images, interrupt efforts. It can also construct a world of abstract conceptions. But when it wishes to return to real and imagined compositions it must return to the fundamental canvas on which reverie works without haste, savouring the forbidden fruit of its lilliputian reveries.[5]

Questions of scale and 'local habitation' in fact provide one of the few links between abstract physics and the physicality of image and dream. It is through attempting to understand the nature of matter at very small levels that one is propelled 'beyond' the conceptions of space that obtain at the scale at which humans live. In his 1937 book, *L'Expérience de l'espace dans la physique contemporaine*, Bachelard had provided a compelling imaging in terms of economics of 'the topological principle of spatial realism', which depends essentially upon 'a simple and poor relation: *the relation of the container to the contained*'.[6] Where are the assets that I am confident I possess? Bachelard outlines the economist's explanation of the three fallacies of the belief that I have money in the bank. The money is not in the bank; it is not mine; and it is not even money:

> A speculator may strive to prove that the content of my wallet is bound up with social conventions – that is, more or less theoretical ideas – that these extrinsic conventions are the only reasons for my fortune, that the financial world is a complex of financial laws, that a financial obligation yields a real benefit only when it is realized and that it is realized outside the safe, at the bank, on the stock exchange, in the temple of fiduciary values.[7]

The confidence that allows what must be understood literally as the confidence trick of money to be perpetuated is that of the realist conception of matter, against which the new scientific spirit must contend:

> The Realist will smile at so many paradoxes and, declining to be astonished at the facility with which we add theoretical themes to the real, will answer: 'The only objective, certain, real basis of your thought about financial reality is that your assets are in the safe, and the safe is in your office. It is there that thieves and inheritors will find it. The subjective reasons for locating an object may well diverge; the localization will nonetheless remain based solely on the convergence of successive interlockings. It is a clearly centripetal operation, methodically organized around a centre. To multiply the envelopes around a reality is to multiply the assurances of its possession, it is to inhibit its emanations, and subtle deficits, it is to fix it solidly in space. *To enclose the real is to stabilize it*.'[8]

The writing to which Bachelard devoted the years of his retirement constitutes a kind of active retreat from the relativistic dissolution of space demanded by the new physics. The first, and most eminent, fruit of this retirement was *The Poetics of Space*, which would become the book by which Bachelard would be most widely known, especially outside France.

The Poetics of Space advances, or, we had better say, *inhabits*, two principal propositions. The first is that the image, in the sense in which it operates in the exercise of imagination, is essentially a matter of corporeally apprehended space. The second is that the condensation of time in space constitutes well-being. In an intriguing phrase in the final pages of *The Dialectic of Duration*, Bachelard had announced that the resonance of human life with 'natural rhythms' produces 'happiness, not thought'.[9] This is a strange doctrine from somebody whose life consisted of the work of thought, indeed who struggled for a large part of his life to make it possible to have a life consisting of that kind of work. Why should happiness be thought to be the abeyance of thought, rather than, say, its accompaniment, or consummation? This is something of the same logical feint that convinces people that feeling is the opposite of reason. The opposite of reason is unreason. Sometimes, though much more rarely than we pretend, the exercise of rationality is cool, sometimes it is impassioned, and usually some streaky mixture of the two, but the temperature of reason has nothing to do with how rational or irrational it is, any more than, say, with how tired or hungry the reasoner may happen to be. Bachelard's deep-laid conviction that thinking is a matter of forceful striving, the retreat of, and from, the condition of happiness, itself seems the product of an arbitrary kind of logical forcing. If by nothing else, the idea that happiness means thoughtless ease is contradicted by the very works of Bachelard that articulate this principle, which provide strong suggestions of the pleasure to be found in restful kinds of cognitive exertion – otherwise, why would anyone curl up with a crossword?

Nevertheless, at the centre of *The Poetics of Space* is the assurance that, as Bachelard writes, 'the poetic image is under the sign of a new being. This new being is happy man.'[10] The conspicuous success of *The Poetics of Space*, which remains the book through which most readers will encounter Bachelard's work, has much to do with the fact that Bachelard confers such philosophical dignity on the ordinary and often overlooked idea of happiness, and manages to make it both simple and interesting (usually by showing the complexity of its simplicity). Readers continue to look to philosophy and literature for accounts of the nobility allegedly conferred by suffering and strife rather than the happiness that is apparently accessible even to ordinary people. This prejudice runs parallel to the epidemically widespread yet snarlingly aristocratic principle that goodness can never be as interesting as evil. Where other writings treat spatial existence in terms of adventure, excitement, exertion and adversity (one of the most widely diffused articles of faith of the social theory of the 1970s was that social existence is made up of 'sites of struggle'), Bachelard's great preoccupation in *The Poetics of Space* is 'topophilia', or '*felicitous space*' (*Poetics of Space*, xxxv). Here, space is contentment, offering containment in place of contention. Bachelard's *Poetics of Space* is really a *Poetics of Cosiness*, and his topophilia is a claustrophilia. In this the book is a sequel and companion piece to the study of *intimité*, or intimate interiority, undertaken almost a decade before in *Earth and the Reveries of Repose*.

Another feature of *The Poetics of Space*, which helps account for its widespread success among readers, is the unembarrassed relaxation of its style. This relaxation is itself modulated through the book, in which Bachelard alternates between a ceremonious scholarly formality, which strives to give the impression that it is carefully working out an elaborate conceptual structure, even as it sometimes approaches teasing parody, and a self-delighting pleasure in the display of items that have been included merely for the purpose of pleasing himself: 'As for myself, in a leisurely book of this kind, in which I enjoy all the images, I was obliged to linger over this monstrous snail' (*Poetics of Space*, 130).

The Poetics of Space is a retirement book in different senses. It is a book written after, and as the confirmation of Bachelard's retirement from his official duties as teacher and writer, largely written in physical retirement from the city of Paris in Bachelard's house in Dijon. The book itself also explores a number of different spaces of recoil, retreat and retraction. And the physical return to the place of Bachelard's childhood is matched by a strong sense of temporal return. To go down, and in, into the cellar, or the nutshell, is also to go back. In stepping aside from every kind of aggression – 'hostile space is hardly mentioned in these pages,' Bachelard reassures (*Poetics of Space*, xxxvi) – the book indeed reaches back to an imaginary space prior to any animosity:

> The nest, quite as much as the oneiric house, and the oneiric house quite as much as the nest – if we ourselves are at the origin of our dreams – knows nothing of the hostility of the world. Human life starts with refreshing sleep, and all the eggs in a nest are kept nicely warm. The experience of the hostility of the world – and consequently, our dreams of defense and aggressiveness – come much later. In its germinal form, therefore, all of life is well-being. Being starts with well-being. (*Poetics of Space*, 103–4)

And yet, something persists of the refusal of merely given being that has characterized all of Bachelard's life, and especially the work of writing in which it has been taken up. Bachelard returns frequently to the idea of condensation, to express the sense of a space that both concentrates time and therefore refuses and redeems its extension. He praises the casket, in which 'the past, the present and a future are condensed. Thus the casket is memory of what is immemorial' (*Poetics of Space*, 84). The writer who did so much to explain the correlation of space and time in theories of relativity reverts here to an absolutism of space, in returning to the stubbornly impossible doctrine of the priority of instants over durations that had animated *Intuition of the Instant*:

> At times we think we know ourselves in time, when all we know is a sequence of fixations in the spaces of the being's stability – a being who does not want to melt away, and who, even in the past, when he sets out in search of things past, wants time to 'suspend' its flight. In its countless alveoli space contains compressed time. That is what space is for. (*Poetics of Space*, 8)

Rather than following through an argument from point to point, Bachelard accumulates examples, as though pulling them from the shelves among which he sits, as he himself is so often pictured in his book-lined burrow. 'Our soul is an abode [une demeure],' writes Bachelard (*Poetics of Space*, xxxvii), and he seems to want to make of his book a kind of abode or abiding, rather than a passage from one place to another.[11] To use the term that Bachelard takes from *Vers une cosmologie* by the phenomenological psychiatrist Eugène Minkowski, the habitat and the inhabitant are joined in the active convolution of a 'reverberation [retentissement]', which Bachelard characterizes as 'the opposite of causality' (*Poetics of Space*, xvi).[12]

But this means that there is in fact a kind of refusal in Bachelard's retirement, almost a kind of antagonism towards the agonistics of life itself. Bachelard refers back constantly to a past that has never been present, that is expressed in a kind of presentness with no past: for 'the poetic act has no past,' as Bachelard declares in bold mendacity (*Poetics of Space*, xv). Bachelard finds in poetry, and, in particular, the function that constitutes the essential work of poetry, the making of images, a special kind of life: 'poetry puts language in a state of emergence, in which life becomes manifest through its vivacity' (*Poetics of Space*, xxvii). Bachelard therefore looks to poetry for 'documents on the intense life of language' (*Poetics of Space*, xxvii). But the life of poetry is a special kind of life, which, in the 'pure sublimation' it brings about (*Poetics of Space*, xxx), goes far beyond mere living. The task of the phenomenologist 'is that of proceeding phenomenologically to images which have not been experienced, and which life does not prepare, but which the poet creates; of living what has not been lived' (*Poetics of Space*, xxx). Such images are profoundly linked in *The Poetics of Space* to memories, and especially the memories of childhood, as they attach in particular to objects and dwelling places. But Bachelard resists the idea that such images allow for the merging of work and life: rather, 'a man's work stands out from life to such an extent that life cannot explain it' (*Poetics of Space*, xxxiii). This is why memory maintains the impatience with biography that is to be found throughout Bachelard's work but grows ever stronger in his final years, as the threat to life grows of turning despite itself into biography:

> Memories are motionless, and the more securely they are fixed in space, the sounder they are. To localize a memory in time is merely a matter for the biographer and only corresponds to a sort of external history, for external use, to be communicated to others. But hermeneutics, which is more profound than biography, must determine the centers of fate by ridding history of its conjunctive temporal tissue, which has no action on our fates. For a knowledge of intimacy, localization in the spaces of our intimacy is more urgent than determination of dates. (*Poetics of Space*, 9)

Bachelard seeks both to retrieve his personal past, and to seal it off from further enquiry. Perhaps remembering the invasiveness of the kind of detailed biographical psychoanalysis practised by Marie Bonaparte with regard to Edgar Allan Poe, of which he reminds himself later in the book, Bachelard repudiates any psychoanalytic method or purpose:

> In all psychological research, we can, of course, bear in mind psychoanalytical methods for determining the personality of a poet, and thus find a measure of the pressures – but above all of the oppressions – that a poet has been subjected to in the course of his life. But the poetic act itself, the sudden image, the flare-up of being in the imagination, are inaccessible to such investigations. (*Poetics of Space*, xvii–xviii)

In the form of the 'archetype', Jungian psychology provides Bachelard with a way of apprehending the intensity of feeling with which poetic images are charged while keeping them impersonal, or 'transsubjective' (*Poetics of Space*, xix). In the opening chapters of *The Poetics of Space*, Bachelard incubates a dream 'of the house we were born in' (*Poetics of*

Space, 7). But, in doing so, he doubles the act of dreaming that it is the function of the house to incubate:

> The places in which we have experienced daydreaming reconstitute themselves in a new daydream, and it is because our memories of former dwelling-places are relived as daydreams that these dwelling-places of the past remain in us for all time. (*Poetics of Space*, 6)

The autobiographical impulse often arises late in the life of writers, at the point at which it begins to seem possible to see the contour of one's life as a whole. But there is always a humiliation that accompanies the impulse to gather oneself together in writing, which arises from the confrontation with the fact that so little of one's life can genuinely or reliably be remembered, especially when it is a matter of one's early years. Because they are almost entirely inaccessible to memory, one's beginnings cannot reliably be accounted among one's belongings. It may be the fact that so much of a life must necessarily have escaped the liver, by reason of the fact that they are living through rather than in it, that energizes the effect to gather memories hastily together for flight.

There is also an unsettling ambivalence in the fact of the timeless abiding of the house that, because it is *sine die*, seems strangely separate from the being who feels that it is their abode:

> Indeed, at times dreams go back so far into an undefined, dateless past that clear memories of our childhood home appear to be detached from us. Such dreams unsettle our daydreaming and we reach a point where we begin to doubt that we ever lived where we lived. Our past is situated elsewhere, and both time and place are impregnated with a sense of unreality. It is as though we sojourned in a limbo of being. (*Poetics of Space*, 57–8)

There is a peculiar mixture of intensity and elusiveness in Bachelard's memories in his final two completed books, *The Poetics of Reverie* and *The Flame of a Candle*, which are humming with emotional tone and texture, but unsupplied with the kind of detail that might place them in relation to the world of others. The being of the well-being on which Bachelard insists depends upon solitude, a solitude that is never lonely because it seems to have such cosmic extent, including everything except the whole of the social world. It may not be exactly that hell is other people for Bachelard, but paradise certainly seems to require their absence. What takes the place of other people – parents, postmen, tobacconists, schoolmates, comrades in arms – is the pseudo-company of other writers, read selectively for the narcissistic society they seem to offer. Bachelard represents the house as a maternal space – a nest, a cradle, a bosom – but there is no actual mother visible or audible in such a scene, for she *is* it. For Mme Bachelard to make an appearance in the house would require her to be distinguishable from the house to which she has been assimilated.

The early chapters of *The Poetics of Space* project a kind of *autonatality*, to venture a term that it is hard to believe has not occurred to Bachelard himself. 'Here', he writes of the act of reading, but also of the present act of writing about it, 'expression creates being' (*Poetics of Space*, xxiii). His reveries of beginning, a beginning that is in fact outside time, so never begins – are not just oneiric, but undisguisedly *onaneiric* – the dream of one dreaming of dreaming himself into being. For Bachelard, one dreams of houses because houses are places in which to dream. To dream is to dream the containing power of dream:

> Daydreaming even has a privilege of autovalorization. It derives direct pleasure from its own being. Therefore, the places in which we have experienced daydreaming reconstitute themselves in a new daydream, and it is because our memories of former dwelling-places are relived as daydreams that these dwelling-places of the past remain in us for all time. (*Poetics of Space*, 6)

There is also nevertheless a kind of anxious melancholy that sometimes makes itself felt in Bachelard's writing. In part it is because of the belatedness that must be a part of every abiding:

> it is not until late in life that we really revere an image, when we discover that its roots plunge well beyond the history that is fixed in our memories. In the realm of absolute imagination, we remain young late in life. But we must lose our earthly Paradise in order actually to live in it, to experience it in the reality of its images, in the absolute sublimation that transcends all passion. (*Poetics of Space*, 33)

The salutation that Bachelard offers to beginnings in *The Poetics of Space* is accompanied by a sense that they constitute some reproach and that some reparation is mysteriously due to them:

> For how forcefully they prove to us that the houses that were lost forever continue to live on in us; that they insist in us in order to live again, as though they expected us to give them a supplement of living. How much better we should live in the old house today! How suddenly our memories assume a living possibility of being! We consider the past, and a sort of remorse at not having lived profoundly enough in the old house fills our hearts, comes up from the past, overwhelms us. (*Poetics of Space*, 56)

Rather than an act of redemption, Bachelard's book is an act of repentance for the fact that 'We did not dream enough in that old house' (*Poetics of Space*, 57). He writes enigmatically that 'today when we discover a nest it takes us back to our childhood or, rather, to a childhood; to the childhoods we should have had' (*Poetics of Space*, 93). At one point, he inserts a parenthesis which indicates that there may even be a conscious avoidance of the actual, biographical experience of childhood:

> we shall never collect enough daydreams, if we want to understand *phenomenologically* how a snail makes its house . . . How can the little snail grow in its stone prison? This is a natural question, which can be asked quite naturally. (I should prefer not to ask it, however, because it takes me back to the questions of my childhood.) (*Poetics of Space*, 118)

Is the self-made man, the professor formed through tireless, self-directed reading and writing, the snail making its own stone prison?

Meanwhile, the external, public world was encroaching, as the electronic media of radio and television continued to cultivate their appetite for intellectual celebrity. At the end of 1955 Bachelard accepted ruefully an invitation to contribute to the radio programme *France-Culture*: 'I have had to agree to radio conversations, which bring me little amusement.'[13] Television was equally quick to grasp the attraction of the bearded sage zoologically on display in the native habitat of his study, with technician-crews crammed into the tiny space off-screen. In the final weeks of his life, he would make clear his low opinion of these interviews, instructing his

Simon Segal, *Gaston Bachelard*, 1956.

daughter Suzanne that 'under no circumstance were texts intended for oral transmission, such as lecture notes or radio interviews' to be reprinted.[14] There was something oxymoronic in the exposure to a mass audience of the cavern of contemplation that Bachelard had made so distinctly his own. In an essay of 1951, he had outlined a reverie of radio that constituted a sort of fantasy defence against exposure to the ravening ear and eye of the mass media. In an era in which 'we all of us speak in the logosphere,' and in which 'radio really does represent the total, daily realization of the human psyche,' Bachelard allowed himself to imagine that radio might be reclaimed for solitary reverie: 'is it possible to set aside radio time and develop subjects for radio aimed at the unconscious, which can then find the principle of reverie on every wavelength'?[15] He even playfully projected a self-invented role for himself, which glanced back at his own early aspirations to a career as an engineer: 'It would be a good thing if we had working alongside the radio engineer – and here again the term must be created to fit the concept – a *psychic engineer*' (*Right to Dream*, 168).

Among the many demands on his time were invitations to contribute prefaces and introductory essays to literary editions and catalogues of the work of artists. He records visiting the studio of Marc Chagall, 'one of the greatest painters of our time', on 7 March 1952, in preparation for an introduction he wrote to a book of Chagall's biblical illustrations.[16] In 1956 Bachelard sat for a portrait by the painter Simon Segal, about whose work he had written, being depicted in front of a wall of books in his study in Paris. Seeing the portrait induced a chronological convolution in Bachelard:

> when I look for any length of time at that portrait Segal painted of me one winter evening, I see over the space of a third of a century – what an astonishing thing is memory! – I see in my own eyes my father looking at me. (*Right to Dream*, 31)

Just as, in his writings about poetry, Bachelard's attention is only rarely drawn to matters of language, so, in his increasingly frequent writings about art and sculpture, he proves oddly unresponsive to the actuality of visual forms – in line, volume, form, colour, composition. He is too eager to read through, and be read by, the images in Chagall's book of Bible illustrations to be delayed, as an art critic might, by their visual form and effect. He is repeatedly drawn from sight to sound, and from images for the eye to pictures of names:

> By illustrating the renown of Laban's daughter, Chagall has hallowed a name. Chagall shows us the very being of a name in the instant of its first appellation. I look upon this volume as a book of names. When we read the Biblical text, the names are sometimes no more than an agglomeration of syllables. We think we know a person because we spell out his name. We are caught up in a great dream of sonority. For a dreamer of words, what splendor of femininity there is in the name Rachel! (*Right to Dream*, 14)

In another essay, Bachelard writes:

> Chagall, in making you see, makes you speak. Prolong your enjoyment in looking at those two stubborn pairs of horns and you will find yourself making up rhymes. The painter's genius will coerce you into a talent for poetry. (*Right to Dream*, 21)

'Chagall has given us a talking picture,' Bachelard writes (*Right to Dream*, 9), and, in an essay about the engravings of his friend Albert Flocon, he informs his reader that 'it is because the engraving "tells" nothing that it obliges you, the musing spectator, to do the talking' (*Right to Dream*, 75). In his writings about art, Bachelard is concerned less with works of art than with the workings of the material imagination in art-making. Rather than bringing the philosophy of material imagination to bear on the work of artists, his tendency is to bring that work into reverberating accord with that philosophy. Art is here the occasion for philosophical allegory: 'Flocon's universe is the Cosmos of Work. Man's function, for him, is to change the face of the world' (*Right to Dream*, 88).

Shortly after his retirement from the Sorbonne, Bachelard accepted an invitation to become one of the forty 'Immortels' who made up the Académie Française, in the Académie des sciences morales section. Bachelard wrote nervously on 14 April 1956 to Daniel Giroux: 'All that confuses me. As you can imagine, I am not made for ceremonies. But my friends have no intention of backing down.'[17] Bachelard was glad to record that the ceremony at the end of June 1956, at which he accepted his ceremonial sword, was held in private, with the press not invited.

Bachelard had written to Ludwig Binswanger on 14 August 1954 apologizing for his long silence, which was to be accounted for by the fact that he had published nothing since *Le Materialisme rationnel*, and had been taken up with his Sorbonne teaching. He remarked that he had not rewritten the last public lecture course he had given, titled 'The Philosophical Life': 'I think I will reflect some more before making a book.' But he does indicate that, the following winter, 'I would like to be able to work on a book of synthesis relating to the five books I have written on the imagination.'[18] This prospect had hardened into a resolution by 24 September, when he wrote in another letter to Binswanger, 'I must now try to integrate all the philosophical points of view spread through my works on the imagination.'[19] *The Poetics of Space* perhaps represented the first attempt at this harvest home, though Bachelard nevertheless wrote in its introduction that, 'full of metaphysical speculations' as they are, the last two chapters of the book

> would tie into another book that I should still like to write. This book would be a condensation of the many public lectures that I gave at the Sorbonne during the three last years of my teaching

> career. But shall I have the strength to write this book? (*Poetics of Space*, xxxix)

The Poetics of Reverie, which appeared in 1960, seems intended to fulfil this ambition. It carries forward the introversive impetus of *The Poetics of Space*, which, directed first of all at space, moves inwards to the intimate space of the house, and then, leaving behind particular spaces and places, ends with tightly coiled reflections on the spatiality of reverie itself. *The Poetics of Reverie* announces a more systematic kind of enquiry and an adherence to phenomenology projected as a kind of method rather than a tendency or complexion, which comes closer than any of Bachelard's earlier enquiries to providing a statement of his philosophy of imagination. Indeed, phenomenology is closely linked to the frankly Romantic idealism of the imagination, as Bachelard proclaims 'a phenomenology of the imaginary where the imagination is restored to its proper, all-important place as the principle of direct stimulation of psychic becoming'.[20]

The opening pages of the book mark an even more decisive break with psychoanalysis than had been articulated before in Bachelard's writing, identified as it is with the exercise of personal biography.

> If you consider poetry in all its fire of human becoming, at the summit of an inspiration which delivers the new world to us, what can be the use of a biography which tells us the past, the heavy past of the poet? If we had the least inclination for polemic, what a dossier we could assemble on the subject of the excesses of biography. (*Poetics of Reverie*, 8)

Bachelard quotes lines from a poem written by Verlaine while in prison at Mons in order to demonstrate that 'It is so difficult to link the life to the work!' (*Poetics of Reverie*, 6). But the lines he quotes instantly conjure a personal identification between himself and Verlaine:

> Who is not in prison in times of melancholy? In my room in Paris, far from the land of my birth, I carry on Verlaine's reverie. A sky from another time spreads out over the city of stone. And through my memory hum the bars of music that Reynaldo Hahn wrote to accompany Verlaine's poems. A whole layer of emotions, reveries and memories grows up out of this poem for me. Above the poem – not beneath in a life which I have not lived, not in the poorly

> lived life of the unhappy poet. Did not the work dominate his life; is not the work a pardon for the man who has lived badly? (*Poetics of Reverie*, 9)

The lines give us a textbook example of the slippage between what Bachelard writes, and what that writing does, as Bachelard's manner of asserting the autonomy of writing from biographical circumstances confirms their reciprocal dependence. It may be true that, for Bachelard, 'One doesn't read poetry while thinking of other things' (*Poetics of Reverie*, 4) – though why on earth not? – but those other things seem to crowd in to the vicinity of the poetry that holds itself apart from everything in life. Bachelard disclaims identification with the 'poorly lived life' of Verlaine, but hints at identification in evoking a writer whose work has dominated his life. Where Verlaine's work is a redemption for his conventionally dissipated poetic life, Bachelard opens the possibility that a life lived entirely for and through its work, without residue, might itself be another mode of living badly. The task of writing may be to seek remission for the sin against life that writing itself commits.

11

Against Biography, 1958–62

If there is a single principle that governs Bachelard's life of writing it might be described as the *dissolution of the object*. His writings on scientific rationality are impelled by the need to escape the mesmerizing dominion of objects and substances in favour of the discursive networks of the city of science. Bachelard wrote that 'through its revolutionary discoveries, contemporary science can be described as the *liquidation of a past*.'[1] His poetic writings, especially the more personal writings of his final five years, are impelled by a movement in the opposite direction, backwards and inwards, towards the cloistered interiorities of the material imagination. But here, too, the liquidating impulse, to refuse the given, reasserts itself. In the intense retrospection of *The Poetics of Reverie*, Bachelard is drawn back to an absent origin, a childhood that had never succeeded in having been lived. Childhood therefore is at once omphalos and void. Ink is often imagined as an ethereal force of self-creation *ex nihilo* in Bachelard's writing:

> An author, whose name escapes me, used to say that the pen point was an extension of the mind. I am completely convinced of it: when my pen leaks, I think awry. And who will give me back the good ink of my school days?[2]

But the seething blackness of ink can also be a terrifying kind of oblivion. In the short passage Bachelard had introduced into the proofs of *Earth and Reveries of Repose*, to point to connections to the work of Binswanger and Kuhn, he alluded to one particular card used in Rorschach tests, which is 'one mass of interior darkness which often causes a "black shock" (*Dunkelschock*), that is to say which gives rise to deep emotion', suggesting to patients 'the powers of embryos or the disordered agitation of larvae'.[3] Bachelard evokes beings who set themselves in dream 'the task of being heroes in the battles of matter', aiming to 'triumph over every "black shock"'.[4] The German term *Dunkelschock* is taken from the work of Hans Binder, a follower of Hermann Rorschach, who proposed that the patterns of chiaroscuro in the inkblots had psychological significance: Bachelard wrote to Roland Kuhn on 28 December 1947 telling him that he had been referred by Jacqueline Verdeaux to Binder's 1932 study on the interpretation of light and dark and asking him where he could obtain a copy of his *Die Helldunkeldeutungen im psychodiagnostischen Experiment von Rorschach*.[5]

Where scientific rationality obviates objects in favour of mathematical structure, poetic expression abnegates the object of the self, in a *sur-être* or over-being that dissolves the having-been of the subject's own objectivity. Increasingly drawn to the thought of death, Bachelard finds his essential image of childhood in the well, which is both source of life and an unsoundable pit of extinction, so that '*childhood is the well of being* [*le puits de l'être*]' (*Poetics of Reverie*, 114).[6]

Bachelard's evocations of childhood from the late 1940s onwards become ever more enigmatic and allusive. A particularly occult passage in *The Poetics of Reverie* gives expression to this sense of the immanence of oblivion:

> A well marked my early childhood. I only approached it with my hand tightly clasped in my grandfather's hand. Who was afraid then, the grandfather or the child? And yet the curb was high. It was in a garden which was soon to be lost . . . [Bachelard's ellipsis] But a dull evil has remained with me. I know what a well of being is. And since one must tell everything when he is evoking his childhood, I must admit that the well of my greatest terrors was always the well of my goose game. In the middle of the softest evenings, I was more afraid of it than of the skull and crossed tibias. (*Poetics of Reverie*, 114–15)

Bachelard alludes here to the *jeu de l'oeil* or 'game of the goose', a popular board game widespread across Europe from the end of the fifteenth century onwards. The earliest surviving game board is in the Metropolitan Museum in New York, and dates from around 1500.[7] The game is a race game resembling snakes and ladders, in which players must roll dice to determine the number of places they move round a board. The board is designed in a spiral, with 63 spaces moving from the outside in to the destination space in the centre. The game has been adapted to simulate many kinds of progress through life, personal, spiritual, moral, military, romantic, economic, geographic and otherwise. Players landing on different squares meet with various kinds of advancement, impediment and reverse. A player landing on a space occupied by a goose, reputed to be lucky in Italy, usually every ninth space on the board, advances beyond it the number of spaces thrown to arrive at it. The well alluded to by Bachelard is one of a number of hazard spaces, including Bridge, Inn, Labyrinth, Prison and Death, which inflict various penalties. Death is usually signified by the skull and crossbones alluded to by Bachelard, though it involves a spiritual rather than physical death, in that the player is sent back to the beginning rather than out of the game altogether. The final square is usually numbered 63, the traditional number of the 'grand climacteric', the product of seven and nine reputed to be a year of particular danger in life.[8] The Well is usually placed at 31, just before halfway through the full course: a player landing here must wait to be 'pulled out' by another player landing on the same space, which sends the first player back to the space

Gaspar ab Avibus, *The Fair and Delightful Game of the Goose*, 1580.

from which the second player has come.[9] As the black hole at the heart of the game, the well seems to have the value of the memory of an '*immobile childhood*, a *childhood without becoming*, liberated from the gearwheels of the calendar' (*Poetics of Reverie*, 116). It signifies a nonextensive duration, time separated from life-time: 'Those great times of non-life dominate life, deepen the past of a person by detaching it, through solitude, from contingencies foreign to his being' (*Poetics of Reverie*, 120). And yet it is also a time buried so deep in life as to be lost to it.

Bachelard began his *Poetics of Reverie* with some reflections on the methods of phenomenology that he proposed to bring to bear on the experience of images. But no sooner has Bachelard introduced the idea of 'the heavy philosophical apparatus of the phenomenological system' than he abandons it, asserting stubbornly of himself, as fabled figure of 'the philosopher', 'when evening has come and he is no longer teaching, he believes he has the right to shut himself up in the system of his choice' (*Poetics of Reverie*, 2). In what follows, Bachelard attempts a strange blend of the impersonal and the personal, the systematic and the arbitrary. In this he seems to arrive at the final stage of the schema he had derived from the work of Ludwig Binswanger, in the pages he had added in haste to the proofs of *Earth and Reveries of Repose* in 1948:

Eugène Minkowski in the 1930s.

> The *Eigenwelt*, the world of personal fantasies, could be linked with psychodrama. The *Mitwelt*, the interhuman world, could be linked with sociodrama. The *Umwelt*, the world described as real, the world declared to be perceived, would have to be worked on with the principles of the material imagination. We would then have the basis of a particular aspect of the psyche to which the term cosmodrama may be taken as appropriate.[10]

The Poetics of Reverie moves towards this cosmodrama in its final chapters. Bachelard had admitted in *Earth and Reveries of Repose* that 'Whenever I have been able to take images up to the cosmic level, I have come to realize that such images give me a happy consciousness, a demiurgic consciousness,' and this consciousness predominates in *The Poetics of Reverie*.[11] Nothing can resist, or survive, the psychocosmic fusion of outer and inner. *The Poetics of Reverie* is governed as *The Poetics of Space* had been by the notion of reverberation that Bachelard had borrowed from Eugène Minkowski (1936), which allows for the idea that the terms of every opposition, of world and word, poet and reader, microcosm and macrocosm, participate in each other. Minkowski's verb *retentir* itself reverberates through *The Poetics of Reverie*:

> The phenomenologist can awaken his poetic consciousness at the contact of a thousand images which lie sleeping in books. He reverberates to the poetic image in the very sense of phenomenological resonance so well described by Eugene Minkowski . . . The poet awakens within us the cosmicity of childhood . . . the poets cause, in Minkowski's sense of the word, a 'resonance' [retentissement] of the archetypes of childhood and cosmicity in us. (*Poetics of Reverie*, 7, 126)[12]

Reverberation implies amplification, to the point where Bachelard can entertain the omnipotence of the child's imagination:

> In every dreamer there lives a child, a child whom reverie magnifies and stabilizes. Reverie tears it away from history, sets it outside time, makes it foreign to time. One more reverie and this permanent, magnified child is a god. (*Poetics of Reverie*, 133)

The poet of reverie actualizes the omnipotence of the child, for 'the poet obliges the world to become . . . the *World of the word*' (*Poetics of Reverie*, 186). In their articulation of exaggerated conceptions, words seem to enact an exaggerated sense of their own power, as 'cosmic words, words which give man's being to the being of things' (*Poetics of Reverie*, 189). Bachelard's extravagantly cosmic evocations come to suggest that reverie should be identified with extravagance itself – for 'images can do anything' (*Poetics of Reverie*, 207) – in an extremity at once of evacuation and of imperious expansion:

> We are touching squarely on one extremity of reverie. Since the poet dares to write this extreme reverie, the reader must dare to read it to the point of a kind of beyond of reader's reveries, without reticence, without reduction, without worry about 'objectivity,' even adding, if it is possible, his own fantasy to the fantasy of the writer. Reading always at the summit of the images, stretched toward the desire to surpass the summits, will give the reader well-defined exercises in phenomenology. The reader will know imagination in its essence since he will be living it in its excess, in the absolute of an incredible image, the sign of an extraordinary being. (*Poetics of Reverie*, 204)

Cosmicity includes everything except events, history and social others, the realm of Binswanger's *Mitsein* always negated by implication in the sovereignty of solitary reverie in Bachelard's writing, and ever more explicitly in *The Poetics of Reverie*. The charge Bachelard lays against psychoanalysis, in his open and systematic preference of phenomenology to it, is that it always returns the dreamer 'to the superficial zone, to the socialized zone' (*Poetics of Reverie*, 148). Accordingly, for dream analysis, 'it is quite essential to take care to desocialize the terms of everyday language' (*Poetics of Reverie*, 70). There are only brief glimpses of the refusal of social life that Bachelard had made his own mythos. To build the possibility, as Bachelard has, of a life lived in writing, through active struggle in and against the social world, is also a way of achieving a worldly adulthood, which can, in its turn, retain the image of childhood that is safe from ever having to be relinquished to the extent that it has never quite been had: 'The child thus enters into the zone of family, social and psychological conflicts. He becomes a premature man. This is the same as saying that this premature man is in a state of repressed childhood' (*Poetics of Reverie*, 107). It takes a lifetime to liquidate the time of one's living, to turn one's life into a kind of fable of life, which Bachelard secures with a line borrowed from a Jean Rousselot poem, 'Je ne suis sûr de rien': 'Then the fable is life itself: "I have lived without knowing that I was living my fable"' (*Poetics of Reverie*, 118).[13]

The child who took his life into his own hands, taking responsibility for making his life from the inside out rather than receiving or accepting it from the outside, must, in the old man's retrospect, himself be remade in a way that replaces and surpasses mere memory, insofar as that memory is contaminated by the biographers who give the child its life: 'Only through the accounts of others have we come to know of our unity. On the thread of our history as told by the others, year by year, we end up resembling ourselves' (*Poetics of Reverie*, 99). To grow to knowledge of oneself is to be, Bachelard contemptuously snorts, 'stuffed with sociability' (*Poetics of Reverie*, 107). To recover childhood is therefore not to rescue its memory, but to rescue it from memory:

> Memory is a field full of psychological ruins, a whatnot [bric-à-brac] full of memories. Our whole childhood remains to be reimagined. In reimagining it, we have the possibility of recovering it in the very life of our reveries as a solitary child. (*Poetics of Reverie*, 100)[14]

Reverie is required to grasp what Bachelard calls the 'antecedence of being'. The childhood that will always need to be retrieved from 'the precisions of the social memory' (*Poetics of Reverie*, 117) will therefore always be alien to datable time, for it will always be both before and after its own assigned moment. Such antecedence perhaps forms a pair with the 'signe du tardif' under which Bachelard said his life had been lived. Being will always be belated, or *nachträglich*, for the being that has always been antecedent to itself. The fact that all humans are born prematurely, because entirely unable to survive without the care of other humans, also means that humans are born too late, because when they are subsequently born to their own sense of themselves it must always be in a precedent world that has prepared a place for them already. The lifelong project of rebirthing or giving rise to himself on which Bachelard set his course intensifies this sense of coming too late. Because it is born before its time, the human child will always arrive late in the day: because Bachelard's coming to himself was in prospect for so long, it could only ever be retrospective when it came.

Much of Bachelard's writing in his final years involves revisitation of old themes, and he returns at the end of *The Poetics of Reverie* to the elements of air and water in particular. But now these elements are dissolved into each other, swimming, for example, becoming a kind of underwater soaring, since both signify dissolution itself, the evaporation of any distinction between self and environment, subject and object. The I and the not-I meet and merge in a cosmic solipsism, in which everything is, and exists in, everything else, and mirror on mirror mirrored is all the show. When the elements that had provided different modes of the material imagination have lost all their density and powers of friction and resistance, material imagination gives way to wholly imaginary matter. Despite Bachelard's continued evocations of 'dynamogeny' (*Poetics of Reverie*, 206), the encounter between psyche and physis progressively loses all energy and tension in favour of a reverberative sonority, with mentality and materiality merely echoing themselves back to each other.

It is perhaps in dread of this consummation-in-dissolution that Bachelard pulls himself up short in the final paragraphs of *The Poetics of Reverie*, as though in an effort of bracing recoil from the oceanic annihilation of a will entirely self-fulfilled, and wills himself to project a new book, which would be devoted once again to the dynamic strivings of the forge and other kinds of craft, reasserting themselves against the soft sift of the *anima*'s cosmic compliancy: 'we would still want to write another book which, this time, would be the work of an *animus*' (*Poetics of Reverie*, 212).

As Bachelard entered his seventies he began to suffer from pains in his legs, which disturbed his sleep and made walking more and more difficult, increasing his already heightened sense of withdrawal into his spaces of intellectual refuge. He records in a letter of late 1957 having his blood pressure taken for the first time and being prescribed medication. He was still unable to walk in February 1958, and, in April, suffered a ruptured artery in his calf.[15] This may indicate a popliteal aneurism, the result of high blood pressure, and perhaps arteriosclerosis, the narrowing of the arteries caused by the build-up of plaque. Bachelard was reduced to a daily walk in the garden of his house in Dijon and was frustrated that he was sometimes unable even to accomplish this. Tormented too by what he called 'rheumatisms', he was forced to refuse invitations and no longer attended meetings of his Institute in Paris. A painful ulcer on his foot developed in late 1960, and a swelling in his right hand made writing as difficult as walking for a while.[16]

He nevertheless insisted on continuing to work as much as he could, and managed to complete *The Poetics of Reverie*, which appeared in 1960. The last two books on which he would work reanimated the fascination with heat and fire that had been apparent from the very beginning of his writing career, in his 1928 dissertation on the propagation of heat. As we have seen, when approaching the end of a book, Bachelard sometimes wrote of his urge to return to the beginning and write it all again, and, in the last two years of his life, he conceived a grandiose return to the subject that had inaugurated his turn from science to the imagination nearly a quarter of a century earlier, in *The Psychoanalysis of Fire*, this time projecting a more comprehensive study of the subject to be called *The Poetics of Fire*.

In *Le matérialisme rationnel*, Bachelard had seized on the explanation of combustion offered by Lavoisier as marking a decisive turn away from unconscious feeling to conscious deliberation:

> When Lavoisier proves that respiration is combustion (a fire without flame), we enter further into the regime of a modern science of matter. In place of the natural phenomenology of the flame that awakens in us the powers of the unconscious, we see the entry into action of a directed phenomenology that needs the assistance of informed consciousness.[17]

It is strange indeed that Bachelard, who issued in his final weeks the statement that '[a] human being is a living pyre', and who should have been better equipped than anyone to see this as an intellectual transformation of vast imaginative potency and reach, should nevertheless have been able so systematically to damp down such an intuition.[18] It would be left to others, such as Michel Serres, to articulate the prodigious incandescence of thermodynamic science, exploding through industry, society, art and dream: 'a sudden change is imposed on the raw elements: fire replaces air and water in order to transform the earth . . . Here comes Turner.'[19] A cultural phenomenology of fire on this scale allows for an enlarged perspective on civilization itself as a sustained sociotechnics of combustion, as articulated by Peter Sloterdijk in his *Die Reue des Prometheus*. Its epigraph from Bachelard's *The Psychoanalysis of Fire* – 'The arsonist is the most dissembling of criminals' – is an indication of how Bachelard has opened up for others the path he vetoed for himself.[20]

Bachelard's final two books give evidence both of undimmed intellectual ambition, as he made plans for a grandly cumulative work on *The Poetics of Fire*, along with a mournful apprehension that the time available to him to complete the task was rapidly running out. In the short, concentrated meditation *The Flame of a Candle*, Bachelard precipitated out one aspect of the poetics of fire, the quiet solitude concentrated in the image of a candle flame, allowing him to continue the work of making himself 'the *author of his solitude*' that he had begun in his previous book (*Poetics of Reverie*, 173). The keynote of *The Flame of a Candle* is sounded in its first sentence, which announces Bachelard's intention to be 'not overburdened by any erudition or imprisoned by a uniform mode of enquiry in this little book of simple reverie'.[21] His aim is a kind of concrete immediacy, avoiding all 'facile generalizations', though nobody could be better equipped than Bachelard to appreciate the complexity of the pure and simple, and the intricacy of the concrete. Thus, as in the image provided by the candle flame of a being entirely consummated in its own self-consuming, Bachelard finds his solitude in the collective solitude of poetic images: 'in total sympathy with the images poets offer me and with others' solitude, I come to be alone by means of their solitude. I become alone, profoundly alone, from the solitude of another' (*Flame*, 36). As usual, this solitude can only be shared if it is in fact unsociable: 'I would be troubled if the dreamer at the center of the image told me the reasons for his solitude, some distant history of life's betrayals. Ah, my own past is enough to burden me. I have no need for someone else's' (*Flame*, 37). As elsewhere in Bachelard's writing, the possibility of reference to religious traditions of sacred flame flares momentarily – 'If I had accorded myself the right to meditate on liturgical themes, I would have no trouble finding documents concerning the symbolism of flames' (*Flame*, 41) – only to be unsentimentally doused: 'I would then have to face scholarship' [Il nous faudrait alors faire face à un savoir] (*Flame*, 41).[22] This eschewal of religion is the more emphatic, given how close *The Flame of a Candle* comes to mysticism, as, for example, in the poeticized piety of the act of contemplation, as imaged in Rembrandt's *The Philosopher in Contemplation*, to which Bachelard alludes via a quotation from George Sand (*Flame*, 6).

The Psychoanalysis of Fire had been driven by the desire 'to cure the mind of its happy illusions' and to reveal 'the futility of those assertions that are constantly being repeated as eternal truths: fire is life, life is a fire'.[23] *The Flame of a Candle* and the sections that survive of *The Poetics of Fire* are no longer focused on the fiery purification of error, but rather on the

Rembrandt, *Philosopher in Contemplation*, 1632, oil on panel.

imagination of immersion and dissolution. Working and dreaming can now coalesce. Bachelard wrote in a letter, 'In solitude I have all the time I need to dream of life, of my life of hard labour.'[24] He worked this paradox up into the opening paragraph of the epilogue to *The Flame of a Candle*, which seems intended to recall Rembrandt's *The Philosopher in Contemplation*:

> one undertakes to live as though he were the sole character in a painting: a room whose walls are hazy and converge toward the center, concentrated around the meditator seated at a table lit by a lamp ... The being who dreams concentrates on it so that he can remember the being who used to work. (*Flame*, 75)

The strange architecture of Rembrandt's painting is recalled again a couple of pages later:

> How many times, living in one of my 'engravings,' I believed that I was deepening my solitude. I believed that I was descending,

Salomon Koninck, *Philosopher with an Open Book*, *c.* 1645, oil on panel.

> spiral after spiral, the stairway of being. But now I see that in such descents, though I believed I was thinking, I was really dreaming. (*Flame*, 77)

Bachelard's solitude coexisted ironically with ever more invasive demands from his own continuing fame. Following the appearance of *The Flame of a Candle*, he was awarded the Grand Prix Nationale des Lettres, a prize awarded under the auspices of the Académie Française between 1951 and 1999 to writers who had made a contribution to the influence of French literature. Bachelard thereby kept company in the roster of prize-winners with figures such as Philippe Soupault, Roger Caillois, Nathalie Sarraute and Jean Genet. Following an exhausting six-hour prize-giving ceremony in early November 1961, Bachelard had to cope with yet more radio and TV interviews.

His daughter Suzanne had obtained a teaching position in Lille, to which she travelled each week, leaving Bachelard to struggle alone to elaborate a shape for the new project, of which *The Flame of a Candle* was a prelude. In late 1960, he recorded in a letter: 'I have written so much that I am rather in confusion.'[25] On 21 April 1961 he wrote to the poet Louis Guillaume:

> When you pass Place Maubert, for example at the end of a Thursday evening, climb my staircase. I am always there, lost amid my projects, agitated by the books I would still like to write. But how can one write still when one has the sense that one should not repeat oneself? One would need to write poems and not books.[26]

Much is concentrated in this somewhat enigmatic suggestion that the way to avoid repetition is through poetry rather than discursive prose. Is this perhaps part of the logic of the attack on linking that provides such paradoxical continuity through Bachelard's life of writing, the sense that to live most intensely is to pull apart from oneself? In the preface to the edition of *Fragments of a Poetic of Fire* she assembled after her father's death, Suzanne Bachelard provides an unusually detailed account of Bachelard's methods of work, which, given the sense that his books on the imagination often give a loose weave of associations rather than

Bachelard in the 1960s.

a closely knit progressive argument, may have become habitual with him. By April 1962, Bachelard seems to have considered splitting the book he was writing into a number of different ones, writing on 25 April: 'I have several books under construction. I am astonished to see so many idle old professors.'[27] Bachelard vacillated in the last nine months or so of writing between the desire for concentrated selection and the desire for plenary dispersal, writing in the introduction he drafted to *The Poetics of Fire*: 'My long tale of methodological torment thus does not end simply. The more work I do, the more diverse I become. To achieve a unified existence one would have to live every age of one's life at once' (*Fragments*, 24).

Bachelard seems to have begun with the idea of a book to be titled *The Experience of Fire*, which he associated with the repose of Jungian *anima*, the self that is happily subject to its experience. But objections to this view of experience seem to have kindled immediately in Bachelard, in his irritable apprehension that '*experience* remains merely ephemeral if it cannot be *experienced again*' (*Fragments*, 18) – in which case, of course, it is no longer experience. For Bachelard, what one experiences in experience is the insufficiency of mere experiencing. Bachelard's inability to make headway with the idea of experience seems to have convinced him that his book should in fact be called *The Poetics of Fire*, falling into place in the sequence set in train in *The Poetics of Space* and *The Poetics of Reverie*. The new problem this posed for Bachelard was that he had already begun to write such a book in *The Psychoanalysis of Fire* in 1938. The danger of the impulse to revisit and revise is that it becomes mere book-keeping, when what Bachelard was seeking, as ever, was to prove the workings of 'a fully autonomous imagination with no connection to reality' (*Fragments*, 36). Bachelard seems to have found a new image for this autonomy in the idea of the Phoenix, for 'The Phoenix's privilege is to be reborn of its own self, not of the "ashes" of others' (*Fragments*, 42).

At the same time, Bachelard was increasingly aware that his end was not far off, and was making provision for his legacy. He dictated to Suzanne the contents of the volumes of essays and prefaces that would be published after his death as *Études* and *Le droit à rêver*. He also proposed that the best way for the incomplete manuscripts of his current work on fire to be published would be as part of a *Complete Works*, an idea that had been broached in 1961 by Paul Angoulvent, then president of Presses Universitaires de France. Difficulties in getting agreement from all Bachelard's publishers meant that this plan stalled in 1961 and again when it was proposed in 1974 and 1981. Only when a *Complete Works* of this kind no longer seemed feasible did Suzanne agree to the publication of these materials separately, as *Fragments d'une poétique du feu*, in 1988.

The book Bachelard was attempting to write was swirling around the idea of death, with the element of fire now being identified with dissolution. But in place of the gentle self-consumption in *The Flame of a Candle* – 'the flame dies a good death; it dies in its sleep' (*Flame*, 17) – Bachelard is taken up with thoughts of a more violent kind of self-immolation. Part of his difficulty came from his impulse to revisit in particular the two mythical motifs which had predominated in *The Psychoanalysis of Fire*, that of Promethean disobedience and Empedoclean self-dissolution.

In the case of the first, Bachelard strove to will himself beyond the psychoanalytic understanding of the Prometheus complex he had offered in 1938, as evidenced in 'all those tendencies which impel us *to know* as much as our fathers, more than our fathers, as much as our teachers, more than our teachers'.[28] In the fragments that he assembled at the end of his life, Bachelard strains to internalize the social drama of 'the Oedipus complex of the life of the intellect'.[29] He proposes that 'Our Promethean dreams are fueled by half conviction that the fire is in us, that our bodies hold their own reserves of inner fire' (*Fragments*, 85). Promethean knowledge goes beyond disputatious rivalry with others and 'the poverty of psychological and psychoanalytical case history' (*Fragments*, 57), in a transcendence of self that is also a kind of supremacism of self. If Bachelard had been able to complete his final book, it might have been a final testament to his personal mythology of knowledge as self-incension:

> a diffuse Prometheanism of a sort associates itself with learning. We learn in general from others and from books; but learning here becomes ours in a deeper sense, uplifting us above ourselves, above ordinary nature. Workers of spirit find themselves invigorated by a sort of prideful power. (*Fragments*, 73)

The theft of fire is really the discovery of 'inflamed speech [langage enflammé]' (*Fragments*, 11).[30] Bachelard presents this as the fictional friction of language chafing itself into self-exceeding: 'Ultimately what maintains and perpetually renews our interest in Promethean imagery is poetic energy, an energy released through a poetics of the mind' (*Fragments*, 83). In making such a definition of poetry as excessiveness itself, one cannot avoid overstatement, though Bachelard's overreach is sometimes silvered with irony: 'the ambitions of those who test the imagination are . . . undoubtedly too vast – for of what use, after all, are ambitions that are not too vast?' (*Fragments*, 31).

The second figure to which Bachelard returned was that of Empedocles, which he reads through the work of Hölderlin, Arnold and Nietzsche. Bachelard blares that 'In the Empedoclean act the individual looms large as fire and becomes the principal actor in a veritable cosmic drama' (*Fragments*, 91), but the will to absolute sublimation is thwarted by the fact that it is impossible for image and act to coalesce in it. Bachelard is drawn to the fact that writers seem unable to bring their versions of the death of Empedocles to completion, as though he were seeing in them the mirror of his own '*hesitation to write*' (*Fragments*, 103).

Bachelard seems to have held out for himself in the figure of the phoenix a kind of alliance of the will to assertion and the will to dissolution. As 'a creature born of the mighty contradiction between life and death' (*Fragments*, 64), the phoenix provides a conflagration devoutly to be wished, dying in a nest that is also a kiln: 'This ideal of fire longed for yet not suffered in the flesh amounts to a maternal preparation of the Phoenix's pyre like a final cradle, a cradle of death' (*Fragments*, 39). Bachelard allows himself a kind of incandescent candour, in his grandiose assertion of his own will-to-power through the phoenix:

> It is in the excess of imagery of the experience of fire that one is able to discover the veritable phenomenologic meaning of the Phoenix, formed in one's earliest consciousness out of flaming desire to take flame [un désir flambant de flamber]. To imagine the legend of the Phoenix sincerely I must always become the Phoenix of myself! (*Fragments*, 39)[31]

Despite his scarcely concealed self-identification with the Phoenix, which 'never ceases to live, to die, and to be born again in poetry, through poetry, and for poetry' (*Fragments*, 25), the writing here approaches liturgical formula. And, though he told himself he was everything, he was not ague-proof. No matter how a human attempts to write himself out of life, by turning his life into writing, the final word can only be that of others, in the afterword of biography.

Bachelard had grown progressively weaker as the autumn of 1962 approached. Suzanne rang Bachelard's publisher and friend José Corti in great distress: her father was not sleeping, could not walk a single step without great effort and was not eating. It was August, and very difficult to find a doctor who had not left Paris for the traditional August holiday. Corti was able to persuade Bachelard to accept a visit from a Dr Amiot, a friend of his who was a hospital anaesthetist, who found him in a very serious condition, with varicose ulcers that had been neglected to the point where gangrene threatened.[32] On 12 October, he was admitted to a clinic and, on the following day, Suzanne rang Bachelard's long-term friend Lescure to tell him that her father was dying. His physician, named 'Dr Mallarmé', confided to Pierre Desvigne that he was caring for a man of the Middle Ages: 'I have seen a man, who has forgotten for twenty years that he had a body.'[33] More and earlier attention to his ills might have kept Bachelard well for longer, though this was not only a result of Bachelard's own self-neglect. Jean Lescure reports that a former doctor had made a diagnosis of leukaemia in Bachelard six years previously but had held off from informing Suzanne. He did however pass on the information two years later in a letter to a third party, whereupon he himself passed over, though the possessor of the letter still could not summon the courage to impart the news of Bachelard's condition. So Bachelard's leukaemia, which may have accounted for some of his symptoms, of swelling, bleeding and long-lasting infections, remained untreated for six years. Though Lescure professes himself 'scandalized' by the doctor's failure to communicate his diagnosis, the long-term prospects for elderly patients with leukaemia were even poorer in the early 1960s than today.[34] To this may be added the fact that in those days, relatively recent though they were, the old were often regarded as unsuited to receive the news of their

Plaque outside 2 rue de la Montagne, Sainte Geneviève, Paris, where Bachelard lived from 1940 until his death in 1962.

mortality. Even today, a terminal diagnosis can be something that pushes you to the side of your own life, in Philip Larkin's phrase, as the management of your dissolution starts to becomes other people's business.[35] Lescure takes the charitable view that 'the doctor used to treating illness often finds themselves at a loss with certain patients who are determined to dispose of their life and their death in their own way.' The judgement that this was a case in which 'the patient prevails over the pathology' might have more force if one were surer that Bachelard's choice in this matter had been informed enough to have been a choice.[36]

Bachelard was buried in Bar-sur-Aube on 19 October 1962, alongside his wife Jeanne, who had died 42 years previously. Suzanne confessed to Lescure that she felt quite at a loss about the kind of ceremony to organize, being aware of her father's lack of religious faith, but not having discussed with him what he wanted. In the end she followed Jean Lescure's advice to do whatever would cause least offence to anyone, with a ceremony that was conventionally but not demonstratively religious.[37] José Corti recalls asking Bachelard what he made of the problem of the hereafter, to which he received the reply, accompanied by an ironic lift of the shoulders, 'There is no problem.' Corti concludes that 'in his quiet certainty, he tranquilly enjoyed the greatest and purest thing a human life can know on earth: the work of the mind and the love of a child.'[38]

Conclusion

What Bachelard discovers in his sequence of books on the imagination, and what proved to be most recognizably 'Bachelardian', is a particular style of heightening, apprehensible as a kind of wilfulness of style itself. *Air and Dreams* brings to the fore the most characteristic feature of Bachelard's new style, in the insistent pressure of hyperbole, enlarged from an occasional habit to a veritable principle of thought. Bachelard had a special fondness and aptitude for the sudden framing of a concept, having the appearance of the 'Augenblicksbegriff', or momentary concept, lying behind Hermann Usener's invention – itself something of a nonce-formulation – of the idea of the Augenblicksgott, or 'momentary god'.[1] A particularly striking group of these are the names of complexes. In *Lautréamont*, we encounter an '*animal life complex*', a '*scalp complex* that is a metaphorical form of *castration complex*' and even, in a puzzling mis-en-abîme, the '*Lautréamont complex*'.[2] Bachelard devises different kinds of 'psychology' in a similarly on-the-wing fashion, abruptly opening up analytic prospects that seem so convincing they leave one with the sensation he has already accomplished them:

> It is amazing that no one has been tempted to do a psychology of bullying and rivalry. An entire book would be needed to clarify it, focus on its individual and social characteristics, and pinpoint the reasons for its persisting and for the indifference or impotence of teachers toward this monstrosity that stamps both bully and bullied with its dual ill-fated marks.[3]

The playful improvisation of different kinds of complex is matched by a coinage like the 'cogito of kneading' introduced in *Earth and the Reveries of Will*.[4]

Clervence Ramnoux points out that Bachelard remained untouched by the infatuation with structuralist analysis that swept across Paris in the final years of his life, and that, for all his deep immersion in poetry, he seems not to have been particularly sensitive to linguistic perspectives: he thought of himself as 'not a linguist, but a "word-dreamer" [rêveur de mots]'.[5] Bachelard's *Lautréamont* sets the visceral force of the cry against formalized language, even the proto-language of the young child:

> The cry is also the antithesis of language. All those who have dreamed while watching a solitary child have been surprised by his linguistic play: the child plays with murmurs, babblings, liquid voices, the tones of fine little bells that ring without resounding – delicate crystals that a breath would break. The linguistic play stops when the cry returns in its initial strength, with its gratuitous anger clear as a sonorous and energetic cogito: I cry out, therefore I am an energy . . . Once more the cry is in the throat before being in the ear.[6]

Among the areas of linguistics to which Bachelard is relatively inattentive is that of phonics, even though his own writing frequently exploits the rhetoric of sound. This is actually a feature in particular of Bachelard's epistemological writing, in which clinching formulations often depend on echoic chiming: 'authentic scientific phenomenology . . . takes instruction from its constructions [La véritable phénoménologie scientifique . . . s'instruit par celle que'elle construit]'.[7] Bachelard's indifference to the analysis of phonic effects is allied to his indulgence of them, and is probably in its service. The concluding chapter of *Water and Dreams* is a celebration of the liquidity of language, which seems determined to dissolve away the materiality of linguistic form – the arrangement of letters that is only ever a prompt to imagine for ourselves a cat's miaow – in favour of the idealized form of his material imagination, which allows him to imagine that, in liquid language, water itself is somehow giving voice to itself. This can lead to brilliant jets of wit, as in his remarks about gargoyles as the visualization of the malice of rain:

> To spit out a storm like an insult, to vomit the water's guttural curses, a gutter would have to be given in monstrous forms, huge-mouthed, thicklipped, horned, and gaping. The gargoyle jokes [plaisante] endlessly with the downpour.[8]

The idea that the gargoyle disports itself with the rain it diverts is the more delicious for the fact that the author is also laughing like a drain. But Bachelard also wilfully decrees that he is transmitting, not translating, the vocality of things: '*liquidity* is, in my opinion, the very desire of language. Language needs to flow.'[9] This results in a determination to countermand linguistics, in the stubbornly immovable conviction (*je sais, mais quand-même*) of feeling:

> I will be accused at this point of accepting as solid proofs mere verbal resemblances; I will be told that *liquid consonants* call up no more than a curious metaphor belonging to the phoneticians. But such an objection seems to me to be a refusal to feel, in its profound life, the *correspondence* of word and reality. Such an objection reflects a will to reject a whole field of creative imagination: imagination through the spoken word, through speaking the imagination that rejoices muscularly in *speaking*, speaks with volubility, and increases the psychic volume of a being.[10]

Pierre Quillet suggests that Bachelard's fondness for neologism and compulsion to a kind of verbal fantasy leads to a delinquent lack of rigour, even when rigour might be his theme.[11] Jean-Claude Margolin takes a different view:

> the picturesque character, even the incongruity of expressions like *sur-stance, ex-stance, géno-analyse, thério-drama, cogito au n*[e] *degré, psychologie exponentielle, bipolarité, topologie philosophique, triangulation des consciences, poésie projective* and other formulae deriving from mathematics, are not only evidence of the humour and playfulness of their author but also his power of linguistic invention, will to scientific precision and pedagogic sense. In playing with suffixes and prefixes, does he not fulfil a function analogous to that of the chemist aiming to design a new chemical compound?[12]

Bachelard's writings on poetry and imagination are much more like anthologies than progressive arguments. It is as though anything that can be regarded as 'pre-scientific' is also without form or significant differentiation. 'In science', he wrote in *Le Rationalisme appliqué*, 'truths form systematic groups, while errors are indistinguishable in an unformed magma.'[13] Cristina Chimisso notices that Bachelard is much more careful about identifying the sources of his quotations in his works on scientific epistemology than in his works on imagination, in which 'his view of the fundamental fixity of the irrational part of our mind allowed and required him to pick his examples from various and diverse sources without being concerned about differences of times and places.'[14] As Chimisso intimates, this is part of Bachelard's reluctance to allow the possibility that imagination might itself be subject to anything like systematic analysis, or historical development:

> If we reject Bachelard's idea that images are immediate, a reflection on them would not necessarily 'destroy' them, even if that reflection exhibits characteristics that Bachelard would have ascribed to rational inquiry. If we accept that works of imagination are social, then they should be subject to the dialectics that Bachelard reserved for science. Imagination and rationality are probably not as antithetical as Bachelard supposed.[15]

Bachelard's instinct in writing of the imagination is to rely on demonstration rather than argument, or a demonstration pressurized into a kind of argument in itself. This tendency is apparent early in his writing, with his use of Gaston Roupnel's book *Siloë* in *Intuition of an Instant* (1932). Bachelard makes it clear that he does not intend in any conventional fashion to reproduce and appraise the argument of Roupnel's book, but rather to 'strive to heed the promptings these intuitions could provide to philosophical meditation'.[16] Viewed generously, this might be seen as a kind of salute to Roupnel's work, and, less generously, as an appropriation of it. Bachelard himself represents the process as a kind of reconstitution, even, frankly, a 'deformation':

> it is through the very deformations to which we have subjected Roupnel's theses that readers may be able to measure their true force. We have thus made free use of the intuitions of *Siloë* and – in a final analysis – more than an objective account, what we offer

> here is our experience of the book . . . Let us now focus on the guiding intuitions of *Siloë* without forcing ourselves to follow the order of the book.[17]

Bachelard even in a sense forces his reverberative method by a kind of induction on to the biographer who might prefer a life 'distorted into intelligibility', in Samuel Beckett's phrase.[18] Biographies of Bachelard are forced by the absence of a calendar into an assembly of quotations, which resemble the collecting of quotations that characterizes his own works on the imagination for the last 25 years of his life. It is as though Bachelard wanted to forestall the writing of biography by making his entire life of writing a kind of autobiography by proxy.

If, in one sense, Bachelard's writings on the imagination represent a kind of relaxation of analytic effort, in another they represent an indulgence of the will to power that is expressed in a more sternly watchful manner in his epistemological writing. Bachelard's hyperbolic tendency is a strange mixture of the relaxation of precaution and the unsupervised exercise of a force. Everywhere in Bachelard's evocations of the material imagination there is self-kindling overstatement: constantly, there is the pressure of, and for, *more*. 'Even when one has included all these legends, all these mental disorders, all these poetic forms under the heading of animism, there is more to be said.'[19] One of the more complex formulations of this exorbitance attempts to explain why only dreams of power will do to embody the will to self-exceeding:

> The destiny of the will for power is, in effect, to dream of power beyond actual power. Without this fringe of dream, the will for power would be powerless. It is through its dreams that the will for power is most aggressive. From this point on, he who would be a superman very naturally rediscovers the same dreams entertained by the child who would be a man. To govern the sea is a superhuman dream. It is both an inspired and a childlike will.[20]

Another of the characteristics of Bachelard's writing, which is more in evidence in his writing about the imagination, but sometimes asserts itself in his epistemological writing too, is the intermittent eruption of absoluteness, laying down laws improbably but for that very reason engrossingly. There is always a libidinal, look-on-my works charge carried by the word 'always' in Bachelard's writing: 'in dream and true myths, one always asks for what is desired. One always knows what one wants to drink, always drinks the same thing. What one drinks in a dream is an infallible clue to the nature of the dreamer.'[21] This is a seductively compelling idea, as long as one does not ask oneself whether it is actually true.

Many of Bachelard's most extravagant utterances can be rescued from their hyperbole by the simple addition of the words 'it is as if'. Transforming a sentence like 'the whole universe is governed by the will and by the imagination of the dreamer' into 'it is as if the whole universe were governed by the will and by the imagination of the dreamer' makes a dubious exaggeration into a judiciously balanced observation on the operations of a particular mode of magical thinking. Nor is this lost on Bachelard himself. Bachelard writes of the child watching clouds and pretending to command them:

> Reverie – as children often practice it – controls a changing phenomenon by giving it a command that has already been carried out or is being carried out. 'Great elephant! Stretch out your trunk,' says the child to the cloud that is growing longer. And the cloud obeys.[22]

When, a page later, Bachelard derives from this process the statement 'Our imaginary desire is attached to an imaginary form filled with imaginary matter,' it is not certain if he is describing the authoritarian operations of the material imagination in the child, or his own projection of those operations.[23] As grandiose statements of how things are in themselves, Bachelard's formulations are childishly easy to puncture: as characterizations of how things often seem, they have familiarity and finesse. It is possible to write of exaggeration without employing it, but in doing so there is always the risk of selling it short. By contrast, Bachelard's overstatement pleasurably underwrites, through participation in it, what it overstates. His willingness to surrender to self-intoxication is itself intoxicating. It is no surprise to find him urging us in *Air and Dreams*, the book in which hyperbolic method is joined to the theme of hyperbole through the idea of sublimation, to 'take the tree as a *theme of exaggeration*'.[24] It would, however, be a mistake to imagine that the ironies of the economy of excess are lost on Bachelard himself, as indicated in the wiry, wily acknowledgement of the centrality of exaggeration with which he concludes the first of his two concluding chapters in *Air and Dreams*:

> In this study I have stressed in several ways the dynamic nature of imaginative exaggeration. Without this exaggeration, life cannot develop. Life always takes too much of everything in order to have enough. The imagination must take too much for thought to have enough. The will must imagine too much in order to realize enough.[25]

Again, in *Earth and the Reveries of the Will*, Bachelard will assert the superlatist principle that 'In imaginary life as in real life, the fate of energies is to go too far. Where the imagination is concerned, one is only strong if one is all-powerful. Reveries of the will to power are reveries of the will to be all-powerful.'[26]

THE GOVERNING PRINCIPLE OF BACHELARD'S LIFE, connecting his two areas of philosophical preoccupation, rationality and imagination, is the ideal of autogeny, or self-origination. Just as, for Bachelard, scientific knowledge comes into being in the absolute, self-generating break with tradition, so the force of the poetic consists in a power of self-making, such that 'the aerial exhilaration of language itself becomes its own authority' (*Fragments*, 19). In their contrasting modes, both science and poetry are, in Bachelard's conception, enactments of this power of self-formation *ex nihilo* – he even playfully projected a 'phenomenology of those words that begin with "ex"'.[27] But the problem of the Philosophy of No through which Bachelard articulated the idea of scientific knowledge is that a kind of servility survives in every refusal, which must remain in debt to what it refuses (*refuse* is from Latin *refundere*, to refund). If thinking for yourself is disobedience, it cannot be all one's own work, for its defiance must depend on what it defies: but if it is really all one's own work, it cannot any more be disobedient.

The biographical matrix for this is the project of pedagogic self-making, or second birth, Bachelard toiled at tenaciously over the first four decades of his life. Despite his avoidance of self-revelation in his own writing and the hostility he maintained until the end, and ever more indignantly as he approached that end, towards biography, one might see this as an essentially autobiographical determination to make himself anew in writing. For writing is the enactment of the power possessed by a biological human to make itself superhuman from its own symbolic resources, always, in an assertion of the *jamais déjà*, and a refusal of whatever is claimed to be given in advance. In Bachelard's writing, being is French *ex-istence* rather than German *Da-sein*, because being is never already, and so always not yet, a being-*there*, but rather a being still in the making, or, better, still to be made. This makes Bachelard an aggressively non-ecological writer, driven always to try to break out of every kind of *Umwelt*, whether natural or social. Even the peaceful states of repose evoked increasingly in his later works tend to centre on self-woven cocoons, hollowed out of social existence by movements of devolution or involution that are themselves powerfully self-impelling.

Nevertheless, by the end of the 1940s, Bachelard had succeeded not only in developing an entirely new style of thought and writing, but had also built a new audience. His circle of correspondents and interlocutors was made up increasingly not of scientists and philosophers of science, but poets and artists. Although Bachelard was strongly attracted to the work of certain writers associated with surrealism, with a particular admiration for the work of Paul Éluard, he never referred to surrealism as a project or programme after his 'Surrationalism' essay. In a sense, Bachelard's relation to surrealism, selective and semi-detached, resembles his relation to psychoanalysis. The two are brought together by the historian of psychoanalysis in France, Elisabeth Roudinesco, who, though saluting Bachelard's work as 'a monument in itself', believes that whatever could be seen as psychoanalytic in it 'emerged from the Surrealist breakthrough . . . [and] owes nothing to the psychoanalytic movement, and that movement does not owe it very much.'[28] One might easily invert these terms: Bachelard's response to surrealism was strongly programmed by his shifting understanding of psychoanalysis, which never extended to sharing the anyway very diffuse surrealist ambitions for political revolution or social transformation. Bachelard's work may have given impetus and intellectual gravity to the surrealist effort to link scientific activity and innovation to socialism in the Popular Front of the 1930s, but Bachelard kept himself fastidiously away from anything that might have looked like allegiance in politics.

In any case, by the time Bachelard had completed his sequence of books on elemental poetics, surrealism was beginning to look rather elderly, as the generational pendulum had begun to swing towards existentialism and then the new forms of language-centred philosophies of structuralism and poststructuralism that established themselves following Bachelard's death in 1962. Nevertheless, for a decade or so following the War, Bachelard was the dominant figure in science and philosophy, with his idea of the 'epistemological break' being embraced with enthusiasm, if also very little engagement with much of the detail of Bachelard's work, by the figure of Louis Althusser, along with followers such as Dominique Lecourt and Étienne Balibar, who wrested the concept of epistemological break away from the history of science to serve as a principle of a Marxist science of history and politics.[29] For a brief period, readers associated with the Sorbonne 'swarmed to him like settlers' as W. H. Auden wrote of Edward Lear: 'He became a land.'[30]

Though he was never taught by Bachelard, the young Michel Foucault felt his influence. Jim Miller records Foucault's memory that 'to be honest, of all the contemporary philosophers alive when I was a student, Bachelard was the one I read the most.'[31] Foucault said of Bachelard's work that

> in his reflections on the discontinuity of the theory of the sciences, and in the idea of the working of reason upon itself in the moment in which it constitutes for itself objects of analysis, there was an entire network of elements that I collected and then used again.[32]

Foucault's first publication was a long introduction (long enough to drown the essay it introduced) to Ludwig Binswanger's essay 'Dream and Existence', which, though it does not mention Bachelard by name, is built around the Bachelardian dynamic of imaginative flight and descent. Foucault had travelled to Switzerland with Jacqueline Verdeaux, the translator of 'Dream and Existence' into French, to consult Binswanger about his work, and had also consulted with Bachelard about it.[33] There is, however, a note of uneasy caution mingled with Foucault's praise of Bachelard's writings on the imagination:

Bachelard commemorative stamp, 1984.

> No one has better understood the dynamic work of the imagination and the incessantly vectorial nature of its movement. But should we also follow Bachelard when he shows this movement culminating in the image, and the thrust of the image installing itself of its own accord within the dynamism of the imagination?[34]

Foucault's uneasiness at the idea of the absolute autonomy of the imagination anticipates the long curve of his subsequent work on the historical conditions that made the constitution of different kinds of subjectivity possible, rejecting the idea that subjectivity could ever assert itself 'of its own accord'. In this respect, he was among the many philosophical writers who have endeavoured since the early 1960s to fill the gap that Bachelard left yawning between imagination and rationality, individual and collective understanding.

In a sense, however, Bachelard himself had suggested the path that Foucault and others would take, in his concept of phenomenotechnique. Foucault himself would write of the act of writing as a kind of self-formation through experiment, the latter term meaning an encounter with an object that transforms both the object and the subject:

> Each book transforms what I thought when I finished the previous book. I am an experimenter, not a theorist. What I call a theorist is one who, whether by deduction or analysis, builds a general system and applies it in a uniform way to different fields, That is not the case with me. I am an experimenter in the sense that I write in order to change myself and no longer to think the same thing as before.[35]

This follows closely the prescription that Bachelard gives in writing of the work of experiment, even if he himself was not able to follow it. As Massimiliano Simons suggests, it is Bachelard's idea of the transformative encounter of subject and object through the mediation of technique and technology that has steadily gained ground, as the sciences of biology and environmentalism have begun to predominate over physics, and the social role of technology has come to be so transformative, impelling the work of writers such as Michel Serres, Bruno Latour, Isabelle Stengers, Bernard Stiegler and Peter Sloterdijk.[36]

In decided contrast with his writings on scientific epistemology, what Bachelard bequeaths in his studies of imagination is not really a body of ideas so much as a style of thought. Though he was no more systematically a follower of phenomenology than he was of surrealism or psychoanalysis, Bachelard developed from phenomenology, and the more phenomenologically inflected psychoanalysis he admired, in his later works especially, from *The Poetics of Space* to the unfinished *Fragments of a Philosophy of Fire*, an ability to intuit systems of phantasmal logic, or, as they might be understood, psychic language games, subtending different areas of ordinary experience. When he evokes the idea of a 'poet of furniture' or a 'phenomenology of roundness', we should recognize behind the playful, mid-air arabesques the seriousness his own writing makes it possible to conceive.[37] He writes, not in defence of lost causes, but in incitement of unsuspected ones. As he grew older, and increasingly beset by the ills and fatigue of old age, he seemed to feel ever more intensely the pressure of new books demanding to be written, in new ways. Like W. B. Yeats lamenting 'decrepit age', it may have seemed to him that 'Never had I more/ Excited, passionate, fantastical/ Imagination, nor an ear and eye/ That more expected the impossible.'[38] Phenomenology is that branch of philosophy that explores, not how things essentially are, but how they essentially seem to us to be; it is a kind of quasi-philosophy or philosophy of the as-if, which explores what arises from the fact that we do not believe in magic, but act as if we did. The richness of Bachelard's late writing is that its reach so far exceeds its grasp, as it constantly throws out hints towards a what-if phenomenology, or phenomenology of the what-if. In an intellectual world that presses ever more irresistibly towards convergence, Bachelard teaches us how to think of new things about which it might still be possible to think. In this, he makes good his principle that what is necessary in a human life is the possibility of going beyond the merely necessary.

REFERENCES

Introduction: A Writing Life

1 Gaston Bachelard, *The Poetics of Reverie: Childhood, Language, and the Cosmos*, trans. Daniel Russell (Boston, MA, 1971), p. 161.
2 François Dagognet, *Gaston Bachelard: Sa vie, son oeuvre, avec un exposé de sa philosophie* (Paris, 1965), p. 1.
3 Jean-Michel Wavelet, *Gaston Bachelard, l'inattendu: Les chemins d'un volonté* (Paris, 2019), p. 23.
4 Gaston Bachelard, *Fragments of a Poetics of Fire*, ed. Suzanne Bachelard, trans. Kenneth Haltman (Dallas, TX, 1990), p. 13.
5 Wavelet, *Gaston Bachelard*, p. 13.
6 Gaston Bachelard, *The Dialectic of Duration*, trans. Mary McAllester Jones (Manchester, 2000), p. 92.
7 Philip Larkin, *Collected Poems*, ed. Anthony Thwaite (London, 1988), p. 153.
8 Bachelard, *Fragments of a Poetics of Fire*, ed. Bachelard, trans. Haltman, p. 3.
9 Léon Brunschvicg, untitled review of Gaston Bachelard, *Essai sur la connaissance approchée*, in *Revue philosophique de la France et de l'etranger*, CVII (1929), p. 95.
10 Gaston Bachelard, *Intuition of the Instant*, trans. Eileen Rizo-Patron (Evanston, IL, 2013), p. 13.
11 Gaston Bachelard, *Lautréamont*, trans. Robert S. Dupree (Dallas, TX, 1968), p. 54.

1 Hostile Novelty, 1884–1919

1 Bruno Belhoste, 'L'enseignement secondaire français et les sciences au début du XXe siècle: La réforme de 1902 des plans d'études et des programmes', *Revue d'histoire des sciences*, XLIII (1990), p. 376.
2 Alan D. Schrift, 'Effects of the *Agrégation de Philosophie* on Twentieth-Century French Philosophy', *Journal of the History of Philosophy*, XLVI (2008), p. 458.
3 André Parinaud, *Bachelard* (Paris, 1996), pp. 58–9.
4 Thomas Hardy, *Jude the Obscure*, ed. Dennis Taylor (London, 1998), pp. 30–31.

5 Hastings Rashdall, *The Universities of Europe in the Middle Ages*, 2 vols (Oxford, 1895), vol. I, p. 250.
6 Gaston Bachelard, *The Formation of the Scientific Mind: A Contribution to a Psychoanalysis of Objective Knowledge*, trans. Mary McAllester Jones (Manchester, 2002), p. 49.
7 Gaston Bachelard, *Le matérialisme rationnel* (Paris, 1953), p. 28.
8 Jean-Michel Wavelet, *Gaston Bachelard, l'inattendu: Les chemins de la volonté* (Paris, 2019), p. 50.
9 Albrecht Fölsing, *Albert Einstein: A Biography*, trans. Ewald Osers (London, 1998), pp. 101–5.
10 Gaston Bachelard, *Essai sur la connaissance approchée* (Paris, 1928), p. 157.
11 Ibid., p. 164.
12 Wavelet, *Gaston Bachelard*, p. 100.
13 Ibid., p. 101.
14 Gaston Bachelard, 'Noumenon and Microphysics', trans. Bernard Roy, *Philosophical Forum*, XXXVII (2006), p. 80.
15 Gaston Bachelard, *Le rationalisme appliqué* (Paris, 1949).
16 Ibid., p. 178.
17 Ibid., pp. 170–93.
18 Gaston Bachelard, *The New Scientific Spirit*, trans. Arthur Goldhammer (Boston, MA, 1984), p. 3.
19 Military register, Archives de l'Aube, quoted in Wavelet, *Gaston Bachelard*, p. 117.
20 Wavelet, *Gaston Bachelard*, p. 117.
21 Gaston Bachelard, *Intuition of the Instant*, trans. Eileen Rizo-Patron (Evanston, IL, 2013), p. 7.
22 Gaston Bachelard, *Lettres à Louis Guillaume* (Paris, 2009), p. 44.
23 Ibid., pp. 48–9.
24 Quoted Parinaud, *Bachelard*, p. 25.
25 Bachelard, *Essai sur la connaissance approchée*, p. 275.
26 Andrew Barnaby, *Coming Too Late: Reflections on Freud and Belatedness* (Albany, NY, 2017), p. 9.
27 Bachelard, *Lettres à Louis Guillaume*, p. 45.

2 Realizations, 1919–32

1 André Parinaud, *Bachelard* (Paris, 1996), p. 67.
2 Gaston Bachelard, *The Flame of a Candle* (Paris, 1988), p. 37.
3 Gaston Bachelard, *Fragments of a Poetics of Fire*, ed. Suzanne Bachelard, trans. Kenneth Haltman (Dallas, TX, 1990), pp. xv–xvi.
4 Gaston Bachelard, *Essai sur la connaissance approchée* (Paris, 1928), p. 15. References abbreviated to *Connaissance* in the text hereafter.
5 Blaise Pascal, *Pensées*, trans. A. J. Krailsheimer (Harmondsworth, 1966), p. 211.
6 Abel Rey, *La théorie de la physique chez les physiciens contemporains: Exposé des théories* (Paris, 1923), p. 291, quoted in *Connaissance*, pp. 247–8.
7 Gaston Bachelard, *Étude sur l'évolution d'un problème de physique: la propagation thermique dans les solides* (Paris, 1928), p. 159.
8 Parinaud, *Bachelard*, p. 66.

9 Jean-Claude Margolin, *Bachelard* (Paris, 1974), p. 169.
10 Parinaud, *Bachelard*, p. 66.
11 Ibid., p. 59.
12 Cristina Chimisso, *Gaston Bachelard: Critic of Science and the Imagination* (London and New York, 1974), p. 74, n. 2.
13 Bachelard, *Flame of a Candle*, p. 37.
14 Gaston Bachelard, *La valeur inductive de la relativité* (Paris, 1929), p. 6.
15 Gaston Bachelard, *Le pluralisme cohérent de la chimie moderne* (Paris, 1932), p. 5. References abbreviated to *Pluralisme* in the text hereafter.
16 Michael D. Gordin, *A Well-Ordered Thing: Dmitrii Mendeleev and the Shadow of the Periodic Table* (New York, 2004), p. 34.
17 Gaston Bachelard, 'Noumenon and Microphysics', trans. Bernard Roy *Philosophical Forum*, XXXVII (2006), p. 80 (translation modified); Gaston Bachelard, *Études*, ed. Georges Canguilhem (Paris, 1970), p. 19.
18 Bachelard, 'Noumenon and Microphysics', p. 79.
19 Ibid., p. 82.
20 Ibid., pp. 83–4.

3 Cadence of Instants, 1932–6

1 Gary Gutting, *French Philosophy in the Twentieth Century* (Cambridge, 2001), p. 39.
2 Ibid., p. 86.
3 Philip Whalen, '"A Merciless Source of Happy Memories": Gaston Roupnel and the Folklore of Burgundian *Terroir*', *Journal of Folklore Research*, XLIV (2007), p. 25.
4 Gaston Roupnel, *Histoire de la campagne française* (Paris, 1932), p. 416.
5 Gaston Bachelard, *The Poetics of Space*, trans. Maria Jolas (Boston, MA, 1994), p. 188.
6 Philip Whalen, 'Gaston Roupnel', in *French Historians, 1900–2000: The New Historical Writing in Twentieth-Century France*, ed. Philip Daileader and Philip Whalen (Oxford, 2010), p. 534.
7 Gaston Bachelard, *Essai sur la connaissance approchée* (Paris, 1928), p. 12.
8 Gaston Bachelard, *Intuition of the Instant*, trans. Eileen Rizo-Patron (Evanston, IL, 2013), p. 11. References, abbreviated to *Instant*, in the text hereafter.
9 Henri Bergson, *Time and Free Will: An Essay on the Immediate Data of Consciousness*, trans. F. L. Pogson (London, 1910), p. 111.
10 Gaston Bachelard, *The Dialectic of Duration*, trans. Mary McAllester Jones (Manchester, 2000), p. 20. References, abbreviated to *Duration*, in the text hereafter.
11 W. R. Bion, 'Attacks on Linking', in *Second Thoughts: Selected Papers on Psycho-Analysis* (London, 1967), pp. 93–109.

4 Spirit of Science, 1934–40

1 Baruch Spinoza, *The Ethics* and *Selected Letters*, ed. Seymour Feldman, trans. Samuel Shirley (Indianapolis, IN, 1982), pp. 51–2.
2 Gaston Bachelard, *Métaphysique des mathématiques*, ed. Charles Alunni and Gerardo Ienna (Paris, 2021), p. 56.
3 Ibid., p. 53.
4 Gaston Bachelard, *The Dialectic of Duration*, trans. Mary McAllester Jones (Manchester, 2000), p. 152.
5 Francis Bacon, *Works*, 14 vols, ed. James Spedding, Robert Leslie Ellis and Douglas Devon Heath (London, 1868–1901), vol. IV, p. 98.
6 Carolyn Merchant, 'Francis Bacon and the "Vexations of Art": Experimentation as Intervention', *British Journal for the History of Science*, XLVI (2012), pp. 551–99.
7 Gaston Bachelard, *The New Scientific Spirit*, trans. Arthur Goldhammer (Boston, MA, 1984), p. 12. References, abbreviated to *New Scientific Spirit*, in the text hereafter.
8 Gaston Bachelard, *Le nouvel esprit scientifique* (Paris, 1934), p. 13.
9 Marie-Louise Gouhier, 'Bachelard et la psychanalyse: la rencontre', in *Bachelard*, ed. Henri Gouhier and Rene Poirier (Paris, 2011), p. 142.
10 Juliette Boutonier, *Contribution à la psychologie et à la métaphysique de l'angoisse* (Paris, 1945).
11 Gaston Bachelard, *Études*, ed. Georges Canguilhem (Paris, 1970), p. 28.
12 Bachelard, *Le nouvel esprit scientifique*, p. 38.
13 Cristina Chimisso, *Gaston Bachelard: Critic of Science and the Imagination* (London and New York, 2001), p. 188.
14 Gaston Bachelard, *The Dialectic of Duration*, trans. Mary McAllester Jones (Manchester, 2000), p. 41. References, abbreviated to *Duration*, in the text hereafter.
15 Michel Serres, 'Reformation and the Seven Sins', trans. Matthew Levine and Paul Cortois, *Parrhesia*, XXXI (2019), p. 34.
16 Ibid., p. 37.
17 Ibid., p. 41.
18 Bernadette Bensaude-Vincent and Jonathan Simon, *Chemistry: The Impure Science* (London, 2008), p. 94.
19 Gaston Bachelard, *Le matérialisme rationnel* (Paris, 1953), p. 22.
20 Ibid., p. 103.
21 Ibid.
22 Chimisso, *Gaston Bachelard*, p. 60.
23 Gaston Bachelard, *The Formation of the Scientific Mind: A Contribution to a Psychoanalysis of Objective Knowledge*, trans. Mary McAllester Jones (Manchester, 2002), p. 21. References abbreviated to *Formation* in the text hereafter.
24 Gaston Bachelard, *Le pluralisme cohérent de la chimie moderne* (Paris, 1932), p. 136.
25 Gaston Bachelard, *Atomistic Intuitions: An Essay on Classification*, trans. Roch C. Smith (Albany, NY, 2018), pp. 97, 101.
26 N. David Mermin, 'What's Wrong with This Pillow?', *Physics Today*, XLII (1989), p. 9.

27 H. G. Wells, *The Open Conspiracy: Blue Prints for a World Revolution* (London, 1928), p. 48.
28 Ibid., p. 70.
29 John S. Partington, *Building Cosmopolis: The Political Thought of H. G. Wells* (Aldershot and Burlington, VT, 2003), pp. 88–9.
30 Wells, *Open Conspiracy*, pp. 65, 64.
31 Gaston Bachelard, *La formation de l'esprit scientifique: Contribution à une psychanalyse de la connaissance objective* (Paris, 1934), p. 9.
32 I. A. Richards, *Science and Poetry* (London, 1926), p. 59.
33 Bachelard, *Études*, pp. 90, 91.
34 Bachelard, *La formation de l'esprit scientifique*, p. 14.
35 Gaston Bachelard, *Essai sur la connaissance approchée* (Paris, 1928), p. 25.
36 W. B. Yeats, *Collected Poems* (London, 1950), p. 388.

5 Fission, 1938–40

1 Gaston Bachelard, *The Psychoanalysis of Fire*, trans. Alan C. M. Ross (Boston, MA, 1964), p. 5. References, abbreviated to *Fire*, in the text hereafter.
2 Caroline Joan S. Picart, 'Metaphysics in Gaston Bachelard's "Reverie"', *Human Studies*, XX (1997), p. 60.
3 Henri Béhar, ed., *Inquisitions: Du surréalisme au front populaire. Fac-similé de la revue augmenté de documents inédits* (Paris, 1990), p. 152.
4 Ibid., p. 153.
5 Quoted and translated, Zbigniew Kotowicz, *Gaston Bachelard: A Philosophy of the Surreal* (Edinburgh, 2016), p. 81.
6 Gaston Bachelard, *L'engagement rationaliste* (Paris, 1972), p. 6.
7 Roger Caillois, *Approaches de l'imaginaire* (Paris, 1974), p. 57.
8 Gavin Parkinson, *Surrealism, Art and Modern Science: Relativity, Quantum Mechanics, Epistemology* (New Haven, CT, and London, 2008), p. 100.
9 Ibid., p. 59.
10 Ibid., p. 69.
11 Ibid.
12 Jean Wahl, *Poésie, pensée, perception* (Paris, 1948), p. 13.
13 Gabriel Kafure da Rocha, 'I Shout, Therefore I Am an Energy: Bachelard and Capoeira Angola, a Phenomenology of the Body', *Philosophy International Journal*, II (2019), p. 2 n. 2.
14 Gaston Bachelard, 'La bestiaire de Lautréamont', *Nouvelle revue française*, XXVII (1939), pp. 711–34.
15 Gaston Bachelard, *Le psychanalyse du feu* (Paris, 1938).
16 José Corti, *Souvenirs désordonnés* (Paris, 2010), pp. 48–9.
17 Gaston Bachelard, *Lautréamont*, trans. Robert S. Dupree (Dallas, TX, 1986), p. 48. References, to *Lautréamont*, in the text hereafter.
18 Francisque Sarcey, *Journal de jeunesse*, ed. Adolphe Brisson (Paris, 1903), pp. 205–12; Luigi de Anna, *Francisque Sarcey, professeur et journaliste: Sa vie et son oeuvre* (Florence, 1919), pp. 47–50.
19 Cristina Chimisso, *Gaston Bachelard: Critic of Science and the Imagination* (London and New York, 2001), p. 7.

20 Roger Caillois, *Le mythe et l'homme* (Paris, 1938), p. 22.
21 Gaston Bachelard, *The Philosophy of No: A Philosophy of the New Scientific Mind*, trans. G. C. Waterston (New York, 1968), pp. 18, 43.
22 Ibid., p. 7.
23 Ibid., p. 9.

6 Occupation, 1940–42

1 Quoted in André Parinaud, *Bachelard* (Paris, 1996), p. 231. References, abbreviated to Parinaud, in the text hereafter.
2 W. H. Auden, *Collected Poems*, ed. Edward Mendelson (London, 1994), p. 275.
3 David Pryce, 'Paris During the German Occupation', in *Collaboration in France: Politics and Culture During the Nazi Occupation, 1940–1944*, ed. Gerhard Hirschfeld and Patrick Marsh (Oxford, New York and Munich, 1989), p. 21.
4 Ibid., p. 17.
5 Julian Jackson, *France: The Dark Years, 1940–1944* (Oxford, 2003), p. 371; Claude Singer, *Vichy, l'université et les juifs: Les silences et la mémoire* (Paris, 1992), pp. 191–2.
6 Gilles Maigron, 'Résistance et collaboration dans l'Université de Paris sous l'occupation', in *Les Facs sous Vichy: Etudiants, Universitaires at Universités de France pendant la Seconde Guerre Mondiale*, ed. André Gueslin (Clermont-Ferrand, 1993), p. 138.
7 Ibid., p. 135.
8 Barbara Will, 'Beckett's French Resistance', in *Revisioning French Culture*, ed. Andrew Sobanet (Liverpool, 2019), p. 110.
9 Simone de Beauvoir, *La force de l'âge* (Paris, 1960), p. 538.
10 Jean-Paul Sartre, 'Paris under the Occupation', trans. Adrian van den Hoven, *Sartre Studies International*, IV (1998), p. 12.
11 Ibid., p. 7.
12 Ibid.
13 Ibid., p. 8.
14 Elizabeth Bowen, *The Heat of the Day* (London, 1998), p. 119.
15 Samuel Beckett, *Molloy. Malone Dies. The Unnamable* (London, 1973), p. 36.
16 Sartre, 'Paris under the Occupation', p. 12.
17 Gaston Bachelard, *The Psychoanalysis of Fire*, trans. Alan C. M. Ross (Boston, MA, 1964), p. 18.
18 Ibid., p. 91.
19 Ibid., p. 89.
20 Sigmund Freud, *The Standard Edition of the Complete Psychological Works of Sigmund Freud*, 24 vols, ed. and trans. James Strachey et al. (London, 1958–74), vol. V, p. 608.
21 Gaston Bachelard, *Water and Dreams: An Essay on the Imagination of Matter*, trans. Edith R. Farrell (Dallas, TX, 2006), p. 11. References abbreviated to *Water and Dreams* in the text hereafter.
22 Gaston Bachelard, *L'eau et les rêves: essai sur l'imagination de la matière* (Paris, 1942), p. 148.

23 Ibid.
24 Gaston Bachelard, *The Dialectic of Duration*, trans. Mary McAllester Jones (Manchester, 2000), p. 146.
25 Bachelard, *The Psychoanalysis of Fire*, p. 99.
26 Beauvoir, *La force de l'âge*, p. 614.
27 Jean-Paul Sartre, *Being and Nothingness: An Essay on Phenomenological Ontology*, trans. Hazel E. Barnes (London, 1984), p. 602.
28 Ibid., pp. 602–3.
29 Gaston Bachelard, *Air and Dreams: An Essay on the Imagination of Movement*, trans. Edith R. Farrell and C. Frederick Farrell (Dallas, TX, 2002), p. 19.
30 Charles Baudouin, *Studies in Psychoanalysis: An Account of Twenty-Seven Concrete Cases Preceded by a Theoretical Exposition*, trans. Eden and Cedar Paul (New York, 1922), p. 378.

7 Tension of Relaxation, 1943–8

1 Sigmund Freud, *The Standard Edition of the Complete Psychological Works of Sigmund Freud*. 24 vols, ed. and trans. James Strachey et al. (London, 1953–74), vol. XIV, pp. 315–30; *Gesammelte Werke*, 18 vols (London, 1991), vol. X, p. 370.
2 Quoted in André Parinaud, *Bachelard* (Paris, 1996), p. 480.
3 Gaston Bachelard, *Water and Dreams: An Essay on the Imagination of Matter*, trans. Edith R. Farrell (Dallas, TX, 2006), p. 159. References abbreviated to *Water and Dreams* in the text hereafter.
4 Gaston Bachelard, *Air and Dreams: An Essay on the Imagination of Movement*, trans. Edith R. Farrell and C. Frederick Farrell (Dallas, TX, 2002), p. 1. References abbreviated to *Air and Dreams* in the text hereafter.
5 Ernest Henry Starling, 'The Chemical Control of the Functions of the Body', in *Source Book in Chemistry, 1900–1950*, ed. Henry M. Leicester (Cambridge, MA, 1968), p. 317.
6 Nicole Fabre, 'Bachelard et la psychanalyse: un compagnonnage houleux', *Bachelard Studies*, II (2021), p. 117 n. 19.
7 Ibid., p. 119.
8 Robert Desoille, *Exploration de l'affectivité subconsciente par la méthode du rêve éveillé dirigé: Sublimations et acquisitions psychologiques* (Paris, 1938), p. 9.
9 Juliette Boutonier, *Contribution à la psychologie et à la métaphysique de l'angoisse* (Paris, 1945), p. 190.
10 Bianca Garufi, 'Reflections on the "Rêve Éveillé Dirigé" Method', *Journal of Analytical Psychology*, XXII (1977), p. 210.
11 Ibid., pp. 208–9.
12 Gaston Bachelard, *Earth and Reveries of Will: An Essay on the Imagination of Matter*, trans. Kenneth Haltman (Dallas, TX, 2002), p. 53.
13 Marta Ples-Bęben, 'La méthode du rêve éveillée dirigé dans l'interprétation de Gaston Bachelard', *Analele Universitatii din Craiova, Seria: Filosofie*, XLI (2018), p. 45.
14 Gaston Bachelard, *Le matérialisme rationnel* (Paris, 1953), p. 18, trans. and quoted in Herbert Marcuse, *One-Dimensional Man: Studies in the*

Ideology of Advanced Industrial Society (London and New York, 2002), p. 254.

15 Marcuse, *One-Dimensional Man*, p. 254.

16 Samuel Beckett, *Disjecta: Miscellaneous Writings and a Dramatic Fragment*, ed. Ruby Cohn (London, 1983), p. 141.

17 Gaston Bachelard, *The Dialectic of Duration*, trans. Mary McAllester Jones (Manchester, 2000), pp. 141, 142.

18 Olivier Leroy, *La lévitation. Contribution historique et critique à l'étude du merveilleux* (Paris, 1928), cited in Gaston Bachelard, *Air and Dreams: An Essay on the Imagination of Movement*, trans. Edith R. Farrell and C. Frederick Farrell (Dallas, TX, 2002), p. 13 n.7.

19 Eugène Caslant, *Passé et avenir de la navigation aérienne* (Paris, 1911); *Méthode de développement des facultés supra-normales* (Paris, 1921). Colette Jacob, 'Approche historique du rêve éveillé en psychanalyse: Les fils rouges depuis l'origine, 1923–1966', *Imaginaire et Inconscient*, XXIII (2009), pp. 13–14.

8 Overcoming, 1947–53

1 Humphry Davy, *Elements of Agricultural Chemistry* (London, 1813), p. 8.

2 Gaston Bachelard, *Earth and Reveries of Will: An Essay on the Imagination of Matter*, trans. Kenneth Haltman (Dallas, TX, 2002), p. 43. References abbreviated to *Reveries of Will* in the text hereafter.

3 Gaston Bachelard, *La terre et les rêveries de la volonté* (Paris, 1947), p. 16.

4 Herman Melville, *Moby-Dick*, ed. Harrison Hayford and Hershel Parker (New York, 1967), p. 348.

5 Ibid., pp. 348, 349.

6 Bachelard, *La terre et les rêveries de la volonté*, p. 80.

7 James Mark Baldwin, *Thought and Things: A Study of the Development and Meaning of Thought, or Genetic Logic*, vol. III: *Interest and Art Being Real Logic. I. Genetic Epistemology* (London, 1911), p. 257.

8 Ibid.

9 Gaston Bachelard, *Air and Dreams: An Essay on the Imagination of Movement*, trans. Edith R. Farrell and C. Frederick Farrell (Dallas, TX, 2002), p. 49 n. 23.

10 Gaston Bachelard, *Earth and Reveries of Repose: An Essay on Images of Interiority*, trans. Mary McAllester Jones (Dallas, TX, 2011), p. 4. References abbreviated to *Reveries of Repose* in the text hereafter.

11 André Bay, *Histoires racontées par les enfants* (Paris, 1938).

12 Gaston Bachelard, *La terre et les rêveries du repos: Essai sur les images de l'intimité* (Paris, 1948), p. 3.

13 Ibid., p. 5.

14 Ibid., p. 299.

15 Ibid., p. 215.

16 Paul de Man, *Allegories of Reading: Figural Language in Rousseau, Nietzsche, Rilke, and Proust* (New Haven, CT, and London, 1979).

17 Medard Boss, *Meaning and Content of Sexual Perversions: A Daseinsanalytic Approach to the Psychopathology of the Phenomenon of Love*, trans. Liese Lewis Abel (New York, 1949), p. 99.

18 Gaston Bachelard and Roland Kuhn, 'Correspondance Gaston Bachelard et Roland Kuhn: 1947–1957', ed. and trans. Elisabetta Basso and Charles Alunni, *Revue de synthèse*, CXXXVII (2016), p. 181.
19 Gaston Bachelard and Ludwig Binswanger, 'Correspondance entre Gaston Bachelard et Ludwig Binswanger (1948–1955)', trans. and ed. Elisabetta Basso and Emmanuel Delille, *Revue germanique internationale*, XXX (2019), https://doi.org/10.4000/rgi.2383.
20 Ludwig Binswanger, 'The Existential Analysis School of Thought', in *Existence: A New Dimension in Psychiatry and Psychology*, ed. Rollo May, Ernest Angel and Henri F. Ellenberger (New York, 1958), p. 211. References abbreviated to 'Existential Analysis' in the text hereafter.
21 Ludwig Binswanger, *Being-in-the-World: Selected Papers of Ludwig Binswanger*, trans. and ed. Jacob Needleman (New York, 1963), p. 346.
22 'Correspondance Gaston Bachelard et Roland Kuhn', p. 181.
23 Ibid., p. 183.
24 Ludwig Binswanger, 'The Case of Ellen West', in *Existence*, ed. Rollo May et al., p. 275.
25 Binswanger, 'Ellen West', pp. 275, 268 n. 18.
26 Roland Kuhn, *Phénoménologie du masque: A travers le test de Rorschach*, trans. Jacqueline Verdeaux (Bruges, 1957).
27 Gaston Bachelard, *The Right to Dream*, trans. J. A. Underwood (Dallas, TX, 1988), pp. 165, 162.
28 Ibid., p. 165.
29 Ludwig Binswanger, *Sigmund Freud: Reminiscences of a Friendship*, trans. Norbert Guterman (New York, 1957), p. 99.
30 Ludwig Binswanger, *Drei Formen missglückten Daseins: Verstiegenheit, Verschrobenheit, Manieriertheit* (Berlin, 1956).
31 'Correspondance entre Gaston Bachelard et Ludwig Binswanger'.

9 City of Science, 1948–53

1 Mary Lydon, *Perpetuum Mobile: A Study of the Novels and Aesthetics of Michel Butor* (Edmonton, 1980), p. 156 n. 31.
2 Leon S. Roudiez, *Michel Butor* (New York, 1965), p. 5; Michel Butor, *Curriculum vitae: entretiens avec André Clavel* (Paris, 1996), p. 37.
3 Gaston Bachelard, *Fragments of a Poetics of Fire*, ed. Suzanne Bachelard, trans. Kenneth Haltman (Dallas, TX, 1990), pp. xv–xvi.
4 Gaston Bachelard, *Earth and Reveries of Repose: An Essay on Images of Interiority*, trans. Mary McAllester Jones (Dallas, TX, 2011), p. 8.
5 'Editorial', *Dialectica*, I (1947), pp. 5–6.
6 Gaston Bachelard, 'The Dialogical Philosophy/La philosophie dialoguée', trans. Gennaro Lauro, *Philosophical Inquiries*, IX (2021), p. 231.
7 Gaston Bachelard, *Le Rationalisme appliqué* (Paris, 1949), p. 178. References abbreviated to *Rationalisme appliqué* in the text hereafter.
8 Gaston Bachelard, *L'engagement rationaliste* (Paris, 1972), p. 52.
9 Ibid., p. 137.
10 Bachelard, 'The Dialogical Philosophy', p. 233.
11 Raymond Ruyer, 'Le Materialisme rationnel selon G. Bachelard', *Revue de métaphysique et de morale*, LVIII (1953), p. 415.

12 Ferdinand and Jean-Paul Gonseth, 'Connaissance objective et connaissance poétique', *Dialectica*, I (1947), p. 117.
13 Ibid., p. 124.
14 Ibid., p. 125.
15 Michel Serres, 'Reformation and the Seven Sins', trans. Matthew Levine and Paul Cortois, *Parrhesia*, XXXI (2019), p. 41.
16 Gaston Bachelard, *Le matérialisme rationnel* (Paris, 1953), p. 43. References, abbreviated to *Matérialisme rationnel*, in the text hereafter.
17 C. G. Jung, *Psychology and Alchemy: Collected Works of C. G. Jung*, vol. XII, 2nd edn, trans. R.F.C. Hull (Princeton, NJ, 1968), pp. 244–5.
18 Jean-Paul Sartre, *Being and Nothingness: An Essay on Phenomenological Ontology*, trans. Hazel E. Barnes (London, 1984), p. 58.
19 Jacob Bronowski, 'A Twentieth-Century Image of Man', *Leonardo*, XVIII 1985), pp. 276, 277.

10 Retirement, 1954–7

1 André Parinaud, *Bachelard* (Paris, 1996), p. 489.
2 Ibid.
3 Gaston Bachelard, *Earth and Reveries of Repose: An Essay on Images of Interiority*, trans. Mary McAllester Jones (Dallas, TX, 2011), p. 70.
4 Quoted in Parinaud, *Bachelard*, p. 485.
5 Gaston Bachelard, *Études*, ed. Georges Canguilhem (Paris, 1970), p. 43.
6 Gaston Bachelard, *L'expérience de l'espace dans la physique contemporaine* (Paris, 1937), p. 11.
7 Ibid., p. 12.
8 Ibid., pp. 12–13.
9 Gaston Bachelard, *The Dialectic of Duration*, trans. Mary McAllester Jones (Manchester, 2000), p. 152.
10 Gaston Bachelard, *The Poetics of Space*, trans. Maria Jolas (Boston, MA, 1994), p. xxix. References, abbreviated to *Poetics of Space*, in the text hereafter.
11 Gaston Bachelard, *La poétique de l'espace* (Paris, 1957), p. 19.
12 Ibid., p. 2.
13 Quoted in Parinaud, *Bachelard*, p. 489.
14 Gaston Bachelard, *Fragments of a Poetics of Fire*, ed. Suzanne Bachelard, trans. Kenneth Haltman (Dallas, TX, 1990), p. xxii.
15 Gaston Bachelard, *The Right to Dream*, trans. J. A. Underwood (Dallas, TX, 1988), p. 168. References abbreviated to *Right to Dream* in the text hereafter.
16 Parinaud, *Bachelard*, p. 487.
17 Quoted ibid., p. 489.
18 Gaston Bachelard and Ludwig Binswanger, 'Correspondance entre Gaston Bachelard et Ludwig Binswanger (1948–1955)', trans. and ed. Elisabetta Basso et Emmanuel Delille, *Revue germanique internationale*, XXX (2019), https://doi.org/10.4000/rgi.2383.
19 Ibid.
20 Gaston Bachelard, *The Poetics of Reverie: Childhood, Language, and the Cosmos*, trans. Daniel Russell (Boston, MA, 1971), p. 8. References, abbreviated to *Poetics of Reverie*, in the text hereafter.

11 Against Biography, 1958–62

1 Gaston Bachelard, *L'engagement rationaliste* (Paris, 1972), p. 137.
2 Gaston Bachelard, *The Poetics of Reverie: Childhood, Language, and the Cosmos*, trans. Daniel Russell (Boston, MA, 1971), p. 6. References abbreviated to *Poetics of Reverie* in the text hereafter.
3 Gaston Bachelard, *Earth and Reveries of Repose: An Essay on Images of Interiority*, trans. Mary McAllester Jones (Dallas, TX, 2011), p. 56.
4 Ibid., p. 57.
5 Gaston Bachelard and Roland Kuhn, 'Correspondance Gaston Bachelard et Roland Kuhn: 1947–1957', ed. and trans. Elisabetta Basso and Charles Alunni, *Revue de synthèse*, CXXXVII (2016), p. 183; Hans Binder, *Die Helldunkeldeutungen im psychodiagnostischen Experiment von Rorschach* (Zürich, 1932).
6 Gaston Bachelard, *La poétique de la rêverie* (Paris, 1960), p. 98.
7 Adrian Seville, *The Cultural Legacy of the Royal Game of the Goose: 400 Years of Printed Board Games* (Amsterdam, 2019), p. 25.
8 Ibid., p. 29.
9 Ibid., p. 14.
10 Gaston Bachelard, *Earth and Reveries of Repose*, trans. McAllester Jones, p. 57.
11 Ibid.
12 Bachelard, *Poétique de la rêverie*, p. 109.
13 Jean Rousselot, *Il n'y a pas d'exil* (Paris, 1954), p. 41.
14 Bachelard, *Poétique de la rêverie*, p. 85.
15 André Parinaud, *Bachelard* (Paris, 1996), p. 491.
16 Ibid.
17 Gaston Bachelard, *Le matérialisme rationnel* (Paris, 1953), p. 41.
18 Gaston Bachelard, *Fragments of a Poetics of Fire*, ed. Suzanne Bachelard, trans. Kenneth Haltman (Dallas, TX, 1990), p. 116. References, abbreviated to *Fragments*, in the text hereafter.
19 Michel Serres, 'Turner Translates Carnot', trans. Marilyn Sides, in *Hermes: Literature, Science, Philosophy*, ed. Josué V. Harari and David F. Bell (Baltimore, MD, 1982), p. 56.
20 Gaston Bachelard, *The Psychoanalysis of Fire*, trans. Alan C. M. Ross (Boston, MA, 1964), p. 13; Peter Sloterdijk, *Die Reue des Prometheus: Von der Gabe des Feuers zur globalen Brandstiftung* (Berlin, 2023), p. 8.
21 Gaston Bachelard, *The Flame of a Candle*, trans. Joni Caldwell (Dallas, TX, 988), p. 1. References, abbreviated to *Flame*, in the text hereafter.
22 Gaston Bachelard, *La flamme d'une chandelle* (Paris, 1961), p. 60.
23 Bachelard, *Psychoanalysis of Fire*, pp. 4, 46.
24 Quoted in Parinaud, *Bachelard*, p. 492.
25 Ibid.
26 Gaston Bachelard, *Lettres à Louis Guillaume* (Paris, 2009), p. 54.
27 Quoted in Parinaud, *Bachelard*, p. 493.
28 Bachelard, *Psychoanalysis of Fire*, p. 11.
29 Ibid., p. 2.
30 Gaston Bachelard, *Fragments d'une poétique du feu*, ed. Suzanne Bachelard (Paris, 1988), p. 37.

31 Ibid., p. 72.
32 José Corti, *Souvenirs désordonnés* (Paris, 2010), pp. 50–51.
33 Quoted in Jean Lescure, *Un été avec Bachelard* (Paris, 1983), p. 222.
34 Ibid., p. 223.
35 Philip Larkin, *Collected Poems*, ed. Anthony Thwaite (London, 1988), p. 121.
36 Lescure, *Un été avec Bachelard*, p. 230.
37 Ibid., p. 224.
38 Corti, *Souvenirs désordonnés*, p. 46.

Conclusion

1 Hermann Usener, *Götternamen: Versuch enier Lehre der religiösen Begriffsbildung* (Bonn, 1896), p. 280.
2 Gaston Bachelard, *Lautréamont*, trans. Robert S. Dupree (Dallas, TX, 1968), pp. 2, 37, 67–82.
3 Ibid., p. 34.
4 Gaston Bachelard, *Earth and Reveries of Will: An Essay on the Imagination of Matter*, trans. Kenneth Haltman (Dallas, TX, 2002), p. 59.
5 Clervence Ramnoux, 'Bachelard à sa table d'écriture', *Revue internationale de philosophie*, XXXVIII (1984), p. 221.
6 Bachelard, *Lautréamont*, p. 64.
7 Gaston Bachelard, *Le nouvel esprit scientifique* (Paris, 1934), p. 15.
8 Gaston Bachelard, *Water and Dreams: An Essay on the Imagination of Matter*, trans. Edith R. Farrell (Dallas, TX, 2006), p. 192; *L'eau et les rêves: essai sur l'imagination de la matière* (Paris, 1943), p. 257.
9 Bachelard, *Water and Dreams*, p. 187.
10 Ibid., p. 189.
11 Pierre Quillet, *Bachelard* (Paris, 1964), p. 48.
12 Jean-Claude Margolin, *Bachelard* (Paris, 1974), p. 86.
13 Gaston Bachelard, *Le rationalisme appliqué* (Paris, 1949), pp. 58–9.
14 Cristina Chimisso, *Gaston Bachelard: Critic of Science and the Imagination* (London and New York, 2001), pp. 222–3.
15 Ibid., p. 45.
16 Gaston Bachelard, *Intuition of the Instant*, trans. Eileen Rizo-Patron (Evanston, IL, 2013), p. 4.
17 Ibid., pp. 4–5.
18 Samuel Beckett, *Proust* and *Three Dialogues with Georges Duthuit* (London, 1970), p. 86.
19 Bachelard, *Water and Dreams*, p. 184.
20 Ibid., p. 179.
21 Ibid., p. 124.
22 Gaston Bachelard, *Air and Dreams: An Essay on the Imagination of Movement*, trans. Edith R. Farrell and C. Frederick Farrell (Dallas, TX, 2002), p. 185.
23 Ibid., p. 186.
24 Ibid., p. 213.
25 Ibid., p. 253.
26 Bachelard, *Earth and Reveries of Will*, p. 278.

27 Gaston Bachelard, *The Poetics of Space*, trans. Maria Jolas (Boston, MA, 1994), p. 201.
28 Elisabeth Roudinesco, *Lacan and Co. A History of Psychoanalysis in France, 1925–1985*, trans. Jeffrey Mehlman (Chicago, IL, 1990), p. xx.
29 Massimiliano Simons, *Michel Serres and French Philosophy of Science* (London and New York, 2022), pp. 37–8.
30 W. H. Auden, *Collected Poems*, ed. Edward Mendelson (London, 1994), p. 183.
31 Quoted in Jim Miller, *The Passion of Michel Foucault* (New York, 1993), p. 60.
32 Michel Foucault, *Remarks on Marx: Conversations with Duccio Trombadori*, trans. R. James Goldstein and James Cascaito (New York, 1991), pp. 67–8.
33 Miller, *Passion of Michel Foucault*, p. 73.
34 Michel Foucault and Ludwig Binswanger, *Dream and Existence*, ed. Keith Hoeller, trans. Forrest Williams and Jacob Needleman (Atlantic Highlands, NJ, 1993), p. 70.
35 Michel Foucault, *Dits et écrits, I: 1954–1988*, 4 vols, ed. Daniel Defert, François Ewald and Jacques Lagrange (Paris, 1994), vol. II, p. 860.
36 Simons, *Michel Serres and French Philosophy of Science*, p. 36.
37 Bachelard, *Poetics of Space*, pp. 78, 232–41.
38 W. B. Yeats, *Collected Poems* (London, 1950), p. 218.

SELECT BIBLIOGRAPHY

Writings by Bachelard

Essai sur la connaissance approchée (Paris, 1928)
Étude sur l'evolution d'un problème de physique: la propagation thermique dans les solides (Paris, 1928)
La valeur inductive de la relativité (Paris, 1929)
La pluralisme cohérent de la chimie moderne (Paris 1932)
L'Intuition de l'instant: Étude sur la Siloë de Gaston Roupnel (Paris, 1932)
    Intuition of the Instant, trans. Eileen Rizo-Patron (Evanston, IL, 2013)
Les intuitions atomistiques: essai de classification (Paris, 1933)
    Atomistic Intuitions, trans. Roch C. Smith (Albany, NY, 2018)
Le nouvel esprit scientifique (Paris, 1934)
    The New Scientific Spirit, trans. Arthur Goldhammer (Boston, MA, 1985)
La dialectique de la durée (Paris, 1936)
    The Dialectic of Duration, trans. Mary McAllester Jones (Manchester, 2000)
L'expérience de l'espace dans la physique contemporaine (Paris, 1937)
La formation de l'esprit scientifique: contribution à une psychanalyse de la connaissance objective (Paris, 1938)
    The Formation of the Scientific Mind: A Contribution to a Psychoanalysis of Objective Knowledge, trans. Mary McAllester Jones (Manchester, 2002)
La psychanalyse du feu (Paris, 1938)
    The Psychoanalysis of Fire, trans. Alan C. M. Ross (Boston, MA, 1964)
Lautréamont (Paris, 1939)
    Lautréamont, trans. Robert S. Dupree (Dallas, TX, 1968)
La Philosophie du non: Essai d'une philosophie du nouvel esprit scientifique (Paris, 1940)
    The Philosophy of No: A Philosophy of the New Scientific Mind, trans. G. C. Waterston (New York, 1968)
L'eau et les rêves: essai sur l'imagination de la matière (Paris, 1942)
    Water and Dreams: An Essay on the Imagination of Matter, trans. Edith R. Farrell (Dallas, TX, 1983)

L'air et les songes: essai sur l'imagination du mouvement (Paris, 1943)
Air and Dreams: An Essay on the Imagination of Movement, trans. Edith R. Farrell and C. Frederick Farrell (Dallas, TX, 1988)
La terre et les rêveries de la volonté: Essai sur l'imagination de la matière (Paris, 1943)
Earth and Reveries of Will: An Essay on the Imagination of Matter, trans. Kenneth Haltman (Dallas, TX, 2002)
La terre et les rêveries du repos: Essai sur les images de l'intimité (Paris, 1948)
Earth and Reveries of Repose: An Essay on Images of Interiority, trans. and ed. Mary McAllester Jones (Dallas, TX, 2011)
Le Rationalisme appliqué (Paris, 1949)
L'activité rationaliste de la physique contemporaine (Paris, 1951)
Le matérialisme rationnel (Paris, 1953)
La poétique de l'espace (Paris, 1957)
The Poetics of Space (New York, 1964)
La poétique de la revêrie (Paris, 1960)
Poetics of Reverie: Childhood, Language, and the Cosmos, trans. Daniel Russell (Boston, MA, 1971)
La flamme d'une chandelle (Paris, 1961)
The Flame of a Candle, trans. Joni Caldwell (Dallas, TX, 1988)
Le droit de rêver (Paris, 1970)
The Right to Dream, trans. J. A. Underwood (Dallas, TX, 1988)
On Poetic Imagination and Reverie: Selections from the Works of Gaston Bachelard, trans. Colette Gaudin (Indianapolis, IN, 1971)
L'engagement rationaliste, ed. Georges Canguilhem (Paris, 1972)
Métaphysique des mathématiques, ed. Charles Alunni and Gerardo Ienna (Paris, 2021)

Writings on Bachelard

Alunni, Charles, *Spectres de Bachelard: Gaston Bachelard et l'école surrationaliste* (Paris, 2018)
Chimisso, Cristina, *Gaston Bachelard: Critic of Science and the Imagination* (London and New York, 2001)
Dagognet, François, *Gaston Bachelard: Sa vie, son oeuvre, avec un exposé de sa philosophie* (Paris, 1965)
Jones, Mary McAllester, *Gaston Bachelard, Subversive Humanist: Texts and Readings* (Madison, WI, 1991)
Kotowicz, Zbigniew, *Gaston Bachelard: A Philosophy of the Surreal* (Edinburgh, 2016)
Lecourt, Dominique, *Marxism and Epistemology: Bachelard, Canguilhem and Foucault*, trans. Ben Brewster (London, 1975)
Lescure, Jean, *Un été avec Bachelard* (Paris, 1983)
Rizo-Patron, Eileen, Edward S. Casey and Jason M. Wirth, eds, *Adventures in Phenomenology: Gaston Bachelard* (Albany, NY, 2017)
Serres, Michel, 'Reformation and the Seven Sins', trans. Matthew Levine and Paul Cortois, *Parrhesia*, XXXI (2019), pp. 33–47
Smith, Roch C., *Gaston Bachelard* (Boston, MA, 1982)
—, *Gaston Bachelard: Philosopher of Science and the Imagination* (Albany, NY, 2016)

Stroud, Joanne H., *Gaston Bachelard: An Elemental Reverie on the World's Stuff*, ed. Robert Sardello (Dallas, TX, 2014)
Tiles, Mary, *Bachelard: Science and Objectivity* (Cambridge, 1984)

Letters

Bachelard, Gaston, *Lettres à Louis Guillaume* (Paris, 2009)
Bourel, Dominique, 'De Bar-sur-Aube à Jérusalem: La correspondance entre Gaston Bachelard at Martin Buber', *Revue Internationale de Philosophie*, XXXVIII (1984), pp. 201–16
'Correspondance entre Gaston Bachelard et Ludwig Binswanger (1948–1955)', ed. and trans. Elisabetta Basso and Emmanuel Delille, *Revue germanique internationale*, XXX (2019), pp. 183–208
Correspondance Gaston Bachelard-Henri Bosco, ed. Christian Morzewski (Arras, 2013)
'Correspondance Gaston Bachelard et Roland Kuhn: 1947–1957', ed. and trans. Elisabetta Basso and Charles Alunni, *Revue de synthèse*, CXXXVII (2016), pp. 177–89

Biography

Parinaud, André, *Bachelard* (Paris, 1996)
Wavelet, Jean-Michel, *Gaston Bachelard, l'inattendu: Les chemins d'une volonté* (Paris, 2019)

Journal

Bachelard Studies/Etudes Bachelardiennes/Studi Bachelardiani, 2020 –
(2020): *Bachelard: An Ecological Thinker?*
(2021/1): *Bachelard the Non-Psychoanalyst*
(2021/2): *Gaston Bachelard's Materialism*
(2022): *Bachelard and Philosophy of Science*

PHOTO ACKNOWLEDGEMENTS

The author and publishers wish to express their thanks to the following sources of illustrative material and/or permission to reproduce it.

© ADAGP, Paris and DACS, London 2024: p. 144; AKG Images (Collection Dupont): p. 161; Alamy: p. 76 (BNA Photographic); Bridgeman Images: pp. 45 (Collection Bourgeron), 52 (Collection Bourgeron), 82 (Tallandier), 93 (Giovanni Coruzzi), 113 (Giovanni Coruzzi), 117 (Archiv/Keystone), 152 (Collection Bourgeron); Public Domain: pp. 151, 159, 160, 165; Shutterstock: p. 175 (wantanddo); Jean-Michel Wavelet: pp. 13, 16, 21.

INDEX

Page numbers in *italics* indicate illustrations